JACK *of* FABLES
AMERICANA

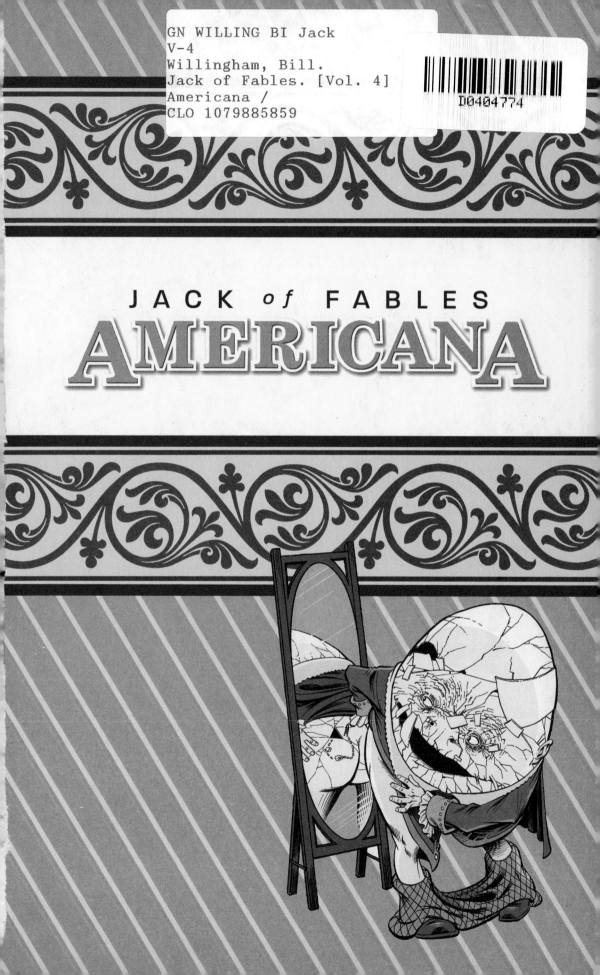

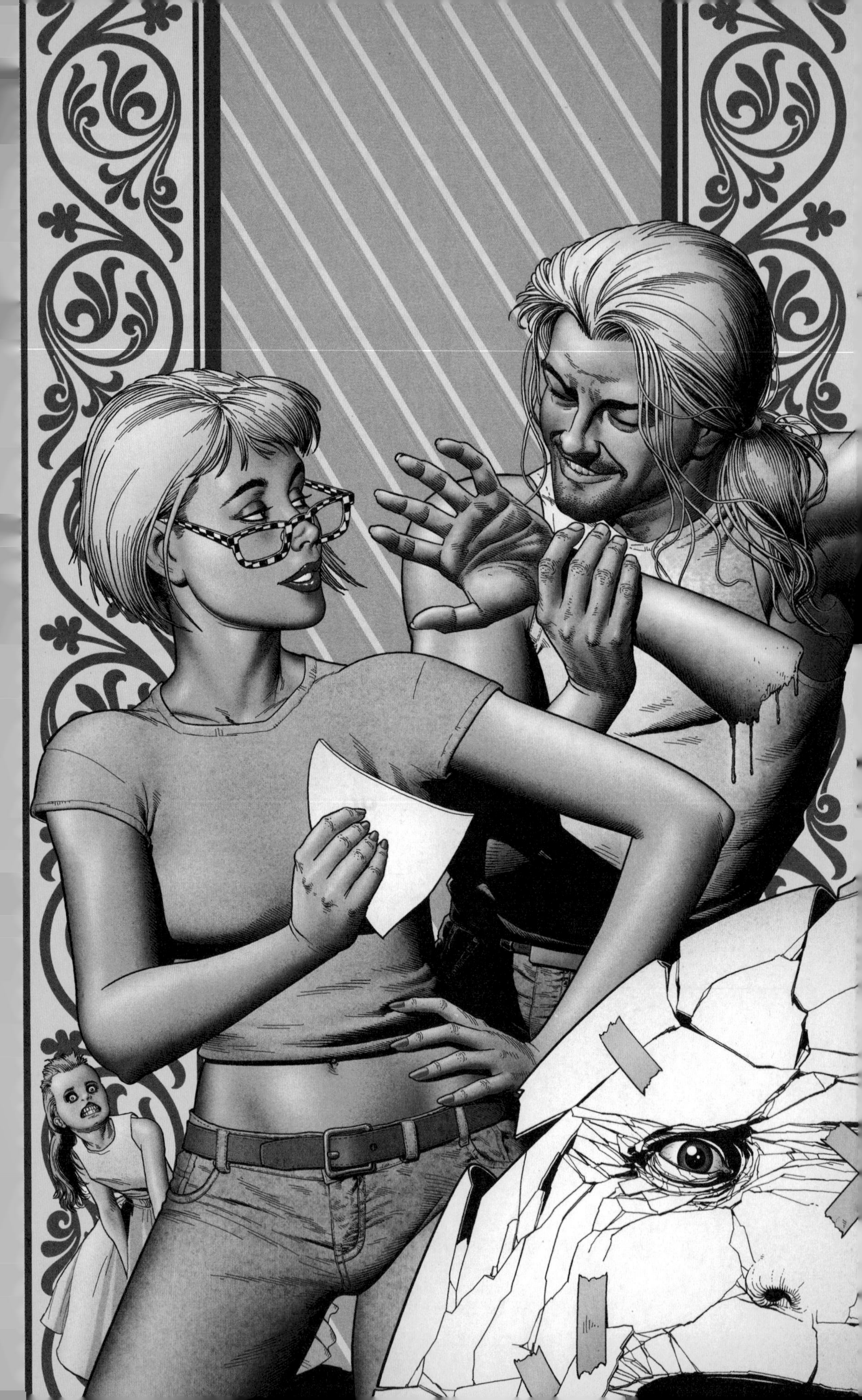

JACK *of* FABLES
AMERICANA

Bill *WILLINGHAM*
Matthew **STURGES**
writers

Russ **BRAUN**
Tony **AKINS**
pencillers

Andrew **PEPOY**
Tony **AKINS**
Steve **LEIALOHA**
inkers

Daniel **VOZZO**
colorist

Todd **KLEIN**
letterer

BRIAN BOLLAND and **ZACHARY BALDUS**
Original Series Covers

Jack of Fables created by **BILL WILLINGHAM**

KAREN BERGER
Senior VP-Executive Editor

ANGELA RUFINO
Editor-original series

SCOTT NYBAKKEN
Editor-collected edition

ROBBIN BROSTERMAN
Senior Art Director

PAUL LEVITZ
President & Publisher

GEORG BREWER
VP-Design & DC Direct Creative

RICHARD BRUNING
Senior VP-Creative Director

PATRICK CALDON
Executive VP-Finance & Operations

CHRIS CARAMALIS
VP-Finance

JOHN CUNNINGHAM
VP-Marketing

TERRI CUNNINGHAM
VP-Managing Editor

AMY GENKINS
Senior VP-Business & Legal Affairs

ALISON GILL
VP-Manufacturing

DAVID HYDE
VP-Publicity

HANK KANALZ
VP-General Manager, WildStorm

JIM LEE
Editorial Director-WildStorm

GREGORY NOVECK
Senior VP-Creative Affairs

SUE POHJA
VP-Book Trade Sales

STEVE ROTTERDAM
Senior VP-Sales & Marketing

CHERYL RUBIN
Senior VP-Brand Management

ALYSSE SOLL
VP-Advertising & Custom Publishing

JEFF TROJAN
VP-Business Development, DC Direct

BOB WAYNE
VP-Sales

Cover illustration by Brian Bolland.
Logo design by James Jean.
Publication design by Brainchild Studios/NYC.

JACK OF FABLES: AMERICANA
Published by DC Comics. Cover and
compilation Copyright © 2008 DC Comics.
All Rights Reserved.

Originally published in single magazine form
as JACK OF FABLES 17-21. Copyright © 2008
Bill Willingham and DC Comics. All Rights
Reserved. All characters, their distinctive like-
nesses and related elements featured in this
publication are trademarks of Bill Willingham.
VERTIGO is a trademark of DC Comics.
The stories, characters and incidents featured
in this publication are entirely fictional. DC
Comics does not read or accept unsolicited
submissions of ideas, stories or artwork.

DC Comics, 1700 Broadway,
New York, NY 10019
A Warner Bros. Entertainment Company.
Printed in Canada. First Printing.
ISBN: 978-1-4012-1979-6

TABLE *of* CONTENTS

DRAMATIS PERSONAE

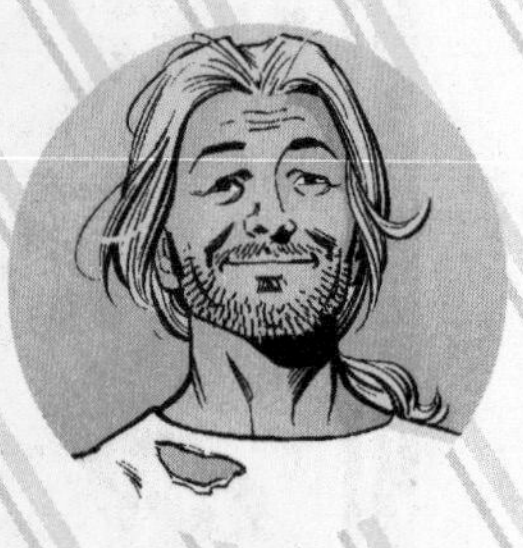

JACK
Also known as Little Jack Horner, Jack B. Nimble, Jack the Giant Killer and by countless other aliases, our hero Jack of the Tales embodies the archetype of the lovable rogue (minus, according to many, the lovability).

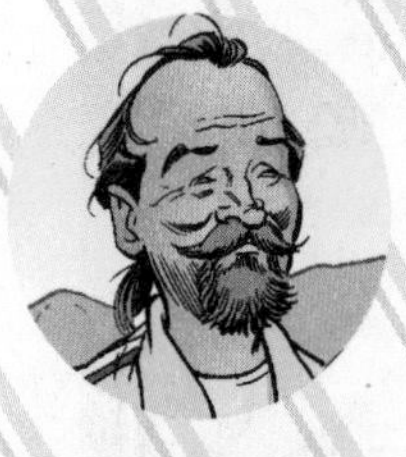

GARY, THE PATHETIC FALLACY
A timid, impressionable and warmhearted fellow whose power over inanimate objects is matched only by his love of Sousa marches.

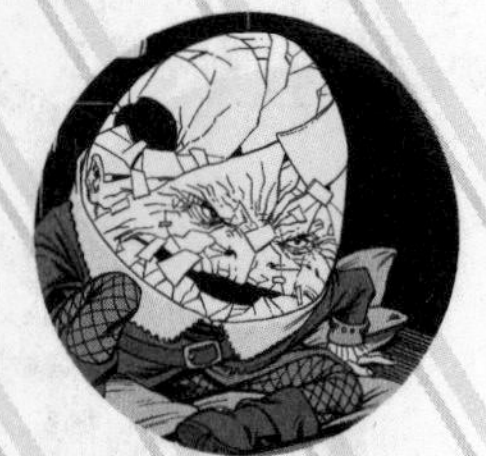

HUMPTY DUMPTY
A stout fellow from Colchester whose ferocious bark belies his brittle nature.

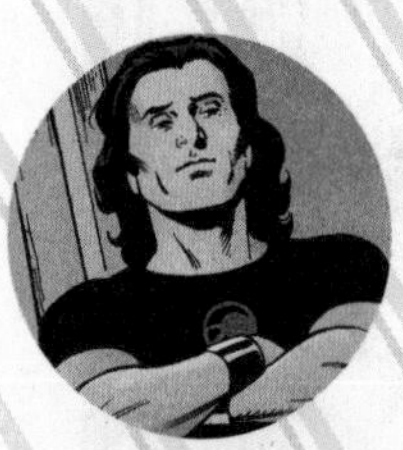

RAVEN
Jack's new Native American companion, blessed with a contrary nature and some surprising abilities.

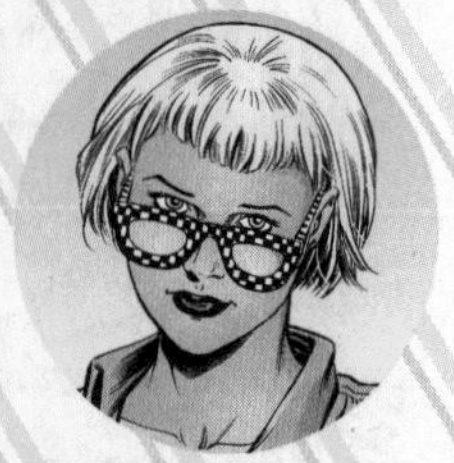

HILLARY PAGE
One of the three Page Sisters, chief librarians and enforcers for the sinister Golden Boughs Retirement Village run by Mr. Revise.

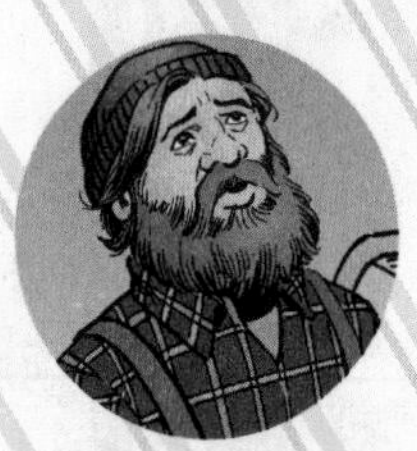

PAUL BUNYAN
A giant of American history, now living in reduced circumstances.

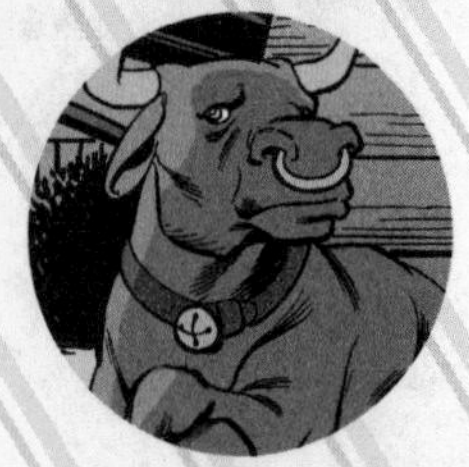

BABE
A blue ox with a rich interior life.

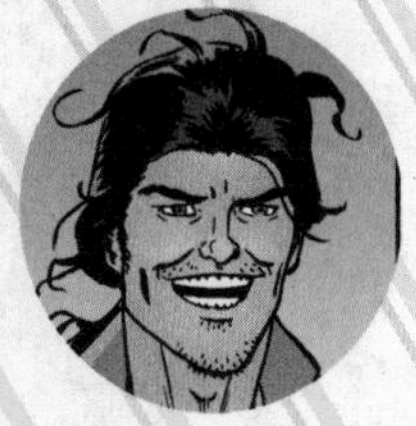

WICKED JOHN
Except for his dark hair, he's the spitting image of Jack — right down to the insufferable air of superiority.

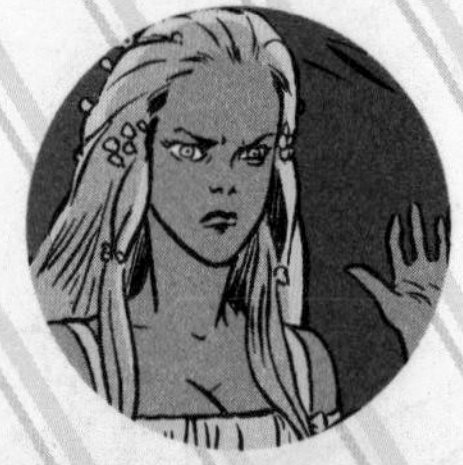

ALICE
A survivor of several adventures through a looking-glass.

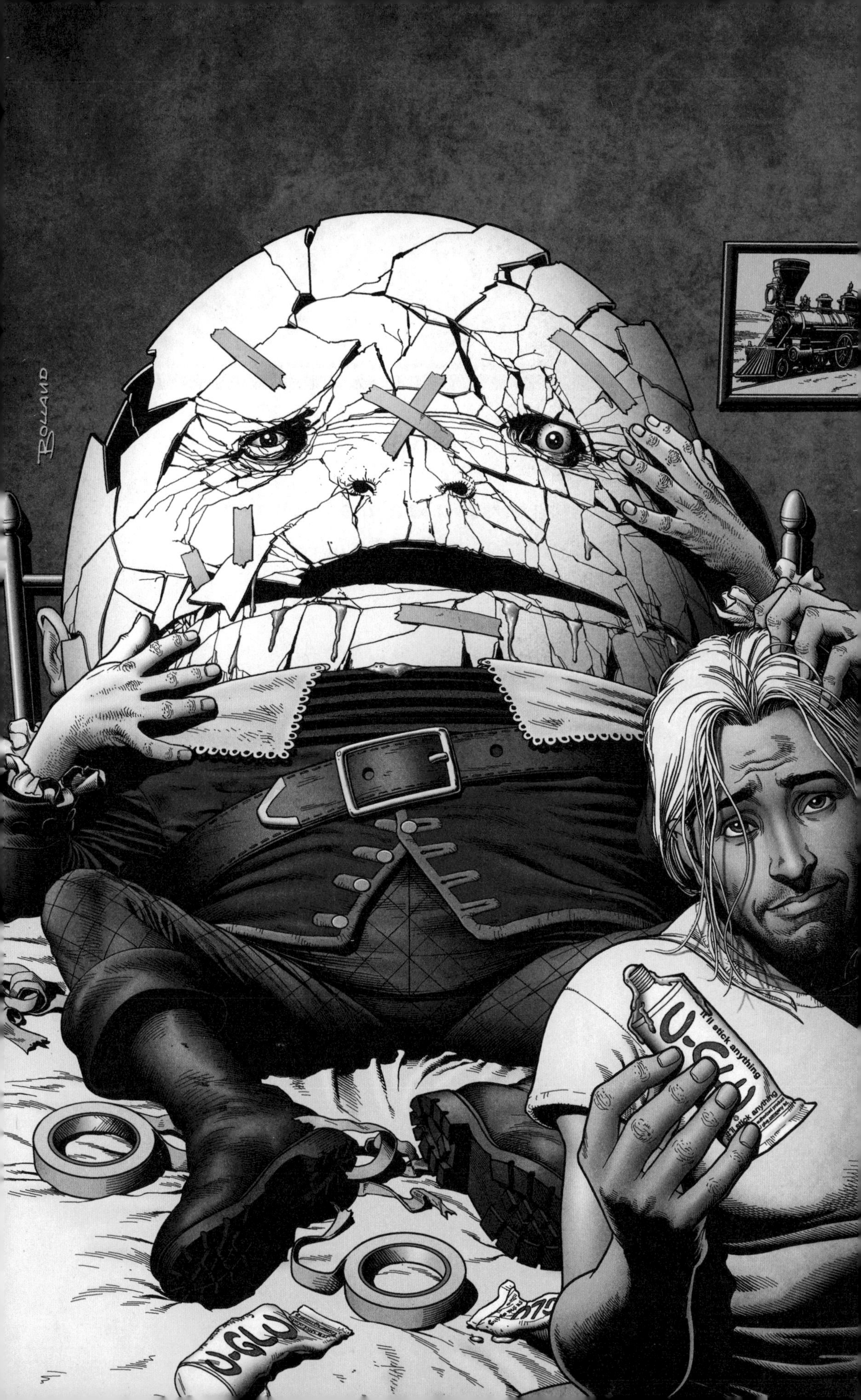
BOLLAND
It'll stick anything
It'll stick anything
U-GLU

*"All the king's horses and all the king's men
got nothin' on Jack of the Tales!"*

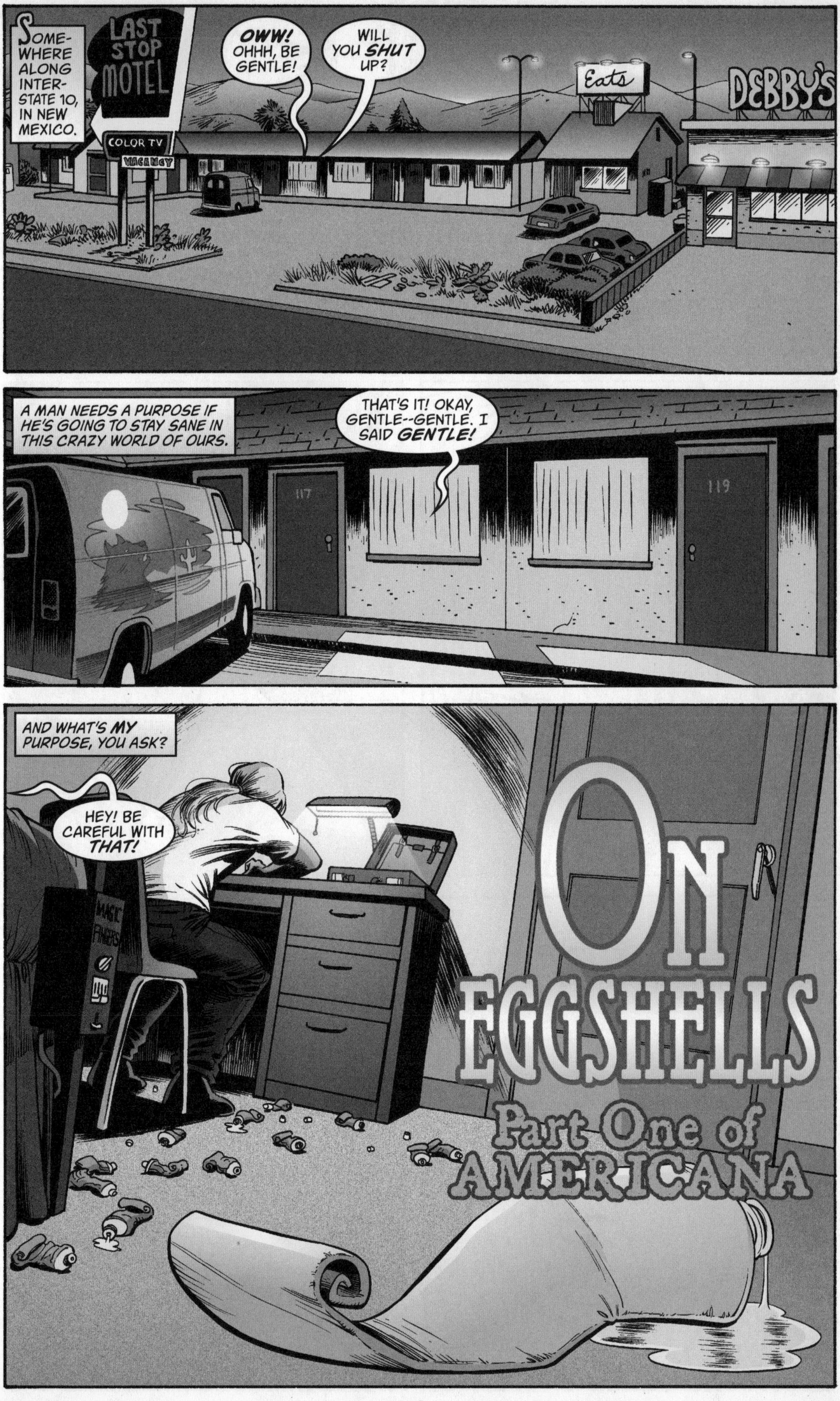
SOMEWHERE ALONG INTERSTATE 10, IN NEW MEXICO.
LAST STOP MOTEL
COLOR TV
VACANCY
OWW! OHHH, BE GENTLE!
WILL YOU SHUT UP?
Eats
DEBBY'S
A MAN NEEDS A PURPOSE IF HE'S GOING TO STAY SANE IN THIS CRAZY WORLD OF OURS.
THAT'S IT! OKAY, GENTLE--GENTLE. I SAID GENTLE!
117
119
AND WHAT'S MY PURPOSE, YOU ASK?
HEY! BE CAREFUL WITH THAT!
MAGIC FINGERS
ON EGGSHELLS
Part One of AMERICANA

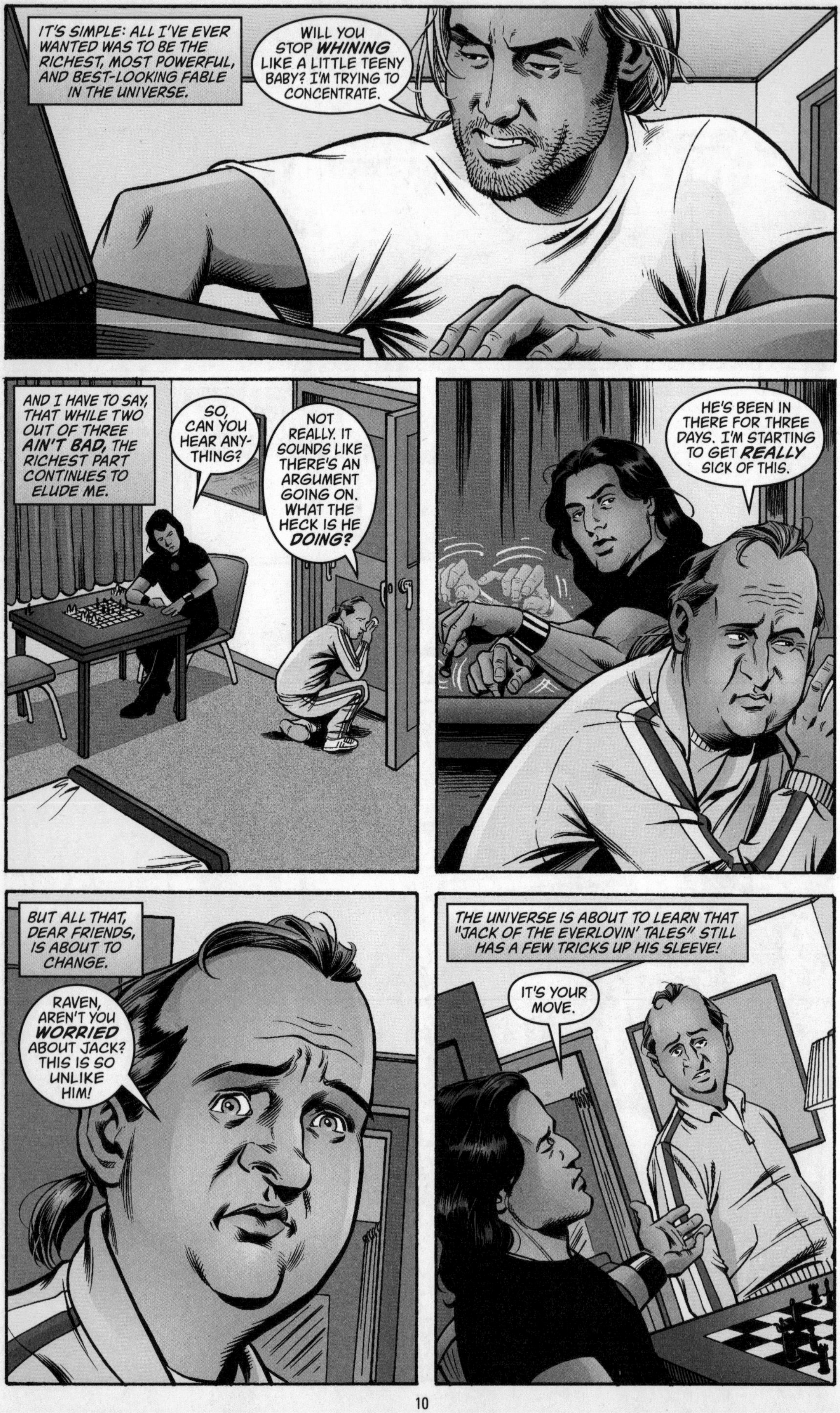
IT'S SIMPLE: ALL I'VE EVER WANTED WAS TO BE THE RICHEST, MOST POWERFUL, AND BEST-LOOKING FABLE IN THE UNIVERSE.
WILL YOU STOP WHINING LIKE A LITTLE TEENY BABY? I'M TRYING TO CONCENTRATE.
AND I HAVE TO SAY, THAT WHILE TWO OUT OF THREE AIN'T BAD, THE RICHEST PART CONTINUES TO ELUDE ME.
SO, CAN YOU HEAR ANY-THING?
NOT REALLY. IT SOUNDS LIKE THERE'S AN ARGUMENT GOING ON. WHAT THE HECK IS HE DOING?
HE'S BEEN IN THERE FOR THREE DAYS. I'M STARTING TO GET REALLY SICK OF THIS.
BUT ALL THAT, DEAR FRIENDS, IS ABOUT TO CHANGE.
RAVEN, AREN'T YOU WORRIED ABOUT JACK? THIS IS SO UNLIKE HIM!
THE UNIVERSE IS ABOUT TO LEARN THAT "JACK OF THE EVERLOVIN' TALES" STILL HAS A FEW TRICKS UP HIS SLEEVE!
IT'S YOUR MOVE.

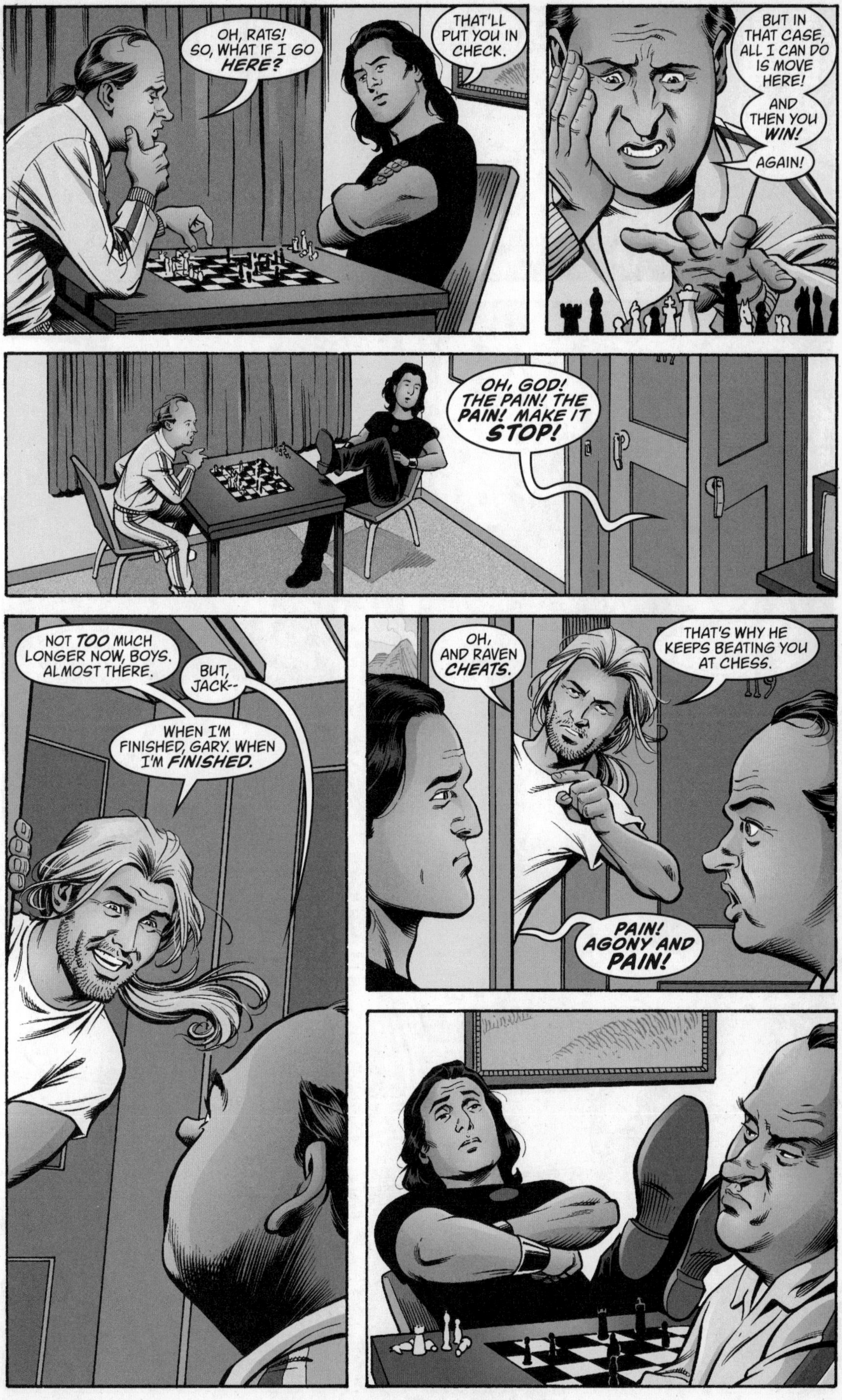
OH, RATS! SO, WHAT IF I GO HERE?
THAT'LL PUT YOU IN CHECK.
BUT IN THAT CASE, ALL I CAN DO IS MOVE HERE!
AND THEN YOU WIN!
AGAIN!
OH, GOD! THE PAIN! THE PAIN! MAKE IT STOP!
NOT TOO MUCH LONGER NOW, BOYS. ALMOST THERE.
BUT, JACK--
WHEN I'M FINISHED, GARY. WHEN I'M FINISHED.
OH, AND RAVEN CHEATS.
THAT'S WHY HE KEEPS BEATING YOU AT CHESS.
PAIN! AGONY AND PAIN!

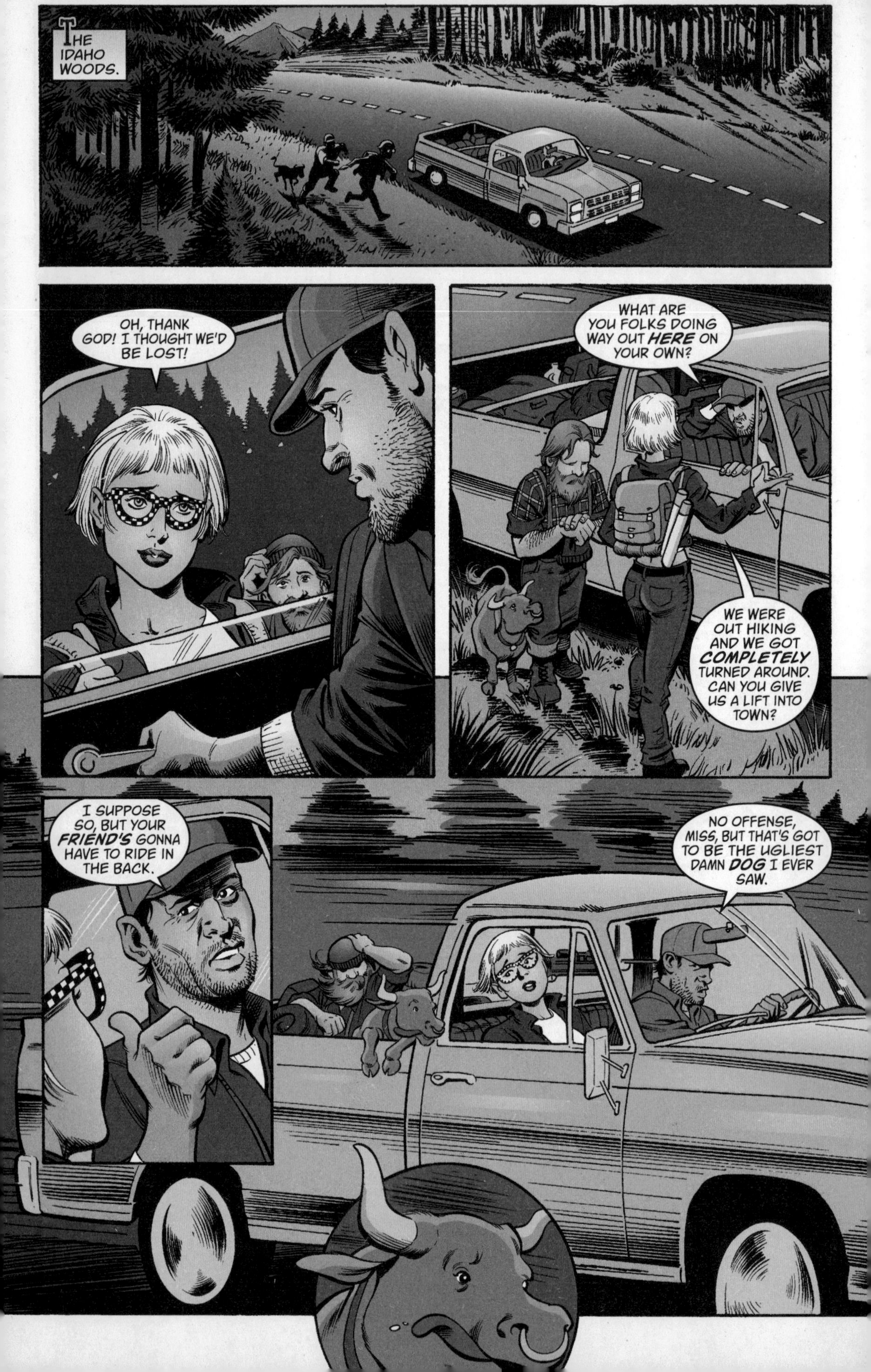
THE IDAHO WOODS.
OH, THANK GOD! I THOUGHT WE'D BE LOST!
WHAT ARE YOU FOLKS DOING WAY OUT HERE ON YOUR OWN?
WE WERE OUT HIKING AND WE GOT COMPLETELY TURNED AROUND. CAN YOU GIVE US A LIFT INTO TOWN?
I SUPPOSE SO, BUT YOUR FRIEND'S GONNA HAVE TO RIDE IN THE BACK.
NO OFFENSE, MISS, BUT THAT'S GOT TO BE THE UGLIEST DAMN DOG I EVER SAW.

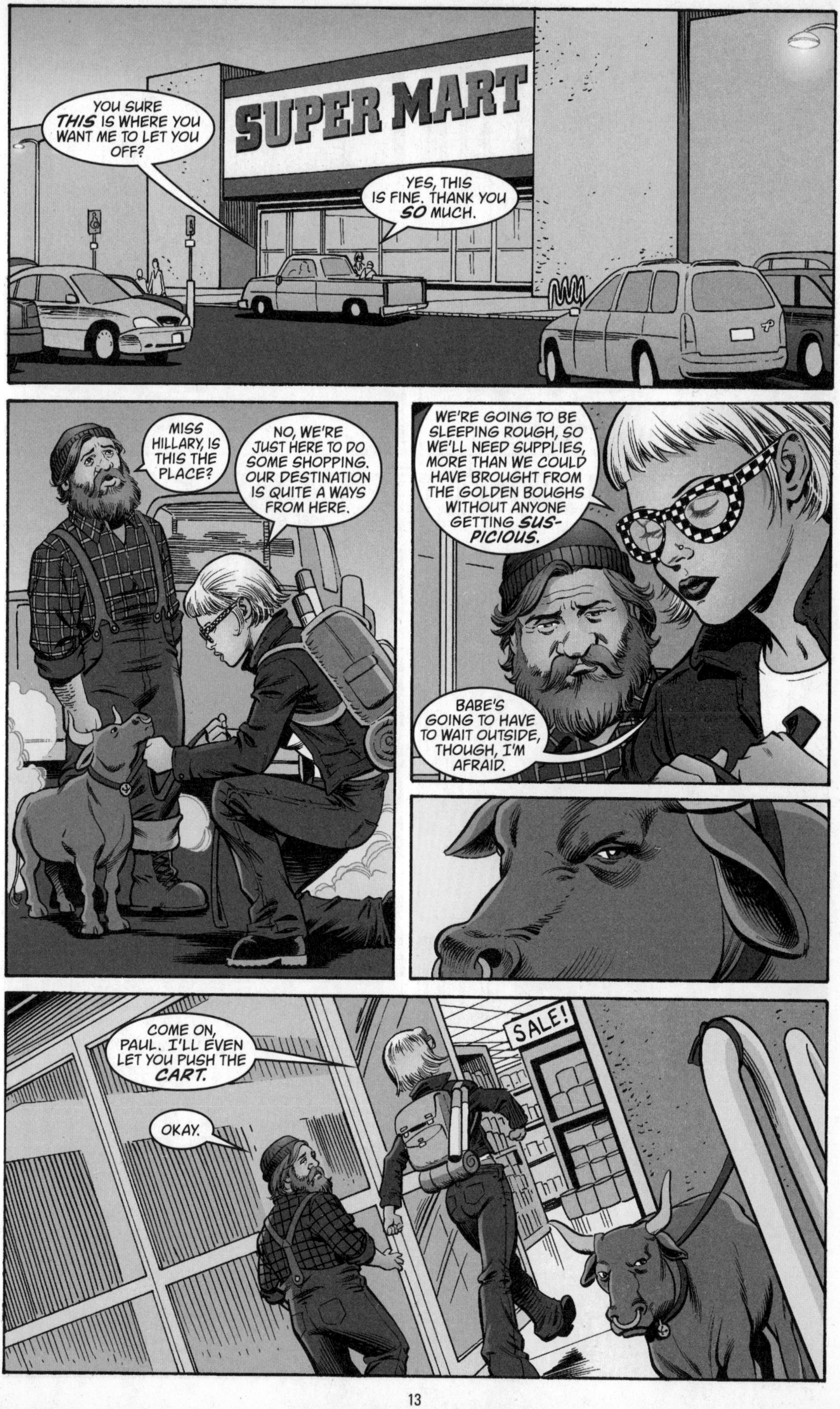
YOU SURE THIS IS WHERE YOU WANT ME TO LET YOU OFF?
SUPER MART
YES, THIS IS FINE. THANK YOU SO MUCH.
MISS HILLARY, IS THIS THE PLACE?
NO, WE'RE JUST HERE TO DO SOME SHOPPING. OUR DESTINATION IS QUITE A WAYS FROM HERE.
WE'RE GOING TO BE SLEEPING ROUGH, SO WE'LL NEED SUPPLIES, MORE THAN WE COULD HAVE BROUGHT FROM THE GOLDEN BOUGHS WITHOUT ANYONE GETTING SUS-PICIOUS.
BABE'S GOING TO HAVE TO WAIT OUTSIDE, THOUGH, I'M AFRAID.
COME ON, PAUL. I'LL EVEN LET YOU PUSH THE CART.
SALE!
OKAY.

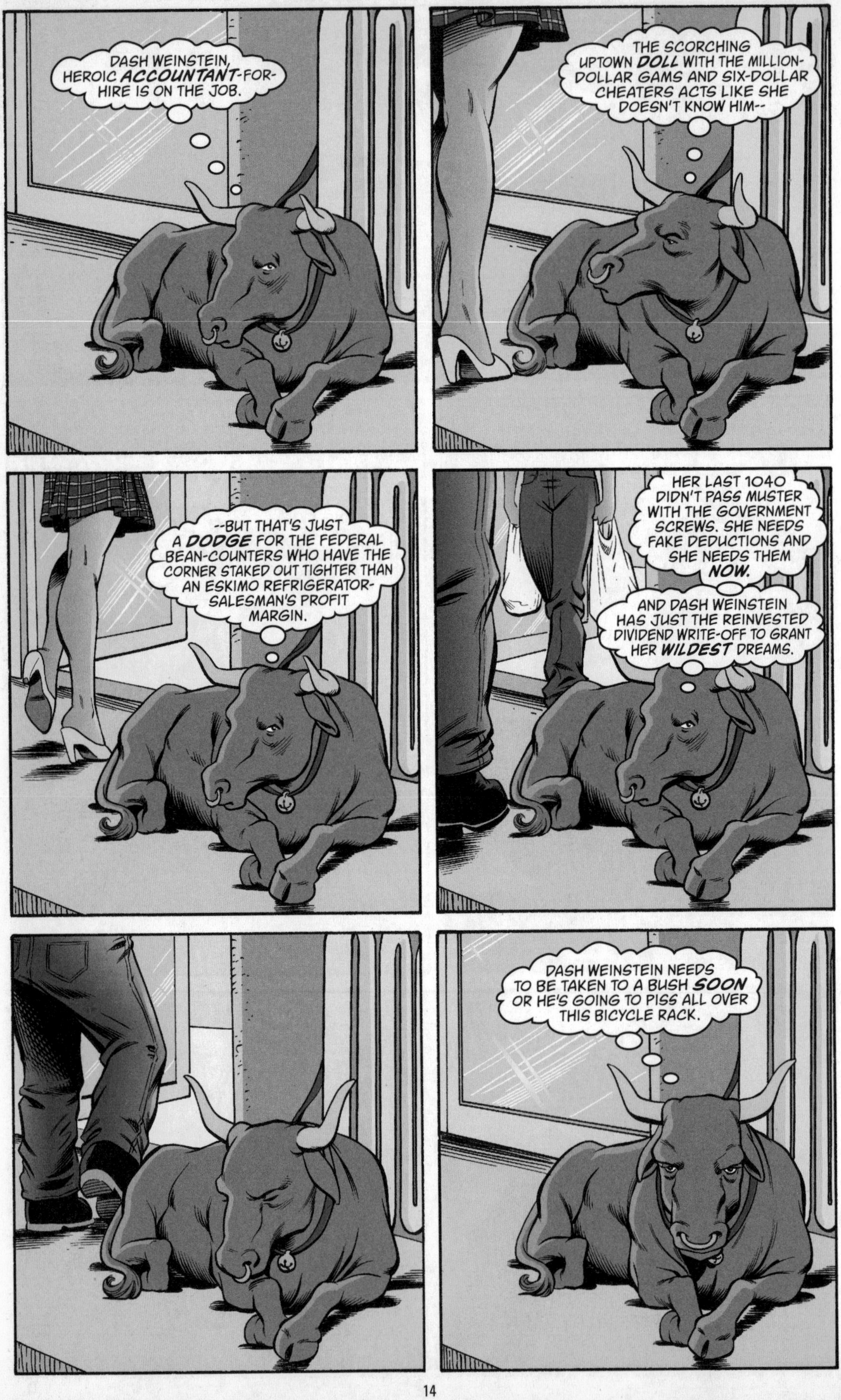
DASH WEINSTEIN, HEROIC ACCOUNTANT-FOR-HIRE IS ON THE JOB.
THE SCORCHING UPTOWN DOLL WITH THE MILLION-DOLLAR GAMS AND SIX-DOLLAR CHEATERS ACTS LIKE SHE DOESN'T KNOW HIM--
--BUT THAT'S JUST A DODGE FOR THE FEDERAL BEAN-COUNTERS WHO HAVE THE CORNER STAKED OUT TIGHTER THAN AN ESKIMO REFRIGERATOR-SALESMAN'S PROFIT MARGIN.
HER LAST 1040 DIDN'T PASS MUSTER WITH THE GOVERNMENT SCREWS. SHE NEEDS FAKE DEDUCTIONS AND SHE NEEDS THEM NOW.
AND DASH WEINSTEIN HAS JUST THE REINVESTED DIVIDEND WRITE-OFF TO GRANT HER WILDEST DREAMS.
DASH WEINSTEIN NEEDS TO BE TAKEN TO A BUSH SOON OR HE'S GOING TO PISS ALL OVER THIS BICYCLE RACK.

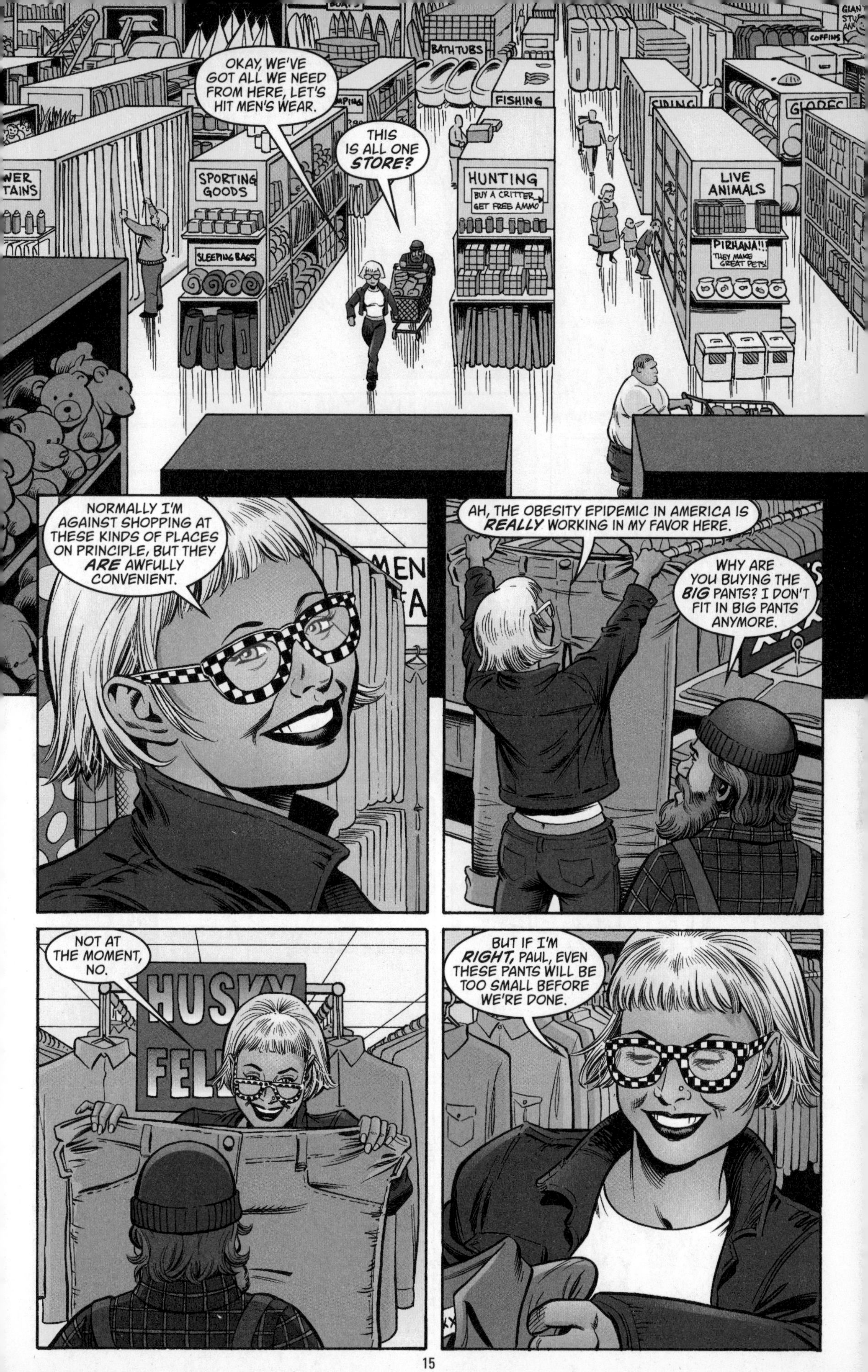
OKAY, WE'VE GOT ALL WE NEED FROM HERE, LET'S HIT MEN'S WEAR.
THIS IS ALL ONE STORE?
BATHTUBS
FISHING
SPORTING GOODS
SLEEPING BAGS
HUNTING
BUY A CRITTER GET FREE AMMO
LIVE ANIMALS
PIRHANA!! THEY MAKE GREAT PETS!
COFFINS
NORMALLY I'M AGAINST SHOPPING AT THESE KINDS OF PLACES ON PRINCIPLE, BUT THEY ARE AWFULLY CONVENIENT.
AH, THE OBESITY EPIDEMIC IN AMERICA IS REALLY WORKING IN MY FAVOR HERE.
WHY ARE YOU BUYING THE BIG PANTS? I DON'T FIT IN BIG PANTS ANYMORE.
NOT AT THE MOMENT, NO.
BUT IF I'M RIGHT, PAUL, EVEN THESE PANTS WILL BE TOO SMALL BEFORE WE'RE DONE.

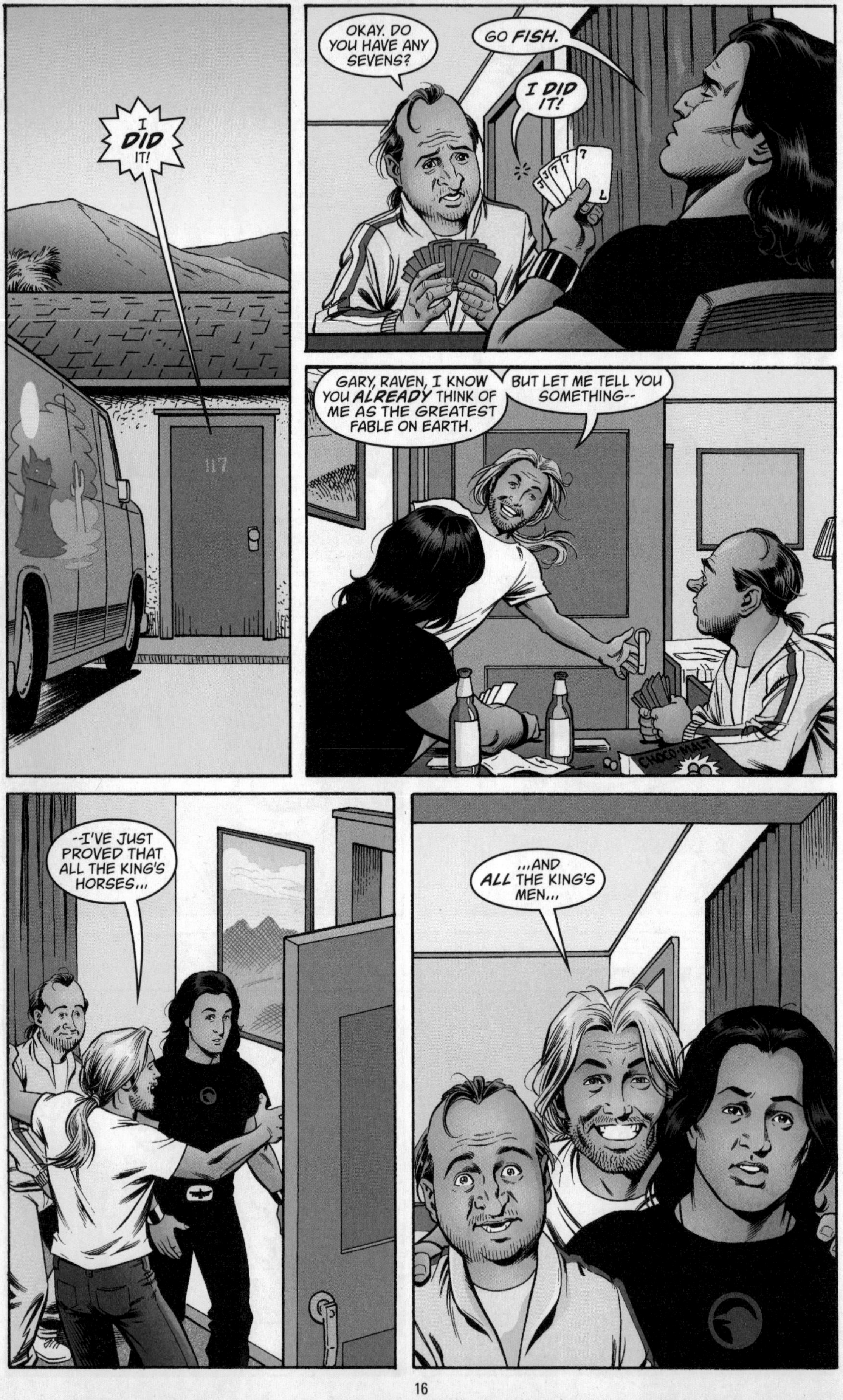
I DID IT!
OKAY. DO YOU HAVE ANY SEVENS?
GO FISH.
I DID IT!
GARY, RAVEN, I KNOW YOU ALREADY THINK OF ME AS THE GREATEST FABLE ON EARTH.
BUT LET ME TELL YOU SOMETHING--
CHOCO-MALT
--I'VE JUST PROVED THAT ALL THE KING'S HORSES...
...AND ALL THE KING'S MEN...

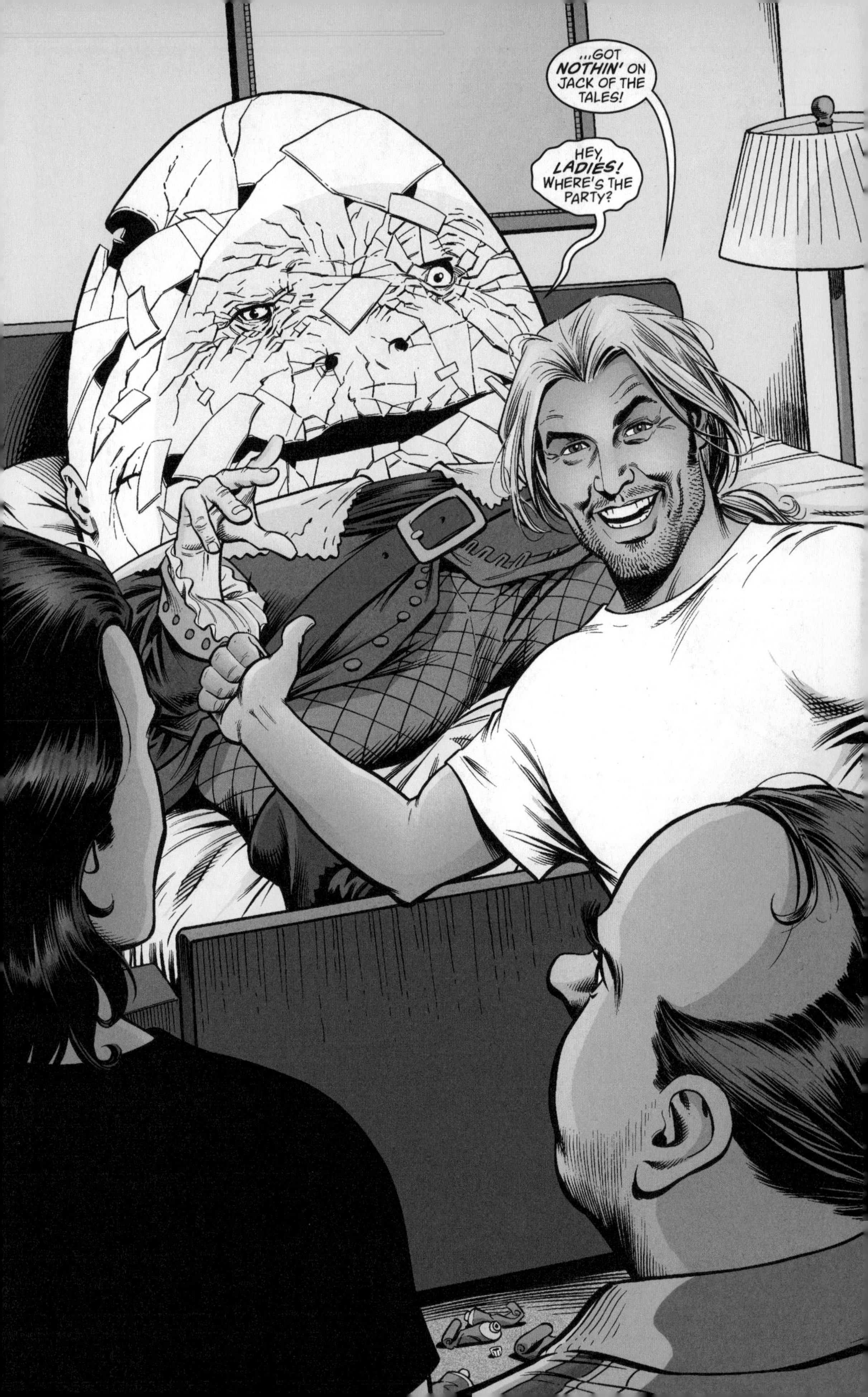
HEY, LADIES! WHERE'S THE PARTY?
...GOT NOTHIN' ON JACK OF THE TALES!

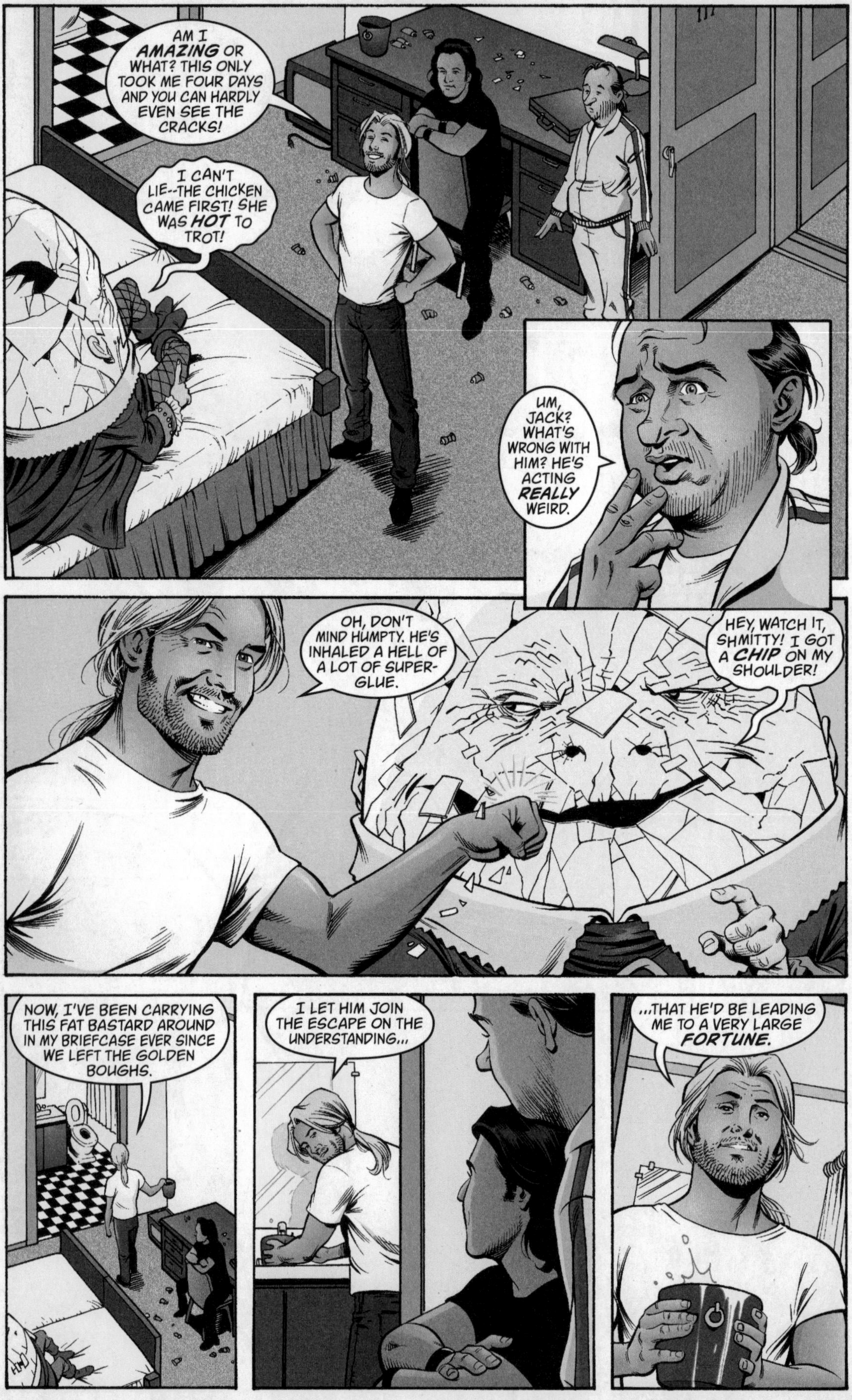
AM I AMAZING OR WHAT? THIS ONLY TOOK ME FOUR DAYS AND YOU CAN HARDLY EVEN SEE THE CRACKS!
I CAN'T LIE--THE CHICKEN CAME FIRST! SHE WAS HOT TO TROT!
UM, JACK? WHAT'S WRONG WITH HIM? HE'S ACTING REALLY WEIRD.
OH, DON'T MIND HUMPTY. HE'S INHALED A HELL OF A LOT OF SUPER-GLUE.
HEY, WATCH IT, SHMITTY! I GOT A CHIP ON MY SHOULDER!
NOW, I'VE BEEN CARRYING THIS FAT BASTARD AROUND IN MY BRIEFCASE EVER SINCE WE LEFT THE GOLDEN BOUGHS.
I LET HIM JOIN THE ESCAPE ON THE UNDERSTANDING...
...THAT HE'D BE LEADING ME TO A VERY LARGE FORTUNE.

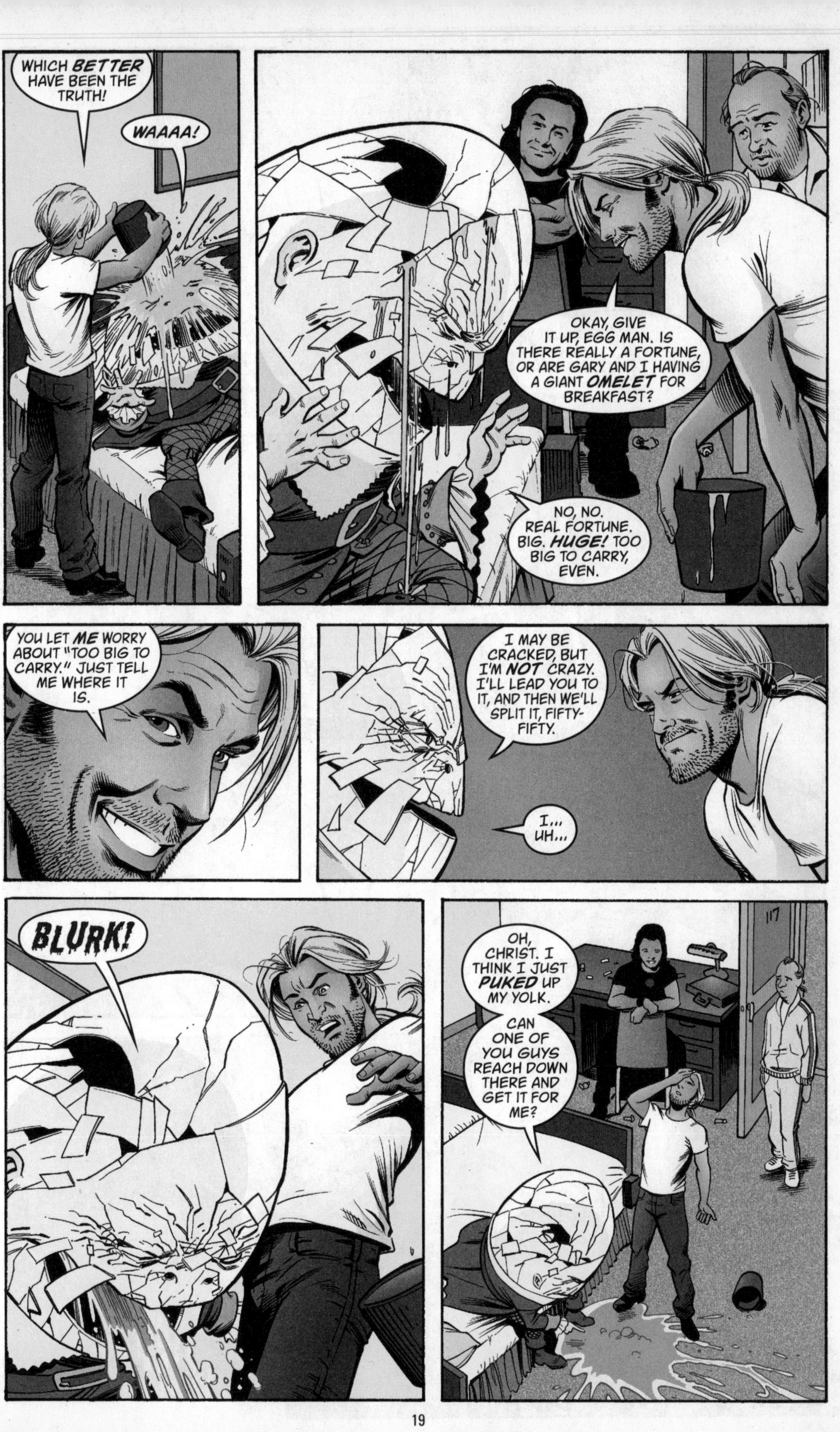
WHICH BETTER HAVE BEEN THE TRUTH!
WAAAA!
OKAY, GIVE IT UP, EGG MAN. IS THERE REALLY A FORTUNE, OR ARE GARY AND I HAVING A GIANT OMELET FOR BREAKFAST?
NO, NO. REAL FORTUNE. BIG. HUGE! TOO BIG TO CARRY, EVEN.
YOU LET ME WORRY ABOUT "TOO BIG TO CARRY." JUST TELL ME WHERE IT IS.
I MAY BE CRACKED, BUT I'M NOT CRAZY. I'LL LEAD YOU TO IT, AND THEN WE'LL SPLIT IT, FIFTY-FIFTY.
I... UH...
BLURK!
OH, CHRIST. I THINK I JUST PUKED UP MY YOLK.
CAN ONE OF YOU GUYS REACH DOWN THERE AND GET IT FOR ME?
117

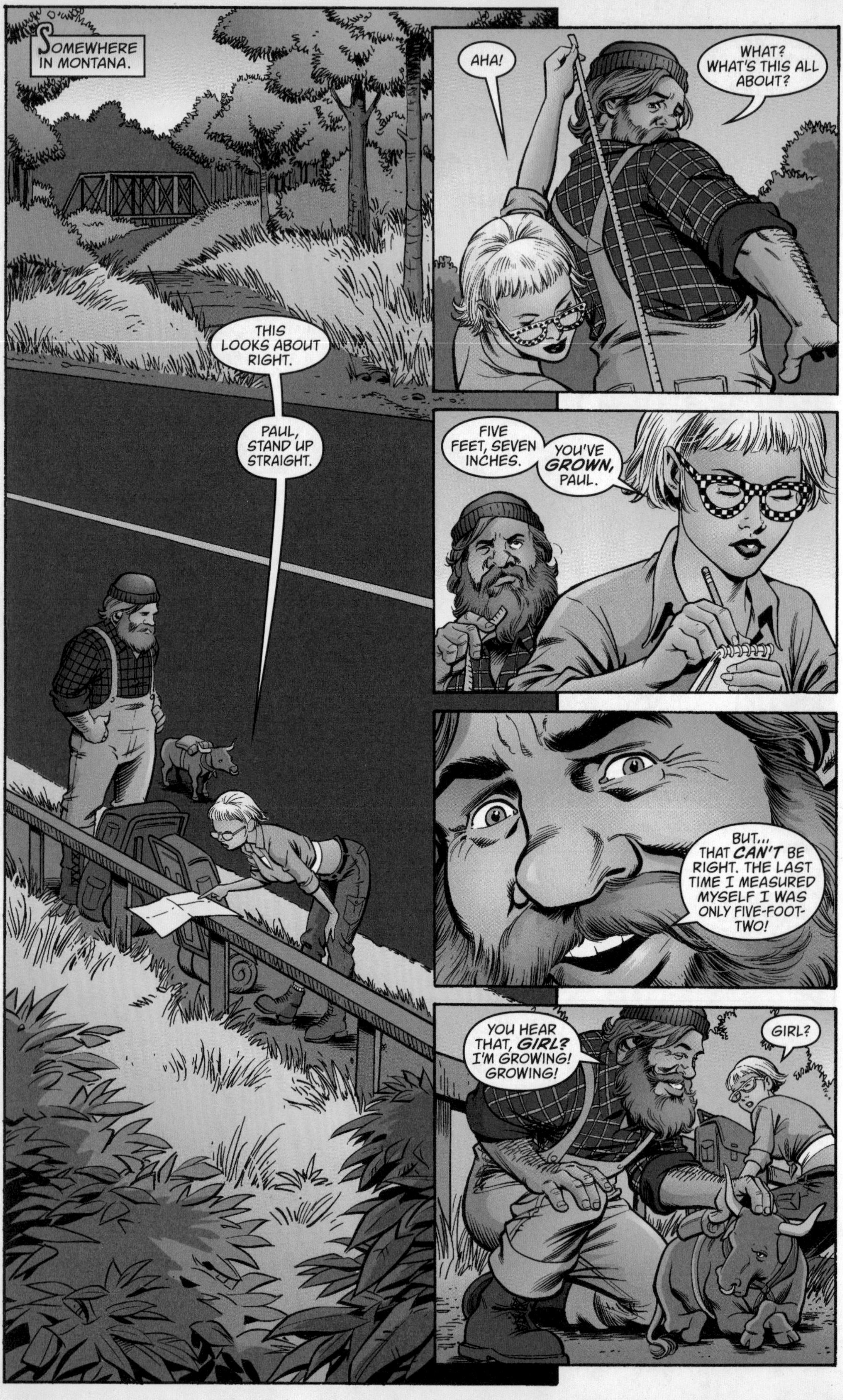
SOMEWHERE IN MONTANA.
THIS LOOKS ABOUT RIGHT.
PAUL, STAND UP STRAIGHT.
AHA!
WHAT? WHAT'S THIS ALL ABOUT?
FIVE FEET, SEVEN INCHES.
YOU'VE GROWN, PAUL.
BUT... THAT CAN'T BE RIGHT. THE LAST TIME I MEASURED MYSELF I WAS ONLY FIVE-FOOT-TWO!
YOU HEAR THAT, GIRL? I'M GROWING! GROWING!
GIRL?

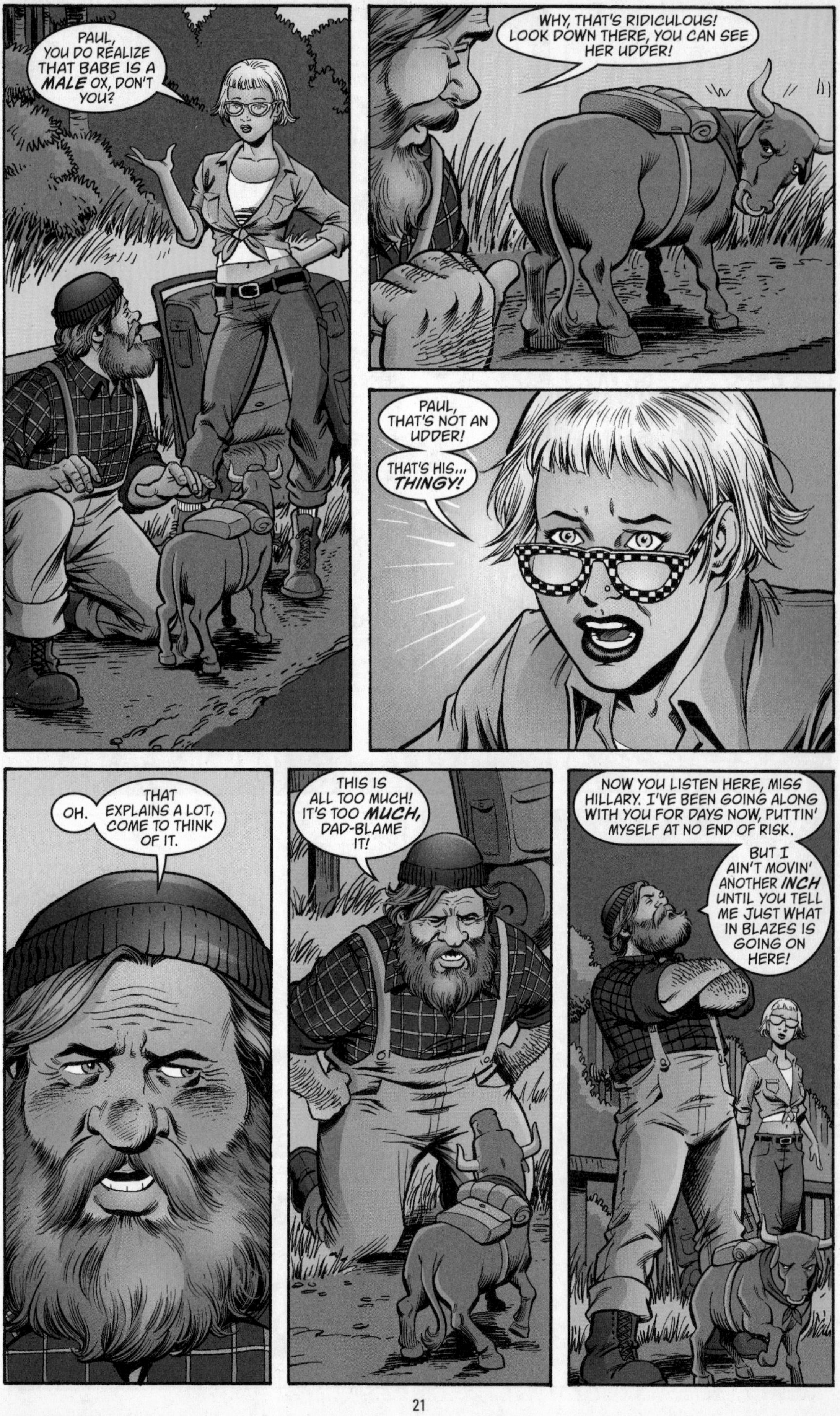
PAUL, YOU DO REALIZE THAT BABE IS A MALE OX, DON'T YOU?
WHY, THAT'S RIDICULOUS! LOOK DOWN THERE, YOU CAN SEE HER UDDER!
PAUL, THAT'S NOT AN UDDER!
THAT'S HIS... THINGY!
OH.
THAT EXPLAINS A LOT, COME TO THINK OF IT.
THIS IS ALL TOO MUCH! IT'S TOO MUCH, DAD-BLAME IT!
NOW YOU LISTEN HERE, MISS HILLARY. I'VE BEEN GOING ALONG WITH YOU FOR DAYS NOW, PUTTIN' MYSELF AT NO END OF RISK.
BUT I AIN'T MOVIN' ANOTHER INCH UNTIL YOU TELL ME JUST WHAT IN BLAZES IS GOING ON HERE!

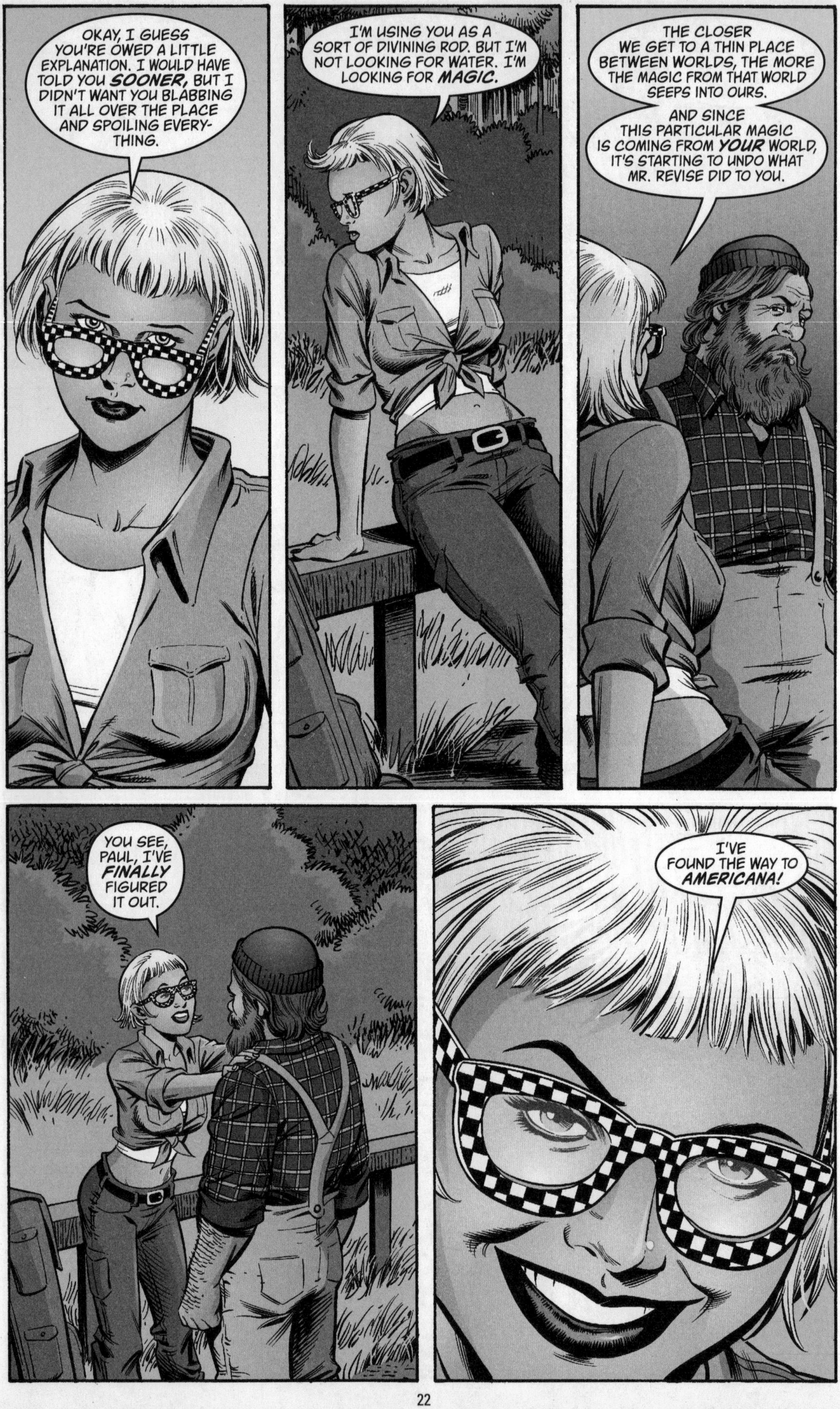
OKAY, I GUESS YOU'RE OWED A LITTLE EXPLANATION. I WOULD HAVE TOLD YOU SOONER, BUT I DIDN'T WANT YOU BLABBING IT ALL OVER THE PLACE AND SPOILING EVERY-THING.
I'M USING YOU AS A SORT OF DIVINING ROD. BUT I'M NOT LOOKING FOR WATER. I'M LOOKING FOR MAGIC.
THE CLOSER WE GET TO A THIN PLACE BETWEEN WORLDS, THE MORE THE MAGIC FROM THAT WORLD SEEPS INTO OURS.
AND SINCE THIS PARTICULAR MAGIC IS COMING FROM YOUR WORLD, IT'S STARTING TO UNDO WHAT MR. REVISE DID TO YOU.
YOU SEE, PAUL, I'VE FINALLY FIGURED IT OUT.
I'VE FOUND THE WAY TO AMERICANA!

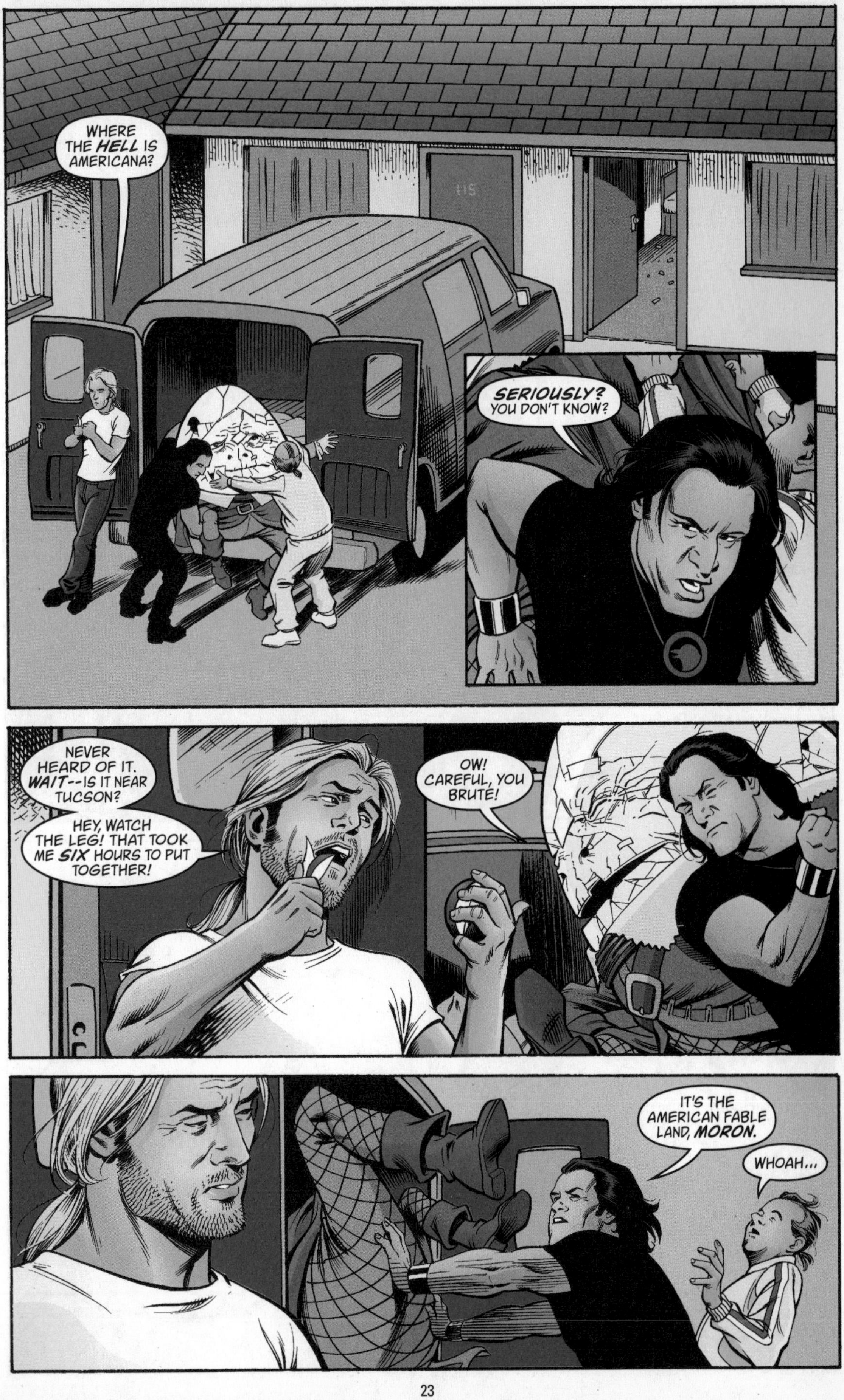
WHERE THE HELL IS AMERICANA?
SERIOUSLY? YOU DON'T KNOW?
NEVER HEARD OF IT. WAIT--IS IT NEAR TUCSON?
HEY, WATCH THE LEG! THAT TOOK ME SIX HOURS TO PUT TOGETHER!
OW! CAREFUL, YOU BRUTE!
IT'S THE AMERICAN FABLE LAND, MORON.
WHOAH...

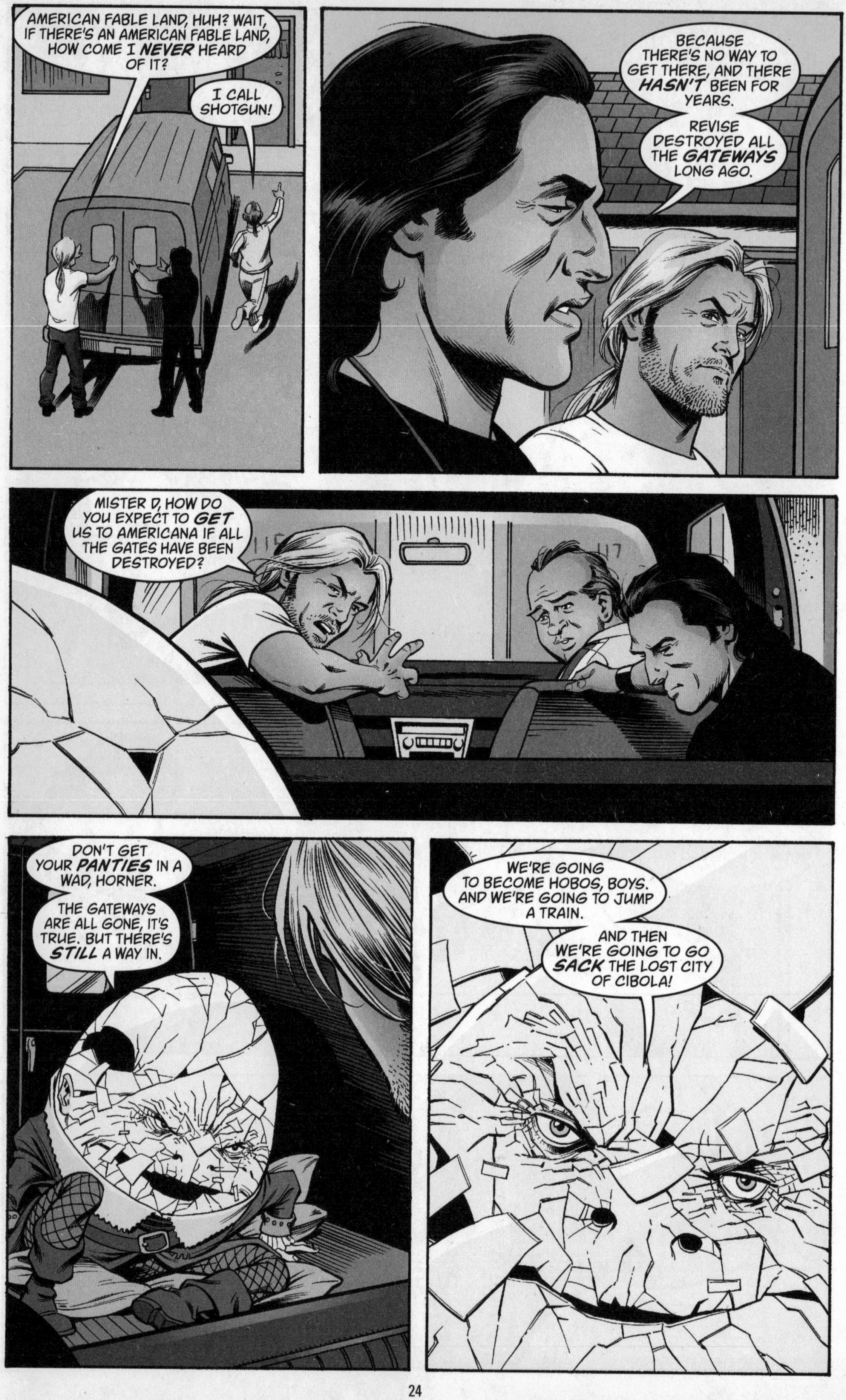

AMERICAN FABLE LAND, HUH? WAIT, IF THERE'S AN AMERICAN FABLE LAND, HOW COME I NEVER HEARD OF IT?
I CALL SHOTGUN!
BECAUSE THERE'S NO WAY TO GET THERE, AND THERE HASN'T BEEN FOR YEARS.
REVISE DESTROYED ALL THE GATEWAYS LONG AGO.
MISTER D, HOW DO YOU EXPECT TO GET US TO AMERICANA IF ALL THE GATES HAVE BEEN DESTROYED?
DON'T GET YOUR PANTIES IN A WAD, HORNER.
THE GATEWAYS ARE ALL GONE, IT'S TRUE. BUT THERE'S STILL A WAY IN.
WE'RE GOING TO BECOME HOBOS, BOYS. AND WE'RE GOING TO JUMP A TRAIN.
AND THEN WE'RE GOING TO GO SACK THE LOST CITY OF CIBOLA!

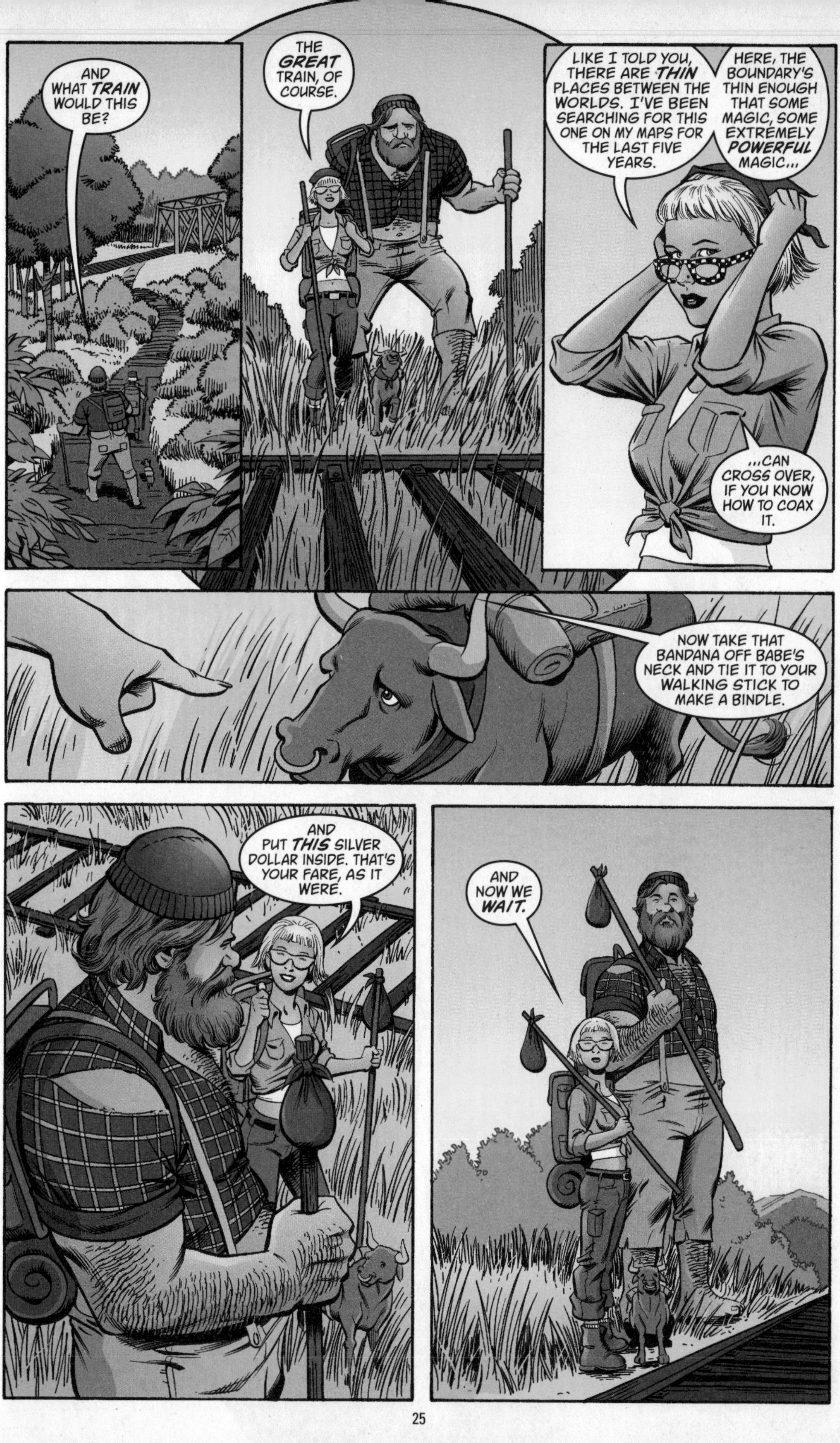
AND WHAT TRAIN WOULD THIS BE?
THE GREAT TRAIN, OF COURSE.
LIKE I TOLD YOU, THERE ARE THIN PLACES BETWEEN THE WORLDS. I'VE BEEN SEARCHING FOR THIS ONE ON MY MAPS FOR THE LAST FIVE YEARS.
HERE, THE BOUNDARY'S THIN ENOUGH THAT SOME MAGIC, SOME EXTREMELY POWERFUL MAGIC...
...CAN CROSS OVER, IF YOU KNOW HOW TO COAX IT.
NOW TAKE THAT BANDANA OFF BABE'S NECK AND TIE IT TO YOUR WALKING STICK TO MAKE A BINDLE.
AND PUT THIS SILVER DOLLAR INSIDE. THAT'S YOUR FARE, AS IT WERE.
AND NOW WE WAIT.

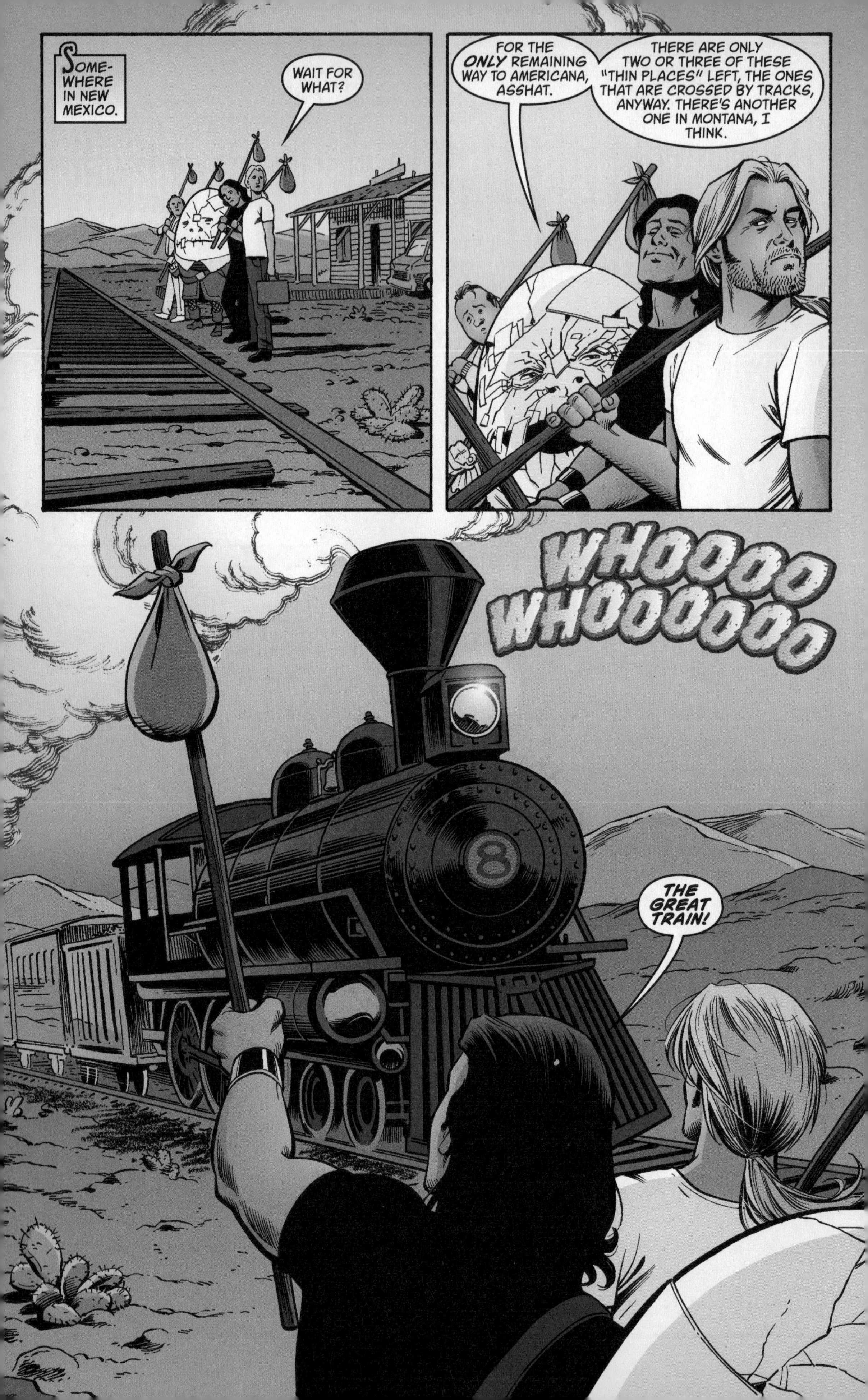
SOMEWHERE IN NEW MEXICO.
WAIT FOR WHAT?
FOR THE ONLY REMAINING WAY TO AMERICANA, ASSHAT.
THERE ARE ONLY TWO OR THREE OF THESE "THIN PLACES" LEFT, THE ONES THAT ARE CROSSED BY TRACKS, ANYWAY. THERE'S ANOTHER ONE IN MONTANA, I THINK.
WHOOOO WHOOOOOOO
THE GREAT TRAIN!

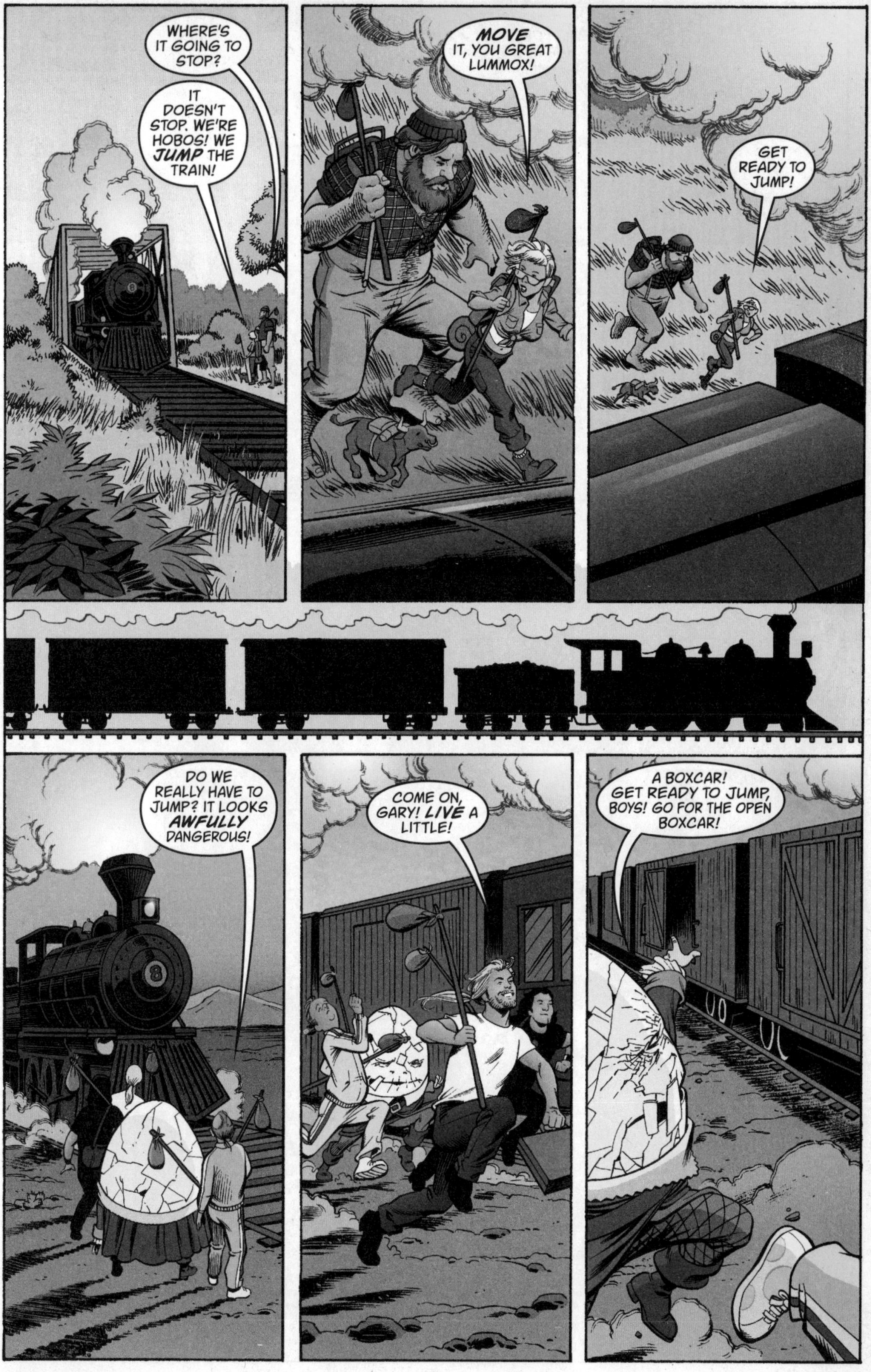
WHERE'S IT GOING TO STOP?
IT DOESN'T STOP. WE'RE HOBOS! WE JUMP THE TRAIN!
MOVE IT, YOU GREAT LUMMOX!
GET READY TO JUMP!
DO WE REALLY HAVE TO JUMP? IT LOOKS AWFULLY DANGEROUS!
COME ON, GARY! LIVE A LITTLE!
A BOXCAR! GET READY TO JUMP, BOYS! GO FOR THE OPEN BOXCAR!

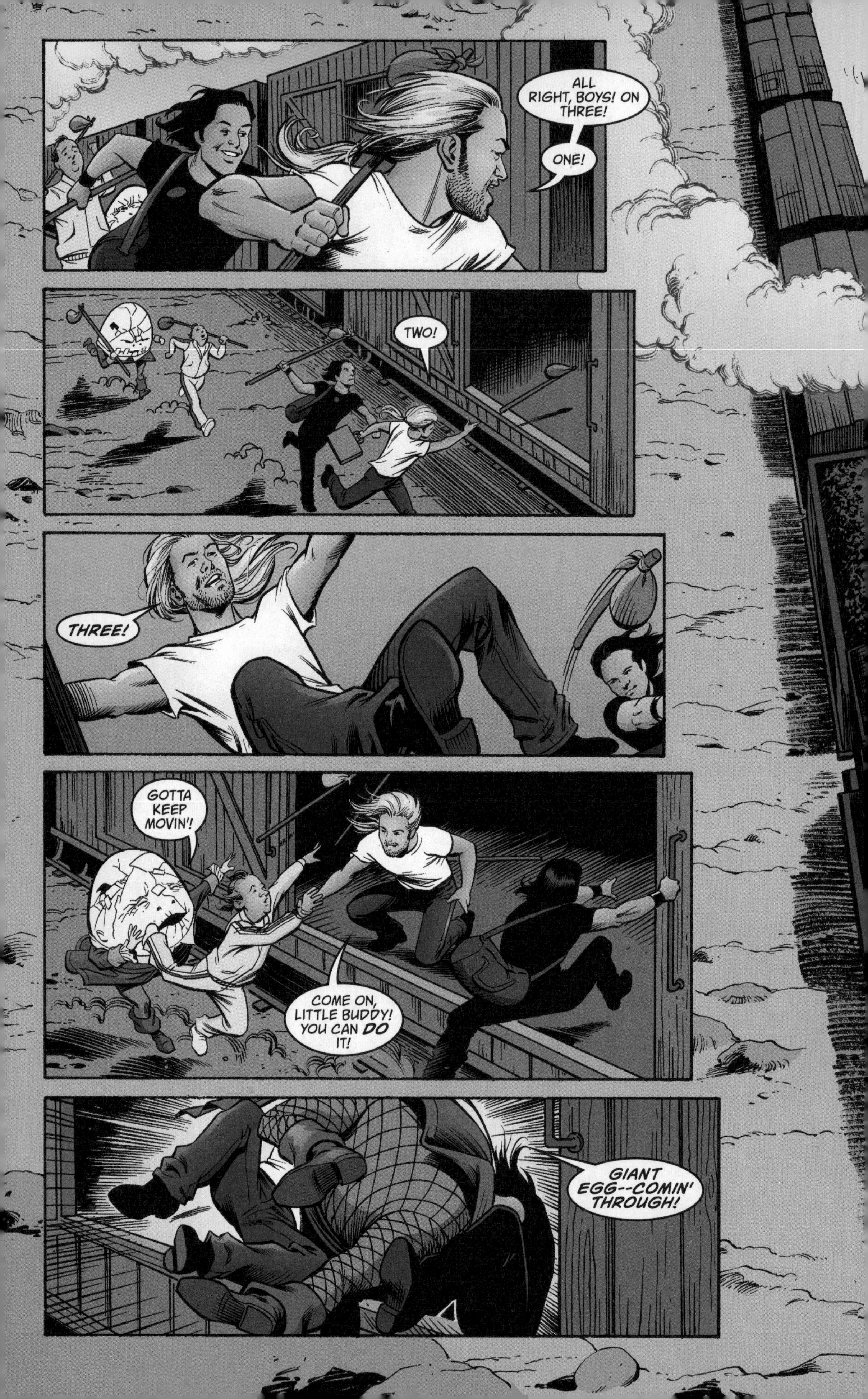
ALL RIGHT, BOYS! ON THREE!
ONE!
TWO!
THREE!
GOTTA KEEP MOVIN'!
COME ON, LITTLE BUDDY! YOU CAN DO IT!
GIANT EGG--COMIN' THROUGH!

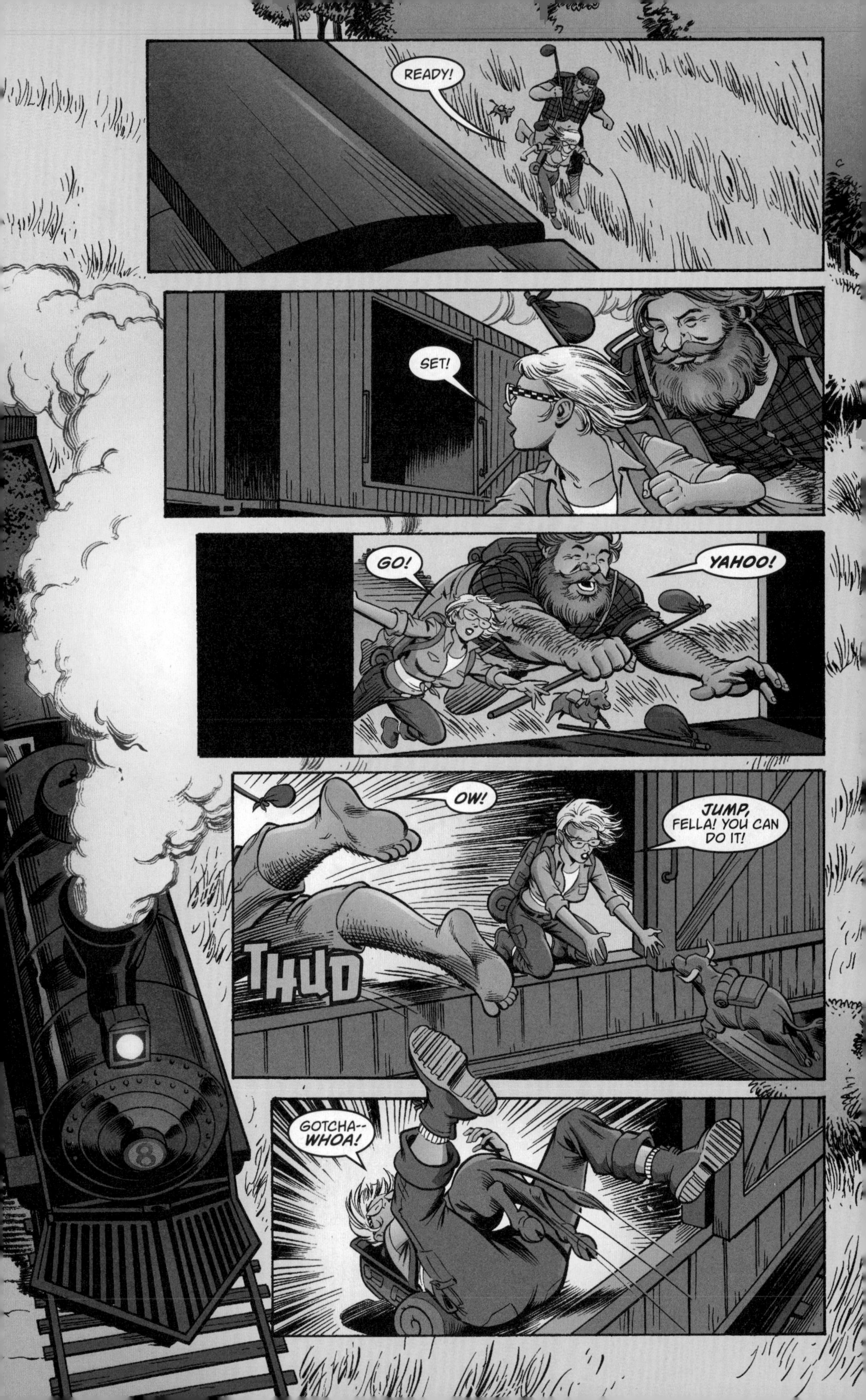
READY!
SET!
GO!
YAHOO!
OW!
JUMP, FELLA! YOU CAN DO IT!
THUD
GOTCHA-- WHOA!

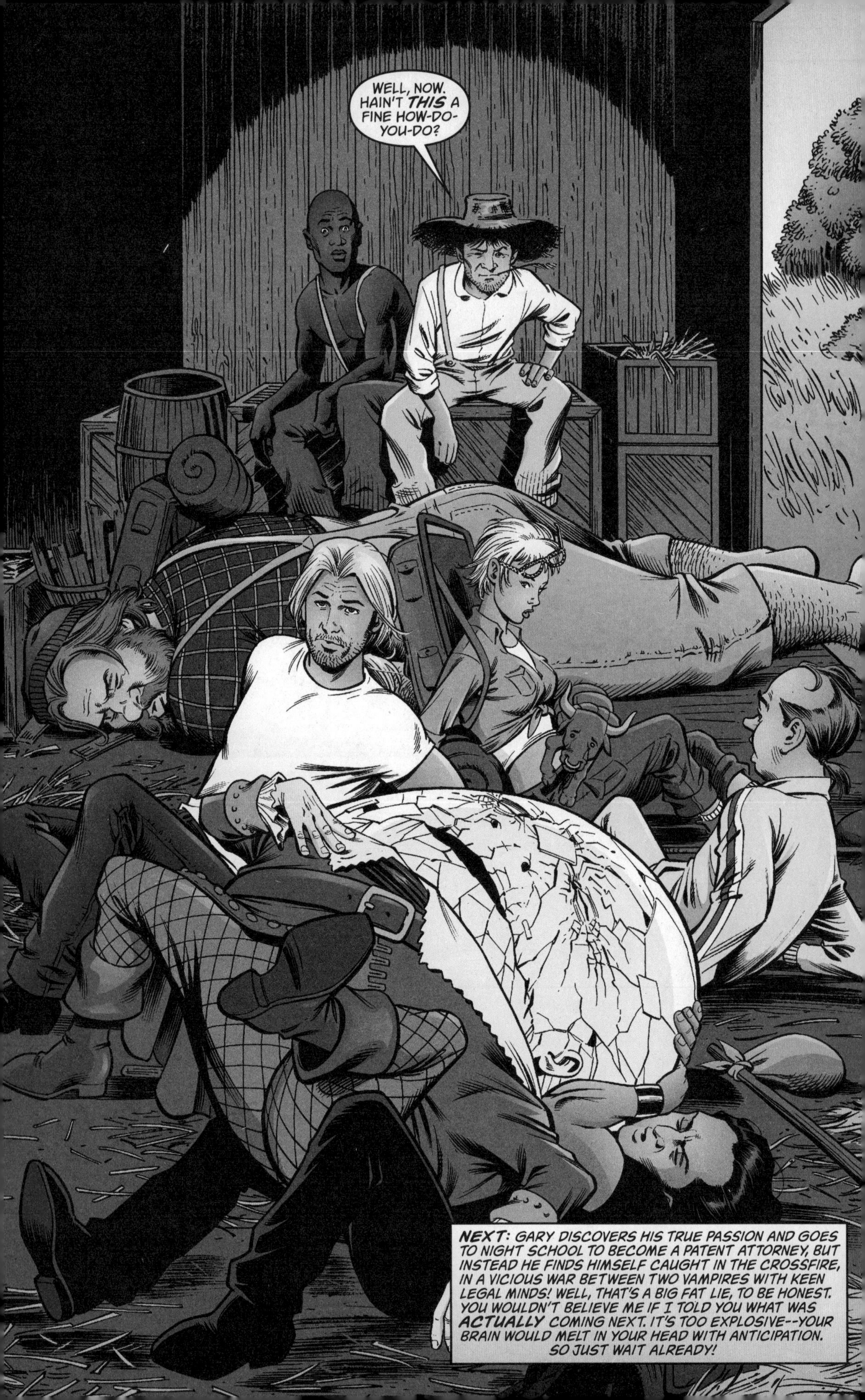
WELL, NOW. HAIN'T THIS A FINE HOW-DO-YOU-DO?
NEXT: GARY DISCOVERS HIS TRUE PASSION AND GOES TO NIGHT SCHOOL TO BECOME A PATENT ATTORNEY, BUT INSTEAD HE FINDS HIMSELF CAUGHT IN THE CROSSFIRE, IN A VICIOUS WAR BETWEEN TWO VAMPIRES WITH KEEN LEGAL MINDS! WELL, THAT'S A BIG FAT LIE, TO BE HONEST. YOU WOULDN'T BELIEVE ME IF I TOLD YOU WHAT WAS ACTUALLY COMING NEXT. IT'S TOO EXPLOSIVE--YOUR BRAIN WOULD MELT IN YOUR HEAD WITH ANTICIPATION. SO JUST WAIT ALREADY!

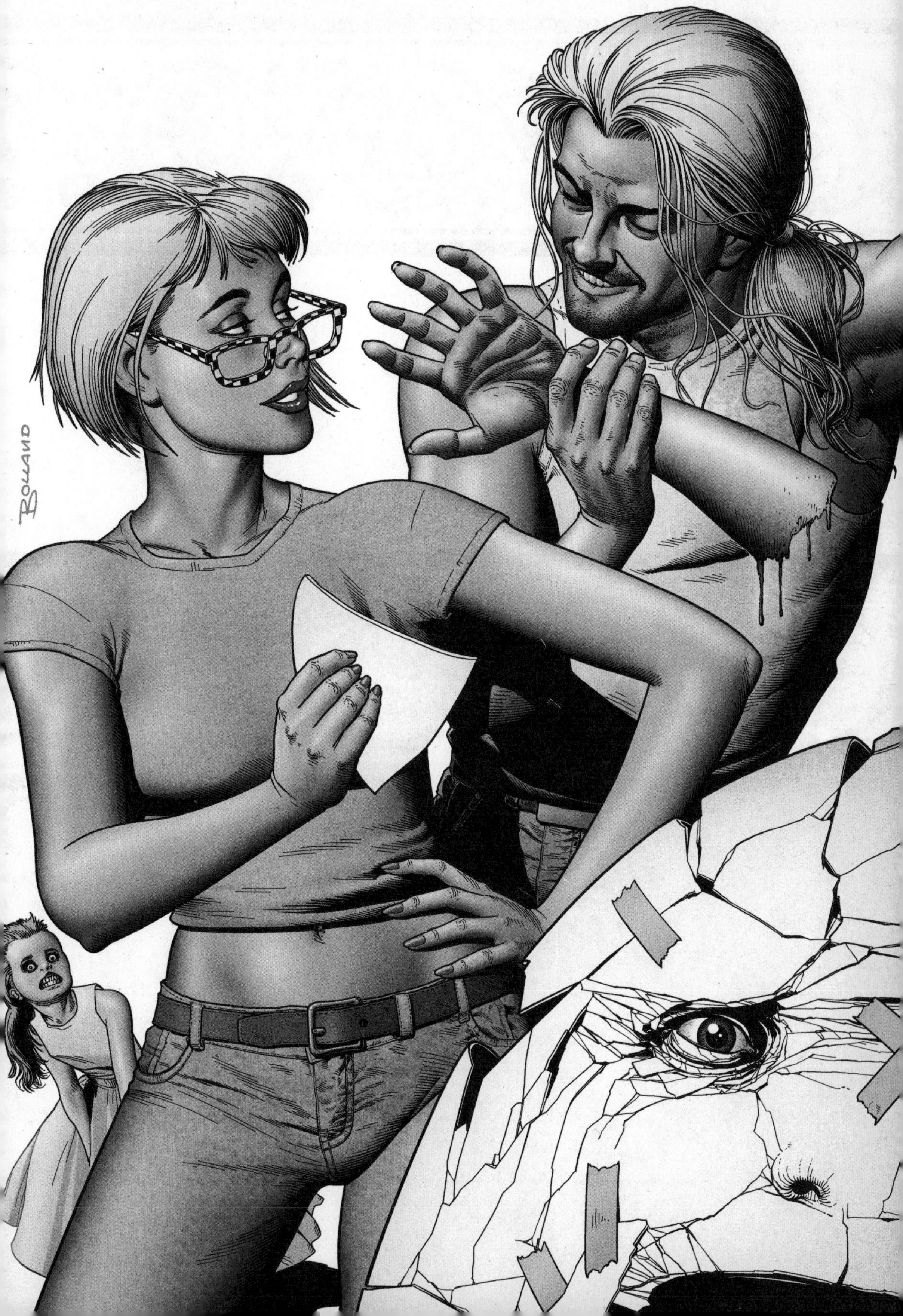
BOLLAND

*"For the eleventieth time, would you mind explaining this **detour**, and why we're taking it instead of going after my **riches**?"*

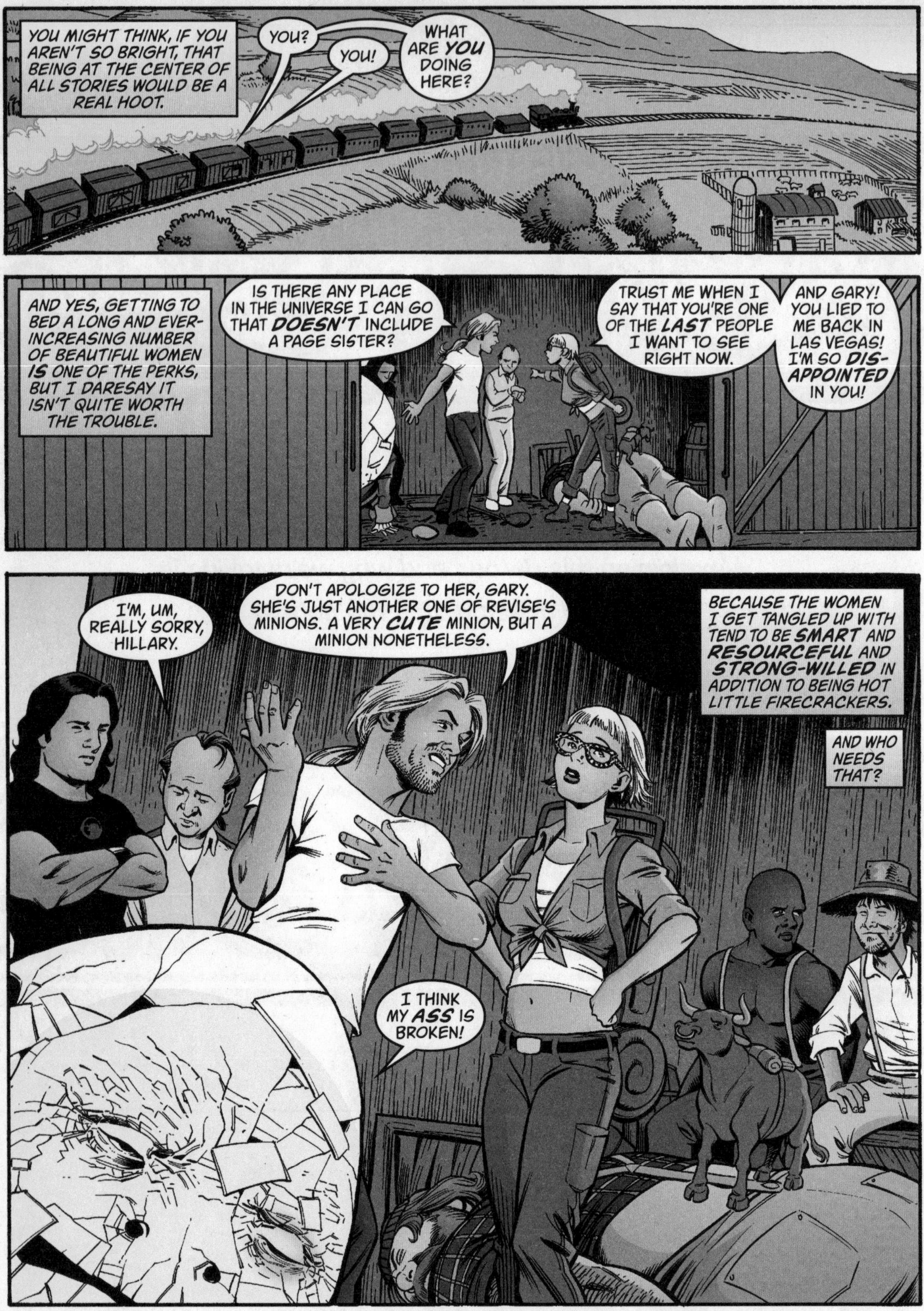
YOU MIGHT THINK, IF YOU AREN'T SO BRIGHT, THAT BEING AT THE CENTER OF ALL STORIES WOULD BE A REAL HOOT.
YOU?
YOU!
WHAT ARE YOU DOING HERE?
AND YES, GETTING TO BED A LONG AND EVER-INCREASING NUMBER OF BEAUTIFUL WOMEN IS ONE OF THE PERKS, BUT I DARESAY IT ISN'T QUITE WORTH THE TROUBLE.
IS THERE ANY PLACE IN THE UNIVERSE I CAN GO THAT DOESN'T INCLUDE A PAGE SISTER?
TRUST ME WHEN I SAY THAT YOU'RE ONE OF THE LAST PEOPLE I WANT TO SEE RIGHT NOW.
AND GARY! YOU LIED TO ME BACK IN LAS VEGAS! I'M SO DIS-APPOINTED IN YOU!
I'M, UM, REALLY SORRY, HILLARY.
DON'T APOLOGIZE TO HER, GARY. SHE'S JUST ANOTHER ONE OF REVISE'S MINIONS. A VERY CUTE MINION, BUT A MINION NONETHELESS.
BECAUSE THE WOMEN I GET TANGLED UP WITH TEND TO BE SMART AND RESOURCEFUL AND STRONG-WILLED IN ADDITION TO BEING HOT LITTLE FIRECRACKERS.
AND WHO NEEDS THAT?
I THINK MY ASS IS BROKEN!

WELCOME TO AMERICANA—MIND THE ZOMBIES

Part Two of AMERICANA

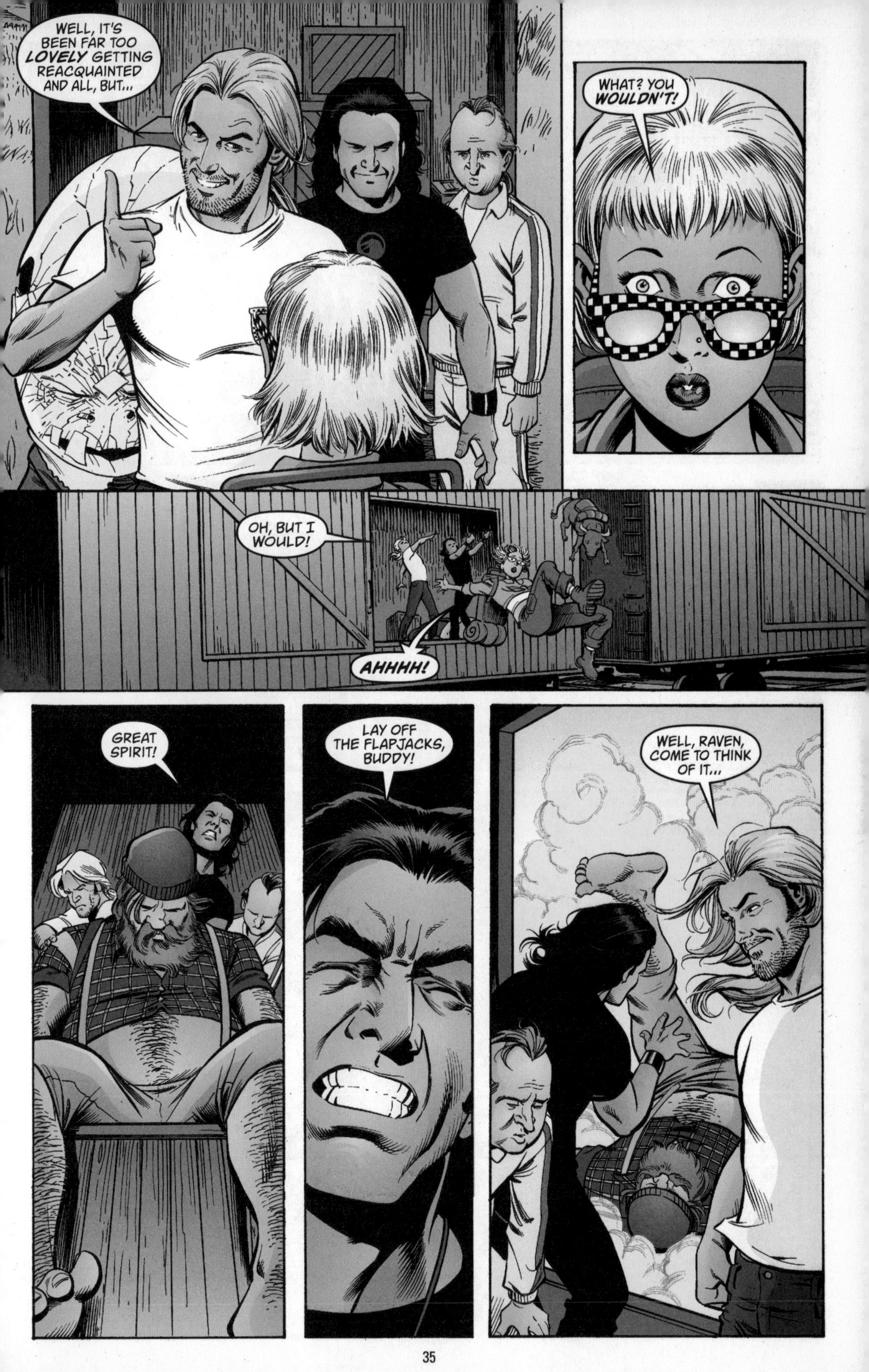
WELL, IT'S BEEN FAR TOO LOVELY GETTING REACQUAINTED AND ALL, BUT...
WHAT? YOU WOULDN'T!
OH, BUT I WOULD!
AHHHH!
GREAT SPIRIT!
LAY OFF THE FLAPJACKS, BUDDY!
WELL, RAVEN, COME TO THINK OF IT...

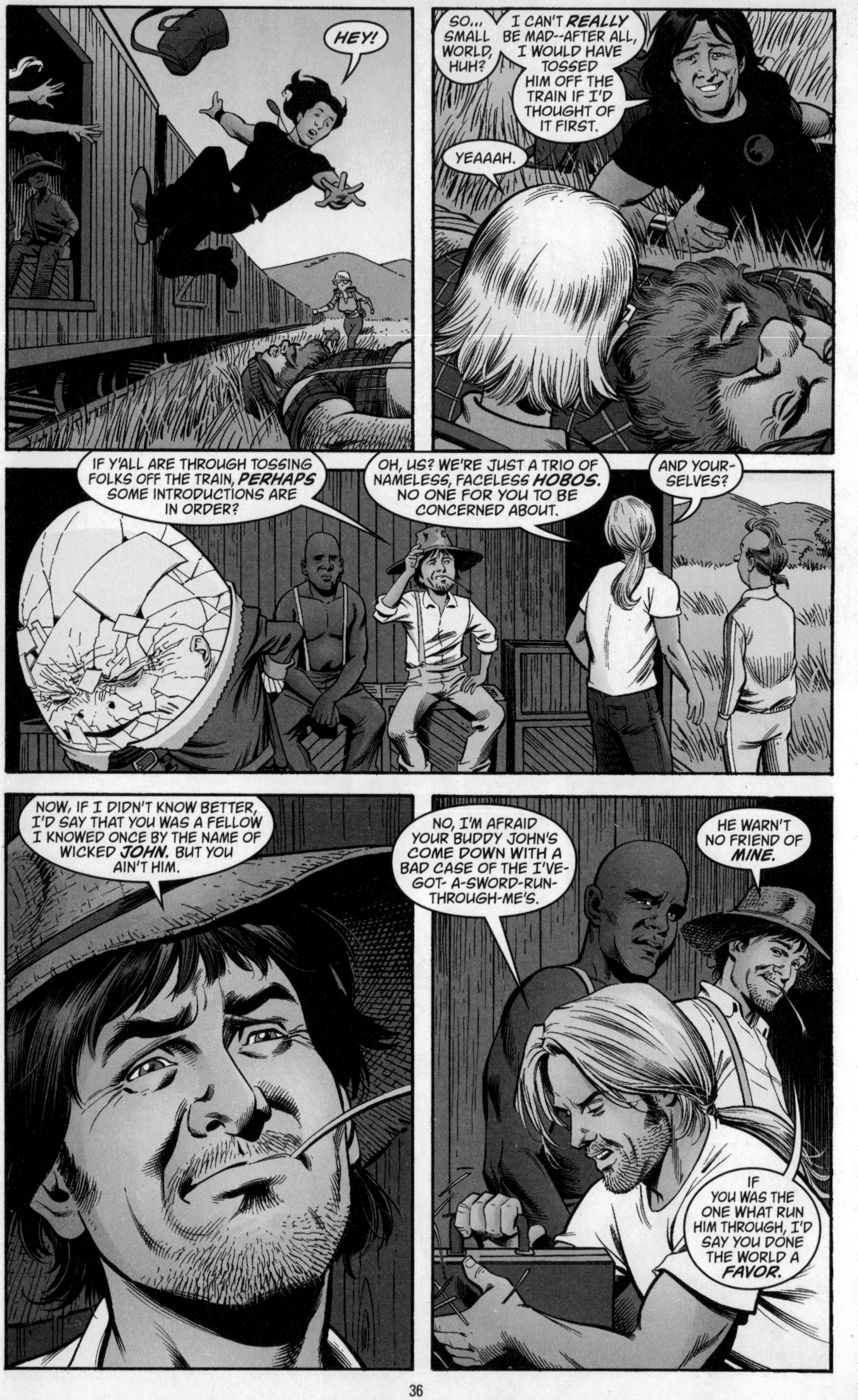
HEY!
SO... SMALL WORLD, HUH?
I CAN'T REALLY BE MAD--AFTER ALL, I WOULD HAVE TOSSED HIM OFF THE TRAIN IF I'D THOUGHT OF IT FIRST.
YEAAAH.
IF Y'ALL ARE THROUGH TOSSING FOLKS OFF THE TRAIN, PERHAPS SOME INTRODUCTIONS ARE IN ORDER?
OH, US? WE'RE JUST A TRIO OF NAMELESS, FACELESS HOBOS. NO ONE FOR YOU TO BE CONCERNED ABOUT.
AND YOUR-SELVES?
NOW, IF I DIDN'T KNOW BETTER, I'D SAY THAT YOU WAS A FELLOW I KNOWED ONCE BY THE NAME OF WICKED JOHN. BUT YOU AIN'T HIM.
NO, I'M AFRAID YOUR BUDDY JOHN'S COME DOWN WITH A BAD CASE OF THE I'VE-GOT- A-SWORD-RUN-THROUGH-ME'S.
HE WARN'T NO FRIEND OF MINE.
IF YOU WAS THE ONE WHAT RUN HIM THROUGH, I'D SAY YOU DONE THE WORLD A FAVOR.

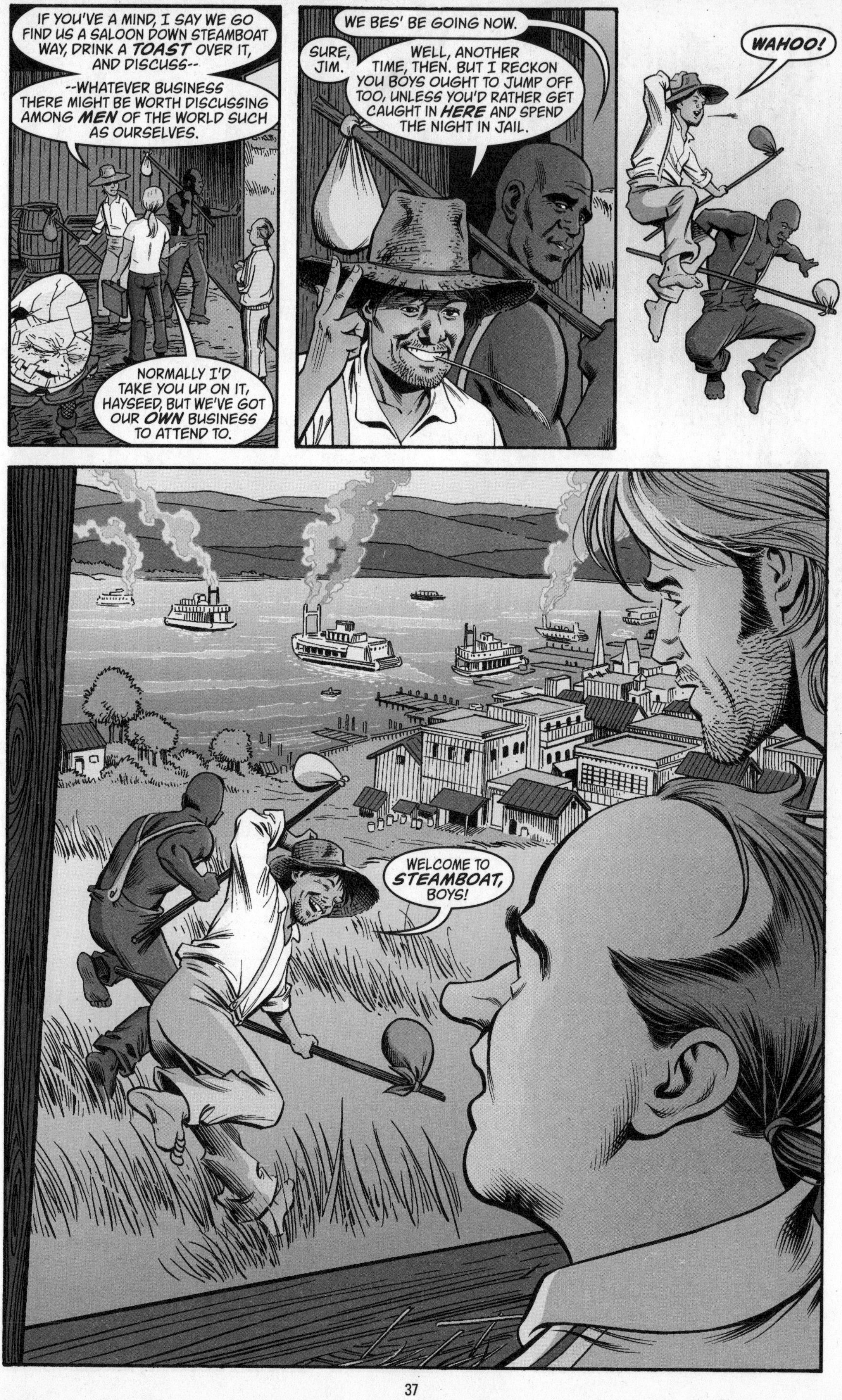
IF YOU'VE A MIND, I SAY WE GO FIND US A SALOON DOWN STEAMBOAT WAY, DRINK A TOAST OVER IT, AND DISCUSS--
--WHATEVER BUSINESS THERE MIGHT BE WORTH DISCUSSING AMONG MEN OF THE WORLD SUCH AS OURSELVES.
NORMALLY I'D TAKE YOU UP ON IT, HAYSEED, BUT WE'VE GOT OUR OWN BUSINESS TO ATTEND TO.
WE BES' BE GOING NOW.
SURE, JIM.
WELL, ANOTHER TIME, THEN. BUT I RECKON YOU BOYS OUGHT TO JUMP OFF TOO, UNLESS YOU'D RATHER GET CAUGHT IN HERE AND SPEND THE NIGHT IN JAIL.
WAHOO!
WELCOME TO STEAMBOAT, BOYS!

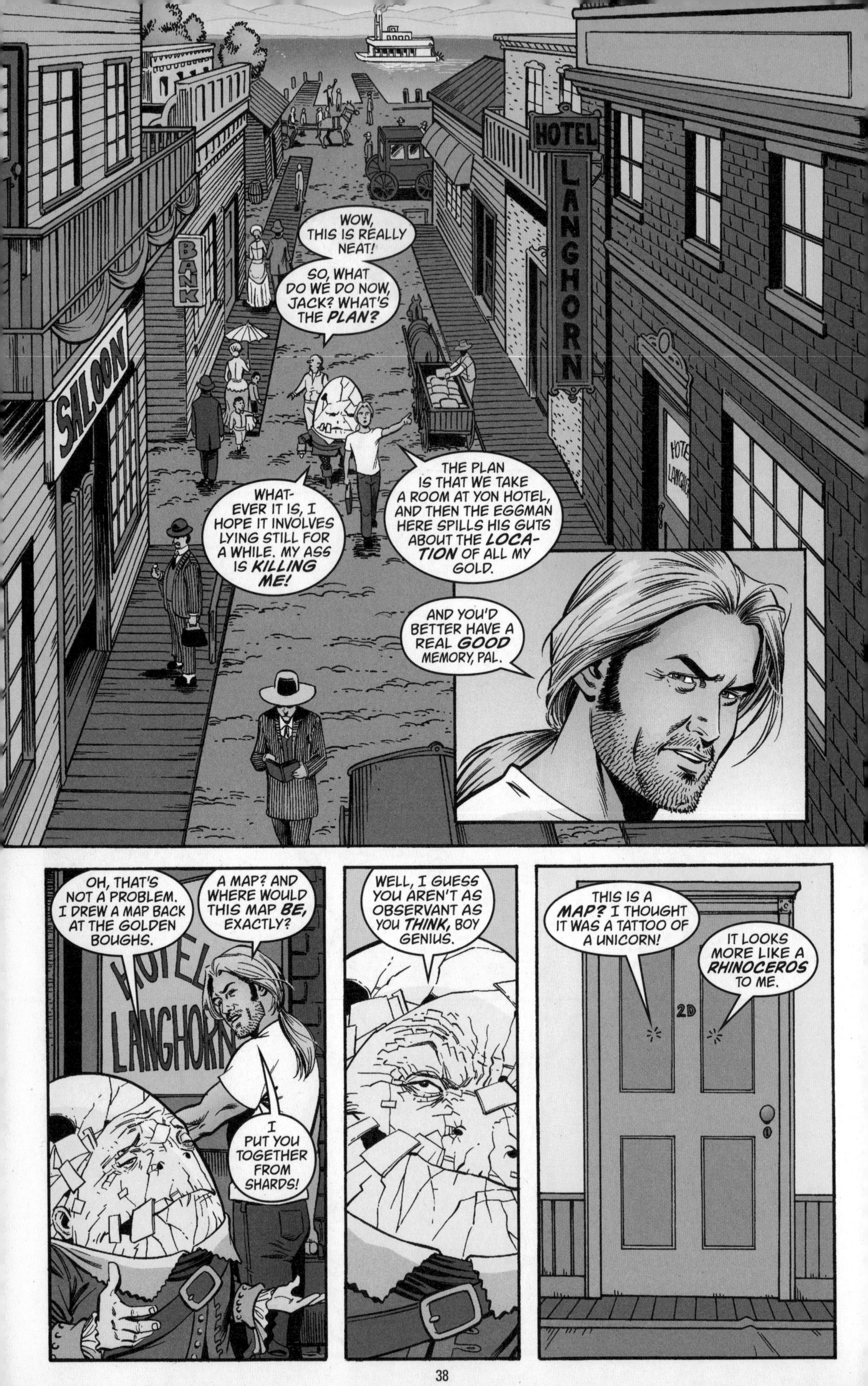
HOTEL
LANGHORN
BANK
SALOON
WOW, THIS IS REALLY NEAT!
SO, WHAT DO WE DO NOW, JACK? WHAT'S THE PLAN?
WHAT-EVER IT IS, I HOPE IT INVOLVES LYING STILL FOR A WHILE. MY ASS IS KILLING ME!
THE PLAN IS THAT WE TAKE A ROOM AT YON HOTEL, AND THEN THE EGGMAN HERE SPILLS HIS GUTS ABOUT THE LOCATION OF ALL MY GOLD.
AND YOU'D BETTER HAVE A REAL GOOD MEMORY, PAL.
OH, THAT'S NOT A PROBLEM. I DREW A MAP BACK AT THE GOLDEN BOUGHS.
A MAP? AND WHERE WOULD THIS MAP BE, EXACTLY?
HOTEL
LANGHORN
I PUT YOU TOGETHER FROM SHARDS!
WELL, I GUESS YOU AREN'T AS OBSERVANT AS YOU THINK, BOY GENIUS.
THIS IS A MAP? I THOUGHT IT WAS A TATTOO OF A UNICORN!
IT LOOKS MORE LIKE A RHINOCEROS TO ME.
2D

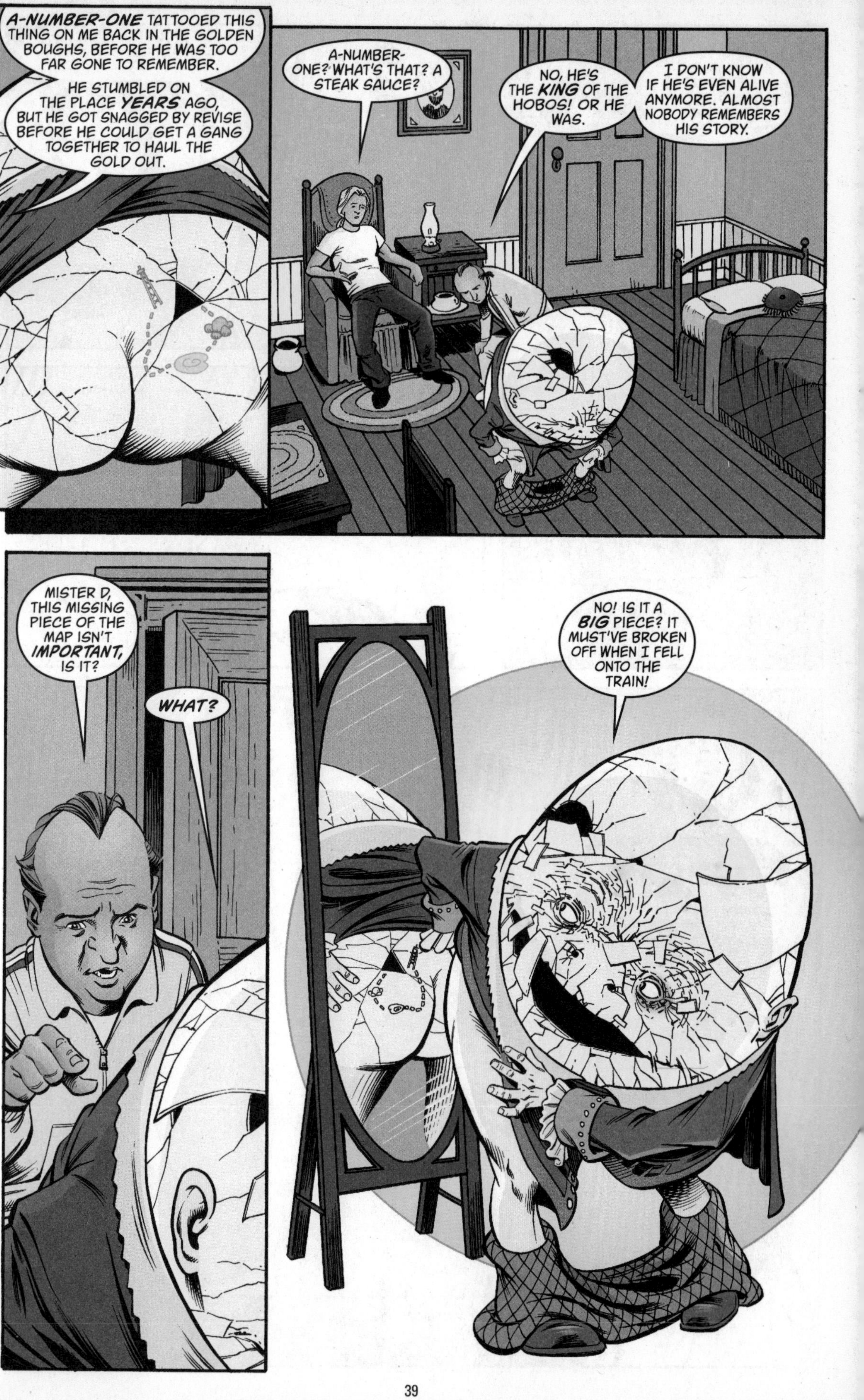
A-NUMBER-ONE TATTOOED THIS THING ON ME BACK IN THE GOLDEN BOUGHS, BEFORE HE WAS TOO FAR GONE TO REMEMBER.
HE STUMBLED ON THE PLACE YEARS AGO, BUT HE GOT SNAGGED BY REVISE BEFORE HE COULD GET A GANG TOGETHER TO HAUL THE GOLD OUT.
A-NUMBER-ONE? WHAT'S THAT? A STEAK SAUCE?
NO, HE'S THE KING OF THE HOBOS! OR HE WAS.
I DON'T KNOW IF HE'S EVEN ALIVE ANYMORE. ALMOST NOBODY REMEMBERS HIS STORY.
MISTER D, THIS MISSING PIECE OF THE MAP ISN'T IMPORTANT, IS IT?
WHAT?
NO! IS IT A BIG PIECE? IT MUST'VE BROKEN OFF WHEN I FELL ONTO THE TRAIN!

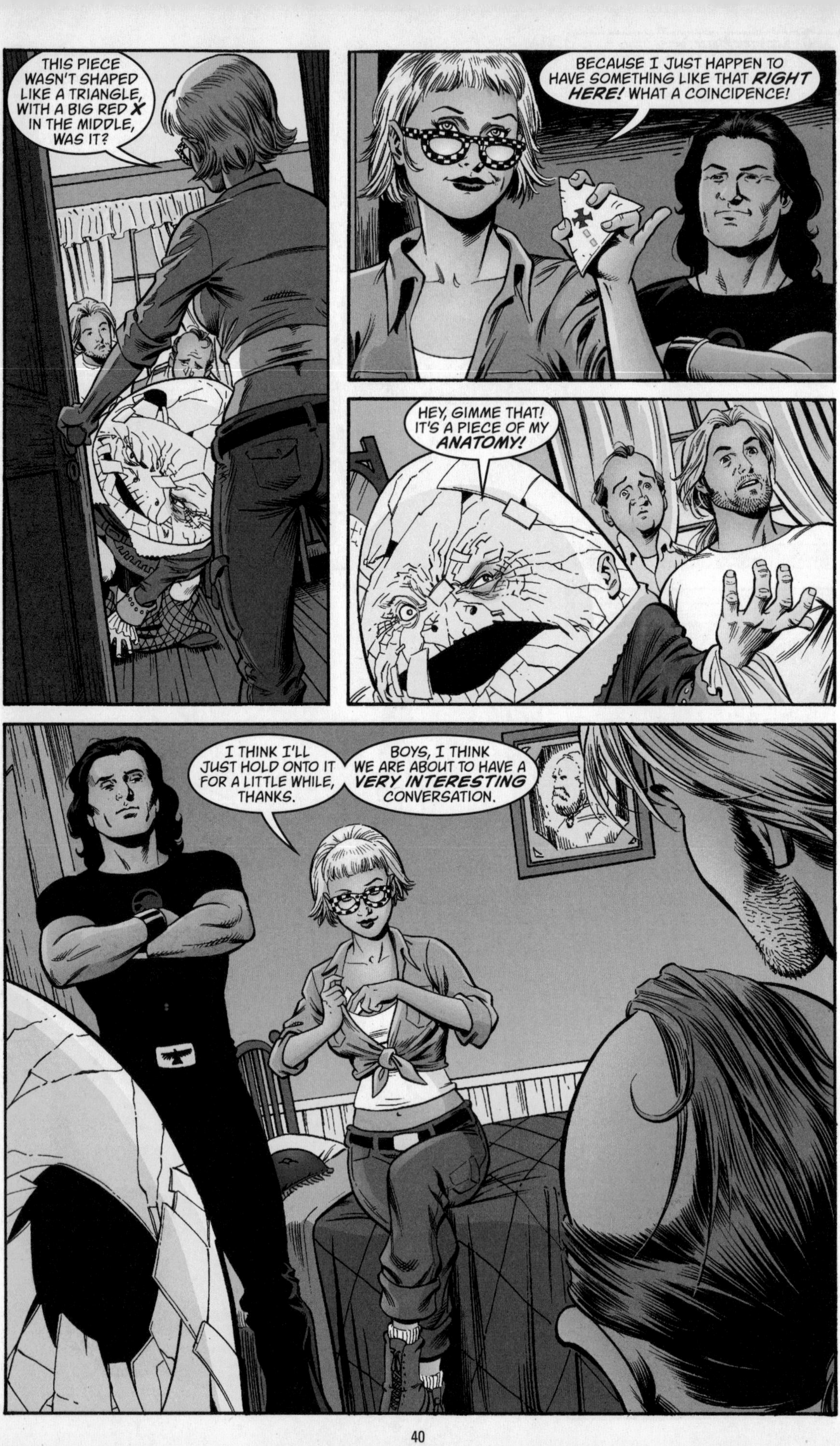
THIS PIECE WASN'T SHAPED LIKE A TRIANGLE, WITH A BIG RED X IN THE MIDDLE, WAS IT?
BECAUSE I JUST HAPPEN TO HAVE SOMETHING LIKE THAT RIGHT HERE! WHAT A COINCIDENCE!
HEY, GIMME THAT! IT'S A PIECE OF MY ANATOMY!
I THINK I'LL JUST HOLD ONTO IT FOR A LITTLE WHILE, THANKS.
BOYS, I THINK WE ARE ABOUT TO HAVE A VERY INTERESTING CONVERSATION.

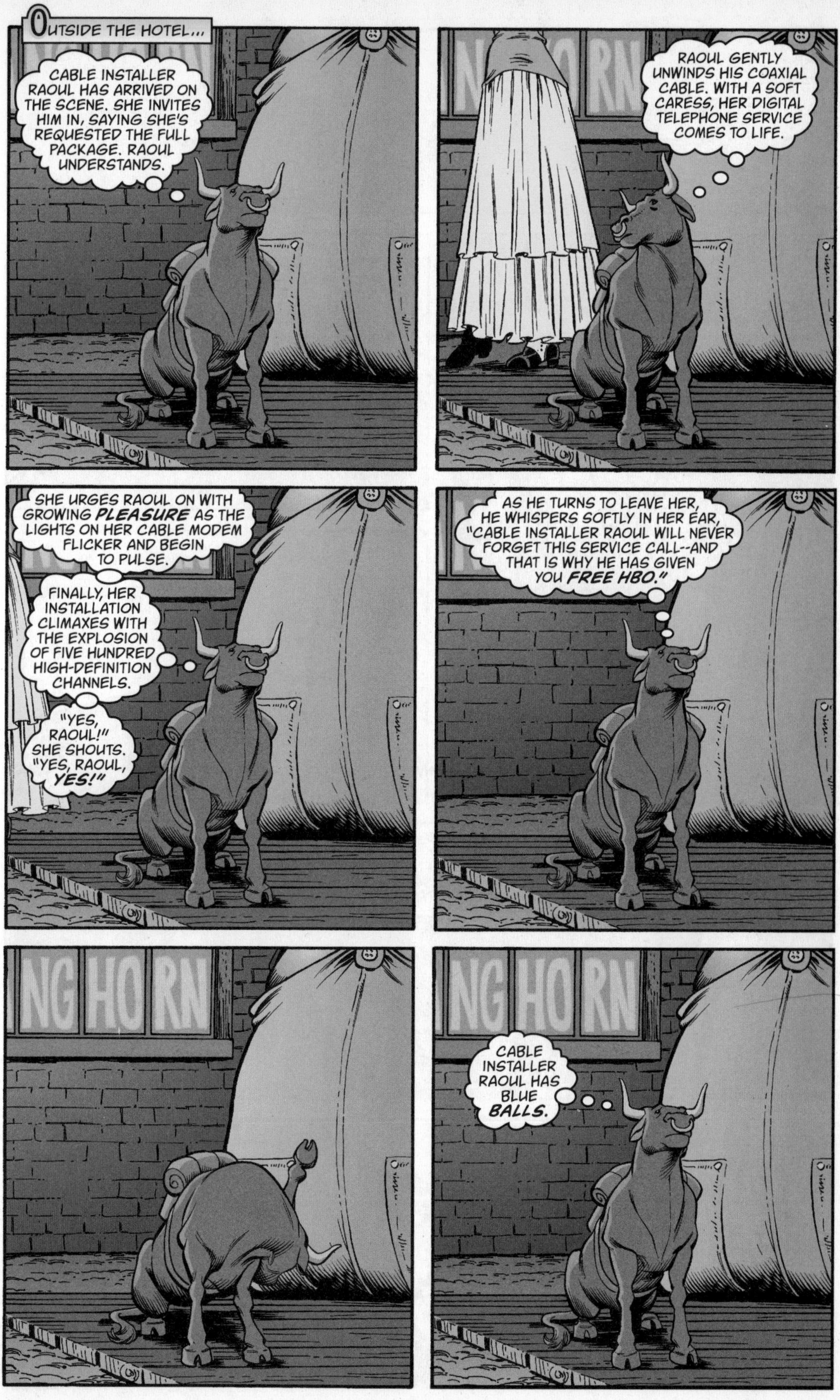
OUTSIDE THE HOTEL...
CABLE INSTALLER RAOUL HAS ARRIVED ON THE SCENE. SHE INVITES HIM IN, SAYING SHE'S REQUESTED THE FULL PACKAGE. RAOUL UNDERSTANDS.
RAOUL GENTLY UNWINDS HIS COAXIAL CABLE. WITH A SOFT CARESS, HER DIGITAL TELEPHONE SERVICE COMES TO LIFE.
SHE URGES RAOUL ON WITH GROWING PLEASURE AS THE LIGHTS ON HER CABLE MODEM FLICKER AND BEGIN TO PULSE.
FINALLY, HER INSTALLATION CLIMAXES WITH THE EXPLOSION OF FIVE HUNDRED HIGH-DEFINITION CHANNELS.
"YES, RAOUL!" SHE SHOUTS. "YES, RAOUL, YES!"
AS HE TURNS TO LEAVE HER, HE WHISPERS SOFTLY IN HER EAR, "CABLE INSTALLER RAOUL WILL NEVER FORGET THIS SERVICE CALL--AND THAT IS WHY HE HAS GIVEN YOU FREE HBO."
NG HORN
NG HORN
CABLE INSTALLER RAOUL HAS BLUE BALLS.

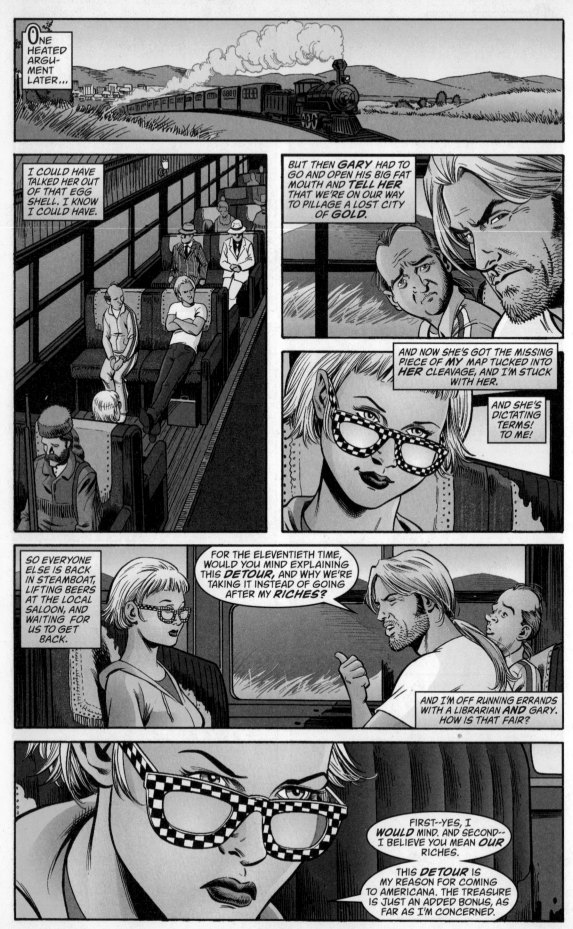

ONE HEATED ARGUMENT LATER...

I COULD HAVE TALKED HER OUT OF THAT EGG SHELL. I KNOW I COULD HAVE.

BUT THEN *GARY* HAD TO GO AND OPEN HIS BIG FAT MOUTH AND *TELL HER* THAT WE'RE ON OUR WAY TO PILLAGE A LOST CITY OF *GOLD*.

AND NOW SHE'S GOT THE MISSING PIECE OF *MY* MAP TUCKED INTO *HER* CLEAVAGE, AND I'M STUCK WITH HER.

AND SHE'S DICTATING TERMS! TO ME!

SO EVERYONE ELSE IS BACK IN STEAMBOAT, LIFTING BEERS AT THE LOCAL SALOON, AND WAITING FOR US TO GET BACK.

FOR THE ELEVENTIETH TIME, WOULD YOU MIND EXPLAINING THIS *DETOUR*, AND WHY WE'RE TAKING IT INSTEAD OF GOING AFTER MY *RICHES*?

AND I'M OFF RUNNING ERRANDS WITH A LIBRARIAN *AND* GARY. HOW IS THAT FAIR?

FIRST--YES, I *WOULD* MIND. AND SECOND-- I BELIEVE YOU MEAN *OUR* RICHES.

THIS *DETOUR* IS MY REASON FOR COMING TO AMERICANA. THE TREASURE IS JUST AN ADDED BONUS, AS FAR AS I'M CONCERNED.

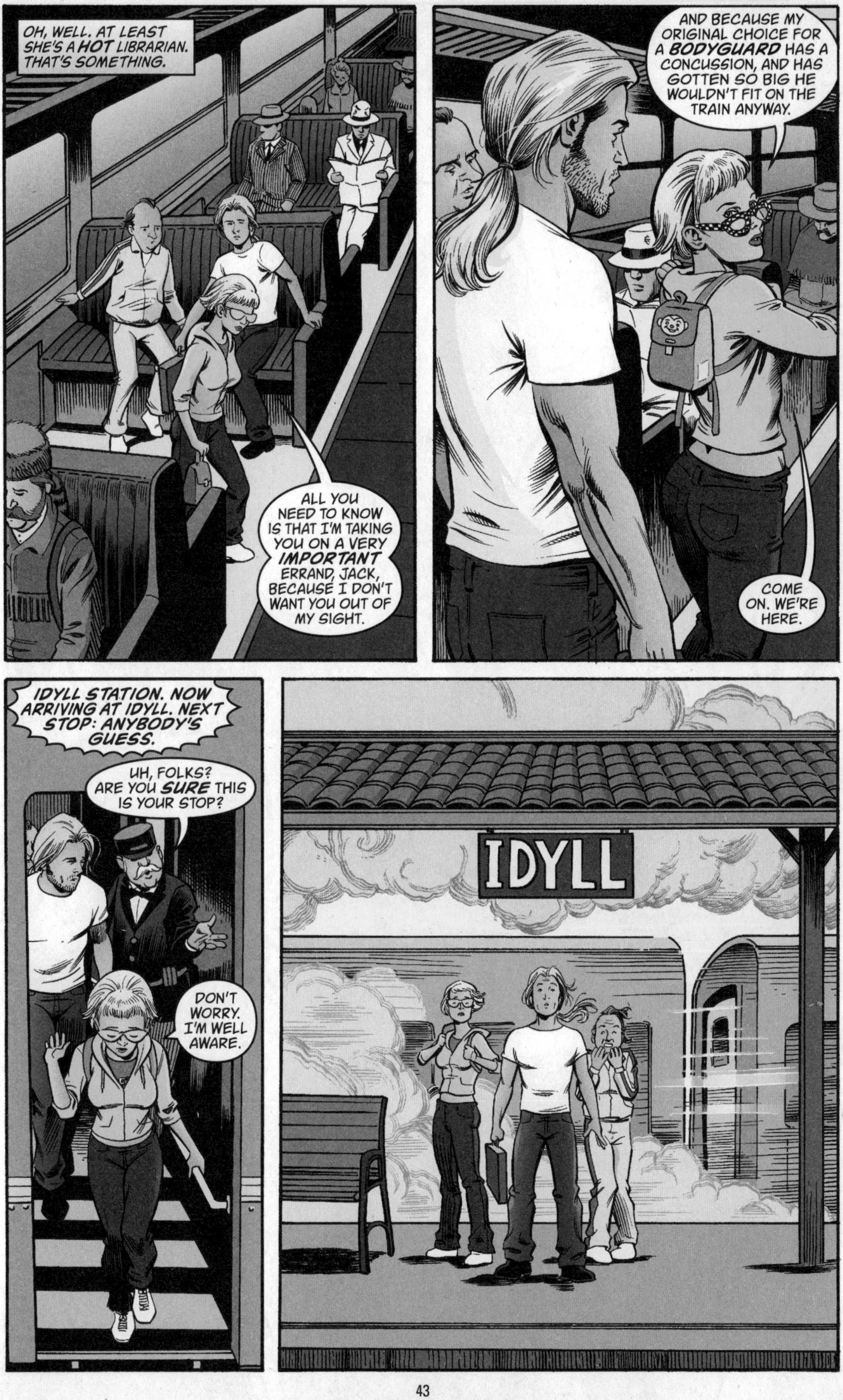
OH, WELL. AT LEAST SHE'S A HOT LIBRARIAN. THAT'S SOMETHING.
ALL YOU NEED TO KNOW IS THAT I'M TAKING YOU ON A VERY IMPORTANT ERRAND, JACK, BECAUSE I DON'T WANT YOU OUT OF MY SIGHT.
AND BECAUSE MY ORIGINAL CHOICE FOR A BODYGUARD HAS A CONCUSSION, AND HAS GOTTEN SO BIG HE WOULDN'T FIT ON THE TRAIN ANYWAY.
COME ON. WE'RE HERE.
IDYLL STATION. NOW ARRIVING AT IDYLL. NEXT STOP: ANYBODY'S GUESS.
UH, FOLKS? ARE YOU SURE THIS IS YOUR STOP?
DON'T WORRY. I'M WELL AWARE.
IDYLL

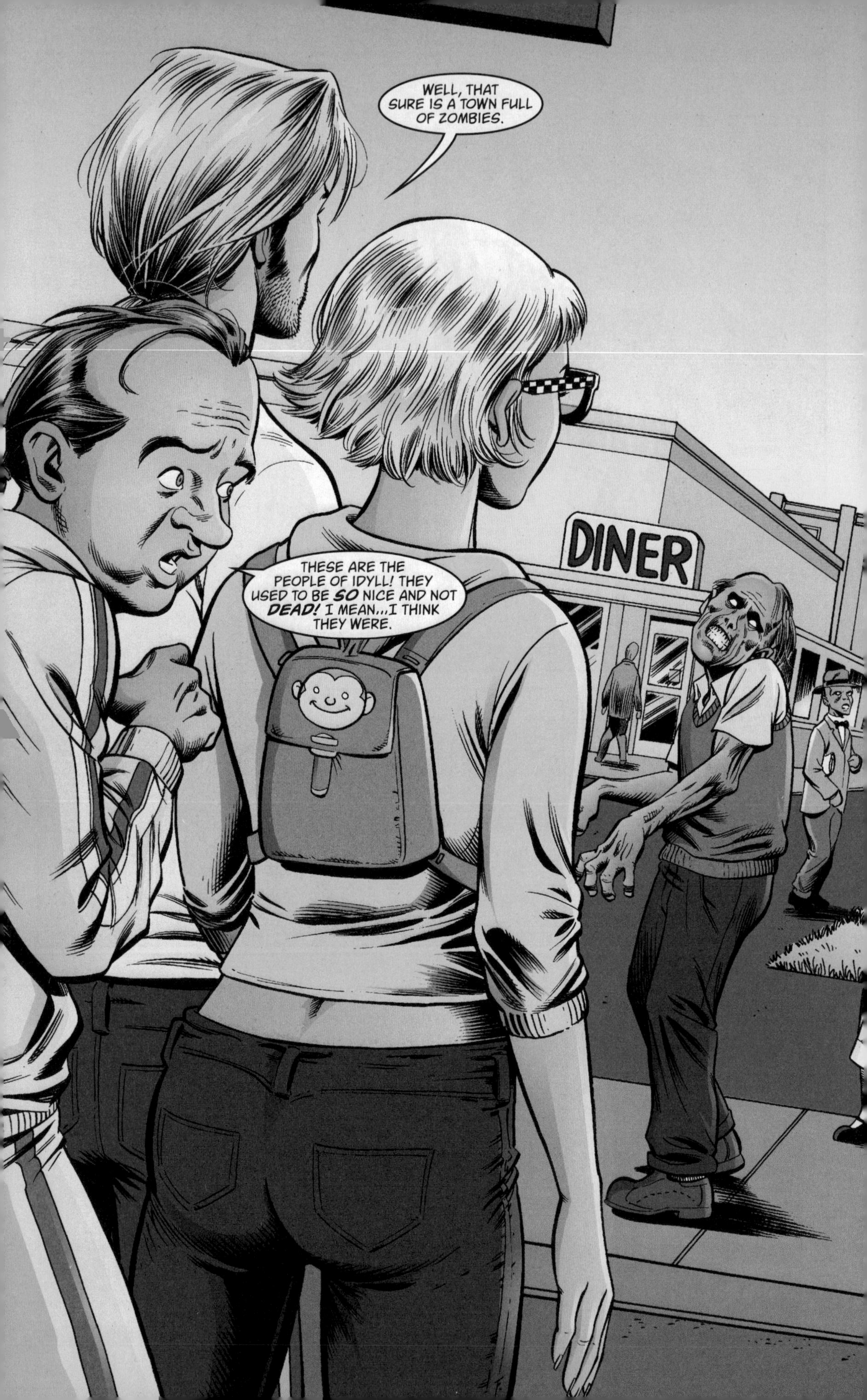
WELL, THAT SURE IS A TOWN FULL OF ZOMBIES.
THESE ARE THE PEOPLE OF IDYLL! THEY USED TO BE *SO* NICE AND NOT *DEAD!* I MEAN...I THINK THEY WERE.
DINER

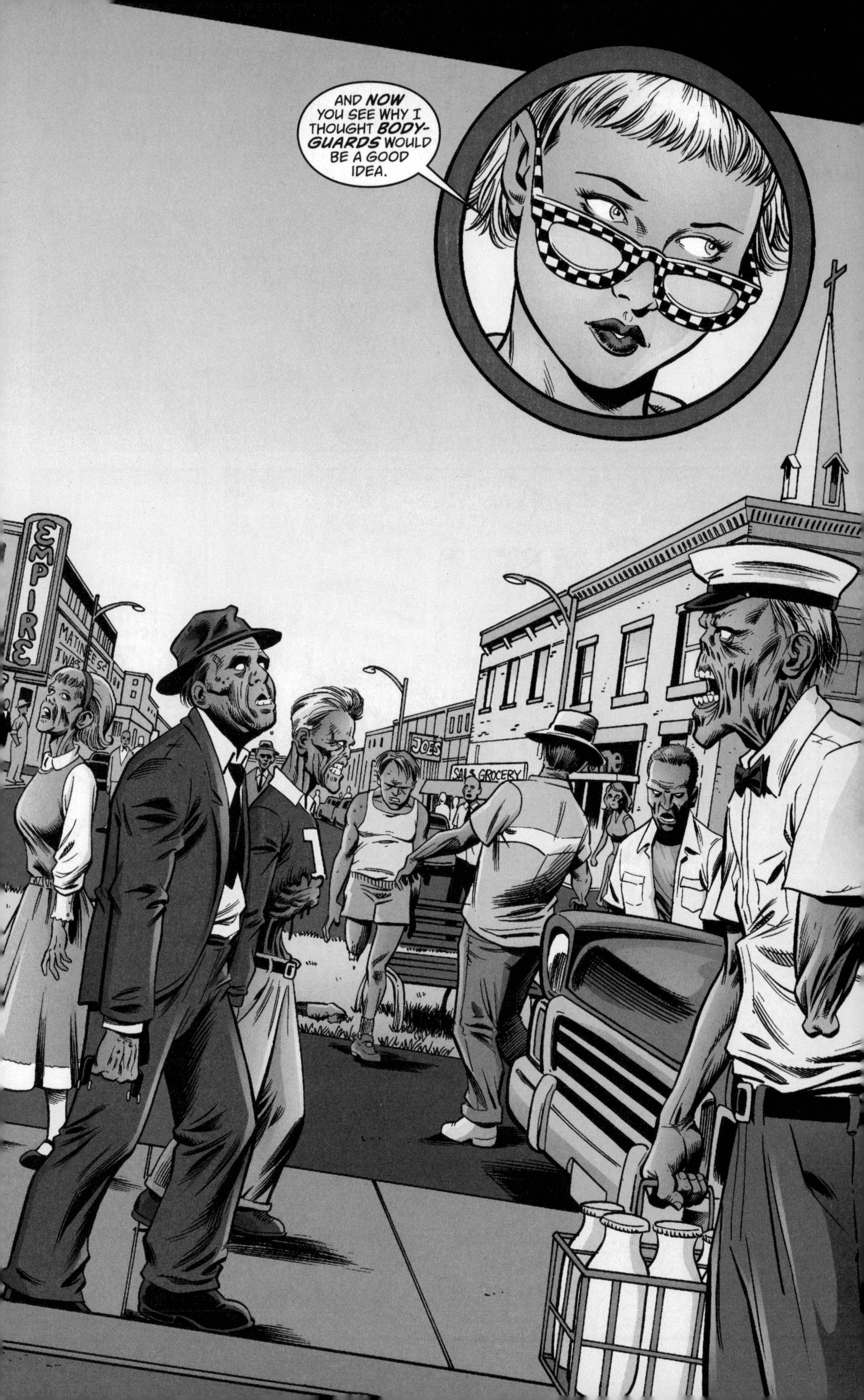
AND NOW YOU SEE WHY I THOUGHT BODY-GUARDS WOULD BE A GOOD IDEA.
EMPIRE
MATINEE 5¢
JOE'S
SAL'S GROCERY

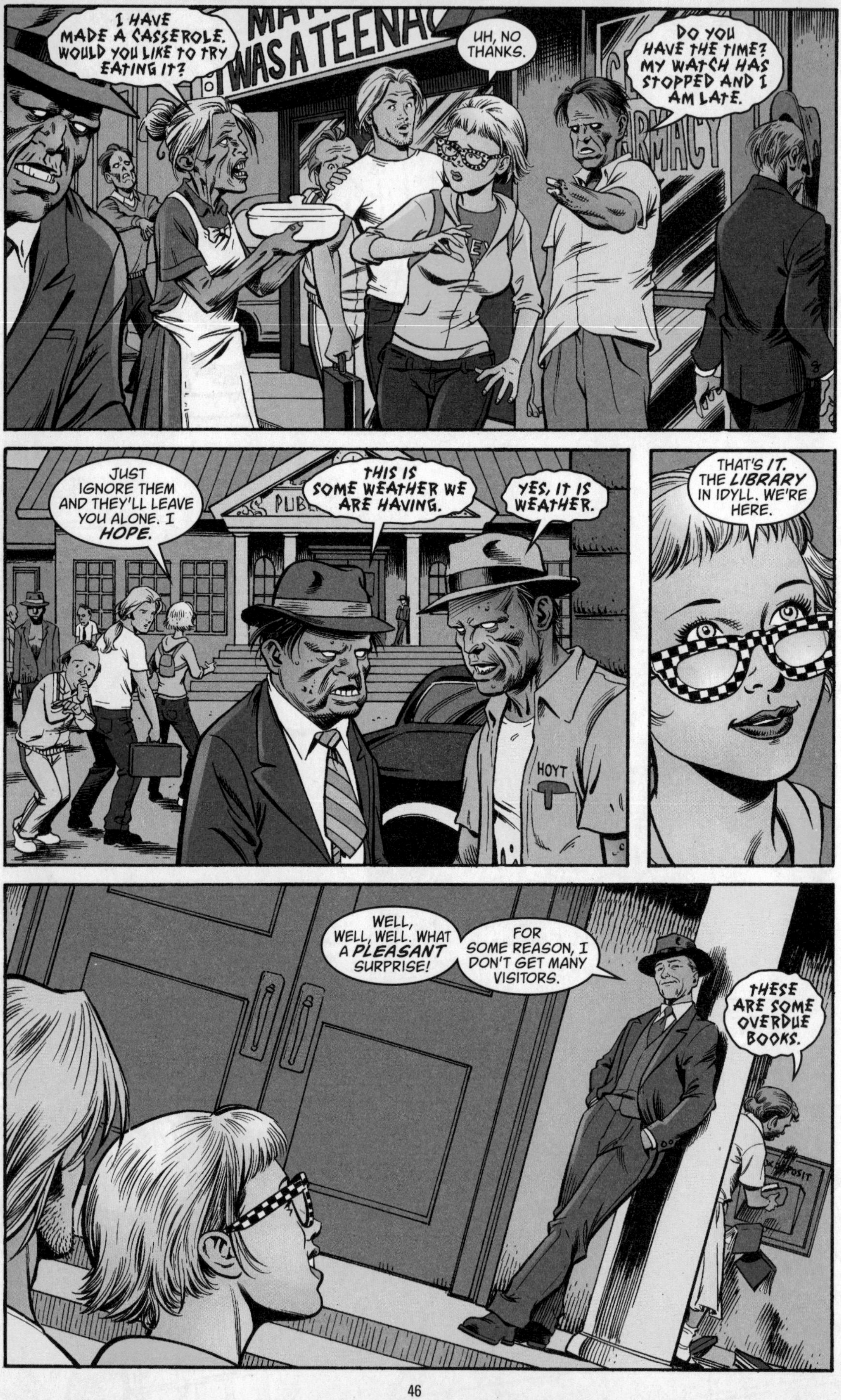
I HAVE MADE A CASSEROLE. WOULD YOU LIKE TO TRY EATING IT?
UH, NO THANKS.
DO YOU HAVE THE TIME? MY WATCH HAS STOPPED AND I AM LATE.
JUST IGNORE THEM AND THEY'LL LEAVE YOU ALONE. I HOPE.
THIS IS SOME WEATHER WE ARE HAVING.
YES, IT IS WEATHER.
HOYT
THAT'S IT. THE LIBRARY IN IDYLL. WE'RE HERE.
WELL, WELL, WELL. WHAT A PLEASANT SURPRISE!
FOR SOME REASON, I DON'T GET MANY VISITORS.
THESE ARE SOME OVERDUE BOOKS.

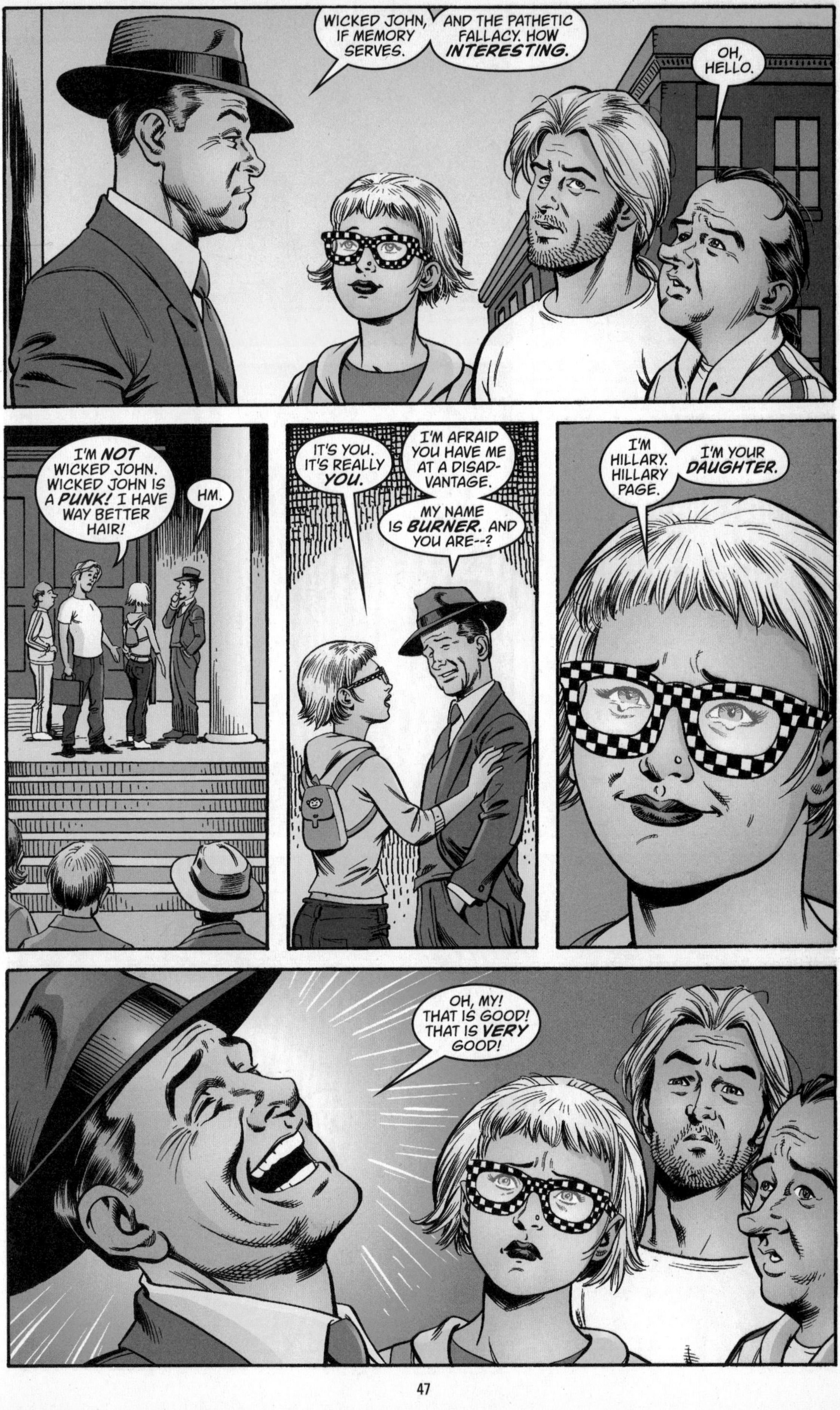
WICKED JOHN, IF MEMORY SERVES.
AND THE PATHETIC FALLACY. HOW INTERESTING.
OH, HELLO.
I'M NOT WICKED JOHN. WICKED JOHN IS A PUNK! I HAVE WAY BETTER HAIR!
HM.
IT'S YOU. IT'S REALLY YOU.
I'M AFRAID YOU HAVE ME AT A DISAD-VANTAGE.
MY NAME IS BURNER. AND YOU ARE--?
I'M HILLARY. HILLARY PAGE.
I'M YOUR DAUGHTER.
OH, MY! THAT IS GOOD! THAT IS VERY GOOD!

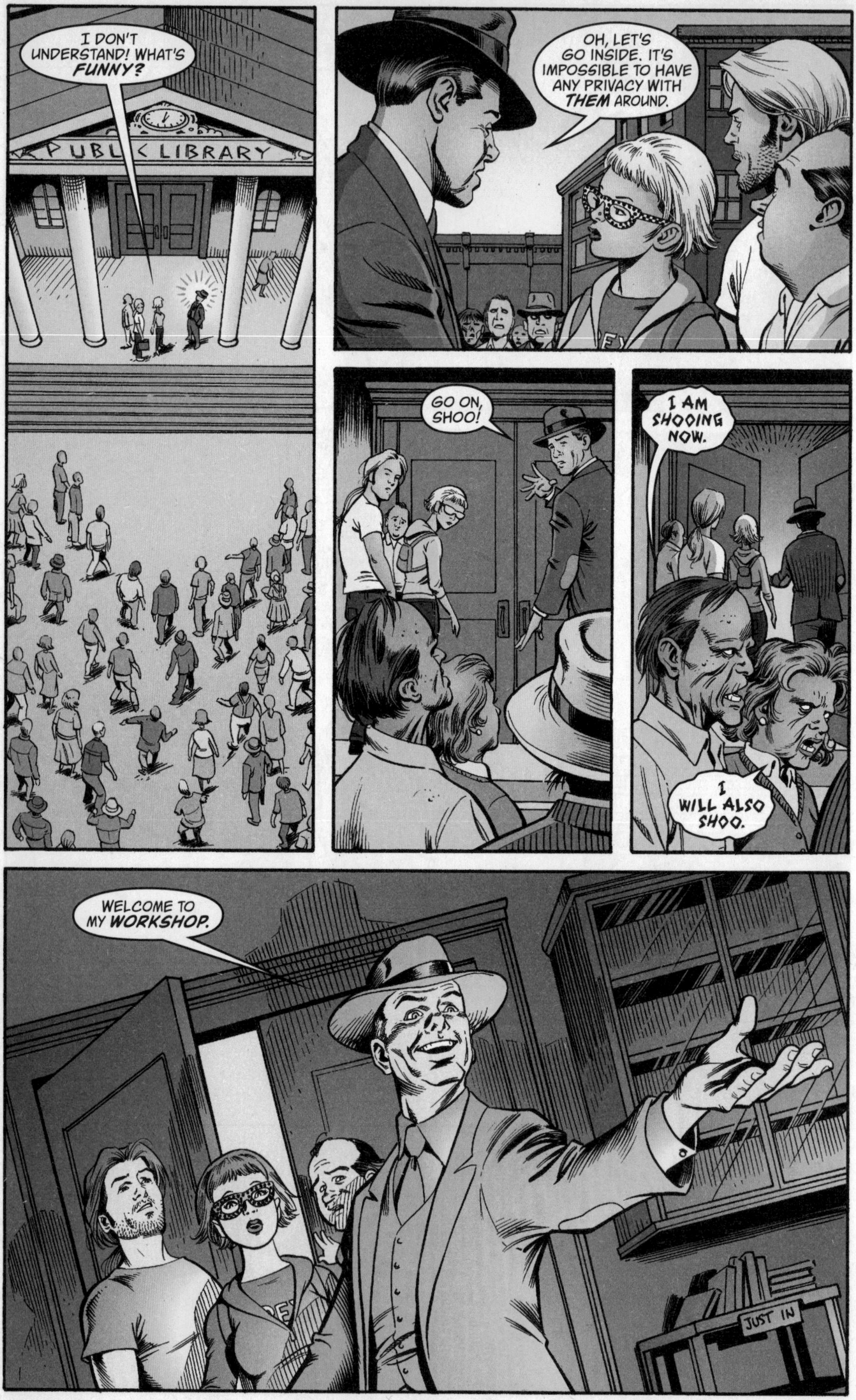

I DON'T UNDERSTAND! WHAT'S *FUNNY?*
OH, LET'S GO INSIDE. IT'S IMPOSSIBLE TO HAVE ANY PRIVACY WITH *THEM* AROUND.
GO ON, SHOO!
I AM SHOOING NOW.
I WILL ALSO SHOO.
WELCOME TO MY *WORKSHOP.*
JUST IN

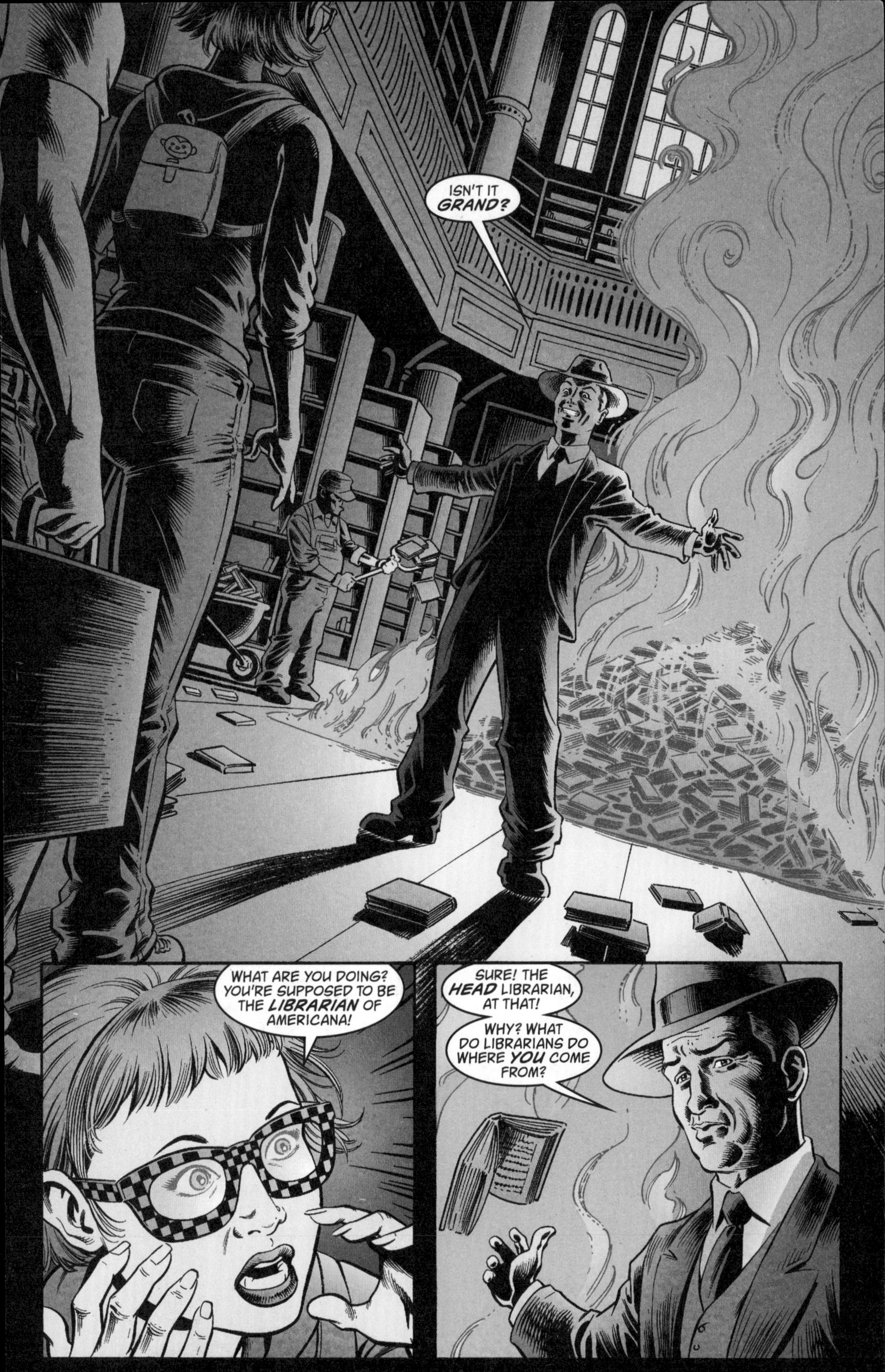
ISN'T IT GRAND?
WHAT ARE YOU DOING? YOU'RE SUPPOSED TO BE THE LIBRARIAN OF AMERICANA!
SURE! THE HEAD LIBRARIAN, AT THAT!
WHY? WHAT DO LIBRARIANS DO WHERE YOU COME FROM?

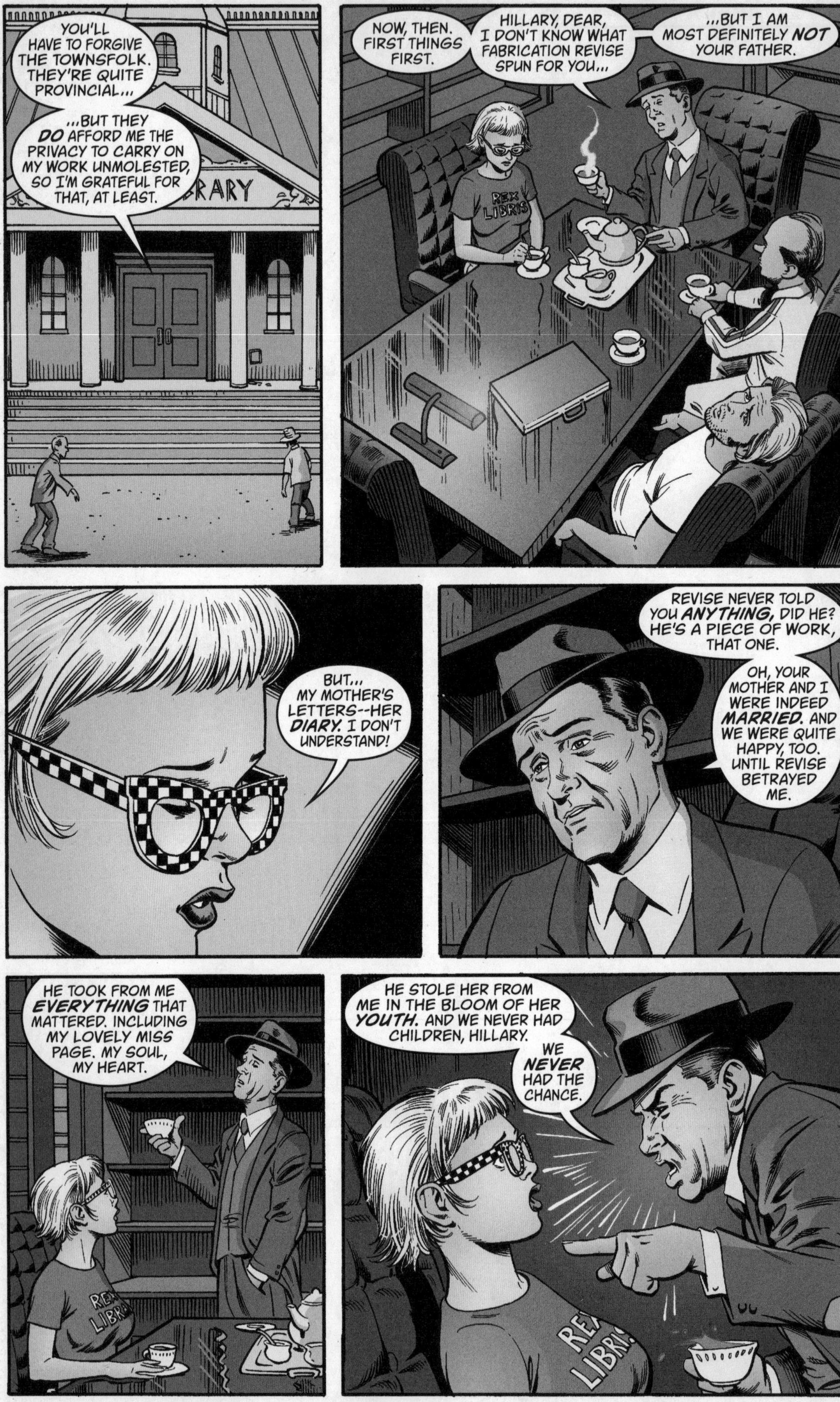
YOU'LL HAVE TO FORGIVE THE TOWNSFOLK. THEY'RE QUITE PROVINCIAL...
...BUT THEY DO AFFORD ME THE PRIVACY TO CARRY ON MY WORK UNMOLESTED, SO I'M GRATEFUL FOR THAT, AT LEAST.
BRARY
NOW, THEN. FIRST THINGS FIRST.
HILLARY, DEAR, I DON'T KNOW WHAT FABRICATION REVISE SPUN FOR YOU...
...BUT I AM MOST DEFINITELY NOT YOUR FATHER.
REX LIBRIS
BUT... MY MOTHER'S LETTERS--HER DIARY. I DON'T UNDERSTAND!
REVISE NEVER TOLD YOU ANYTHING, DID HE? HE'S A PIECE OF WORK, THAT ONE.
OH, YOUR MOTHER AND I WERE INDEED MARRIED. AND WE WERE QUITE HAPPY, TOO. UNTIL REVISE BETRAYED ME.
HE TOOK FROM ME EVERYTHING THAT MATTERED. INCLUDING MY LOVELY MISS PAGE. MY SOUL, MY HEART.
HE STOLE HER FROM ME IN THE BLOOM OF HER YOUTH. AND WE NEVER HAD CHILDREN, HILLARY.
WE NEVER HAD THE CHANCE.

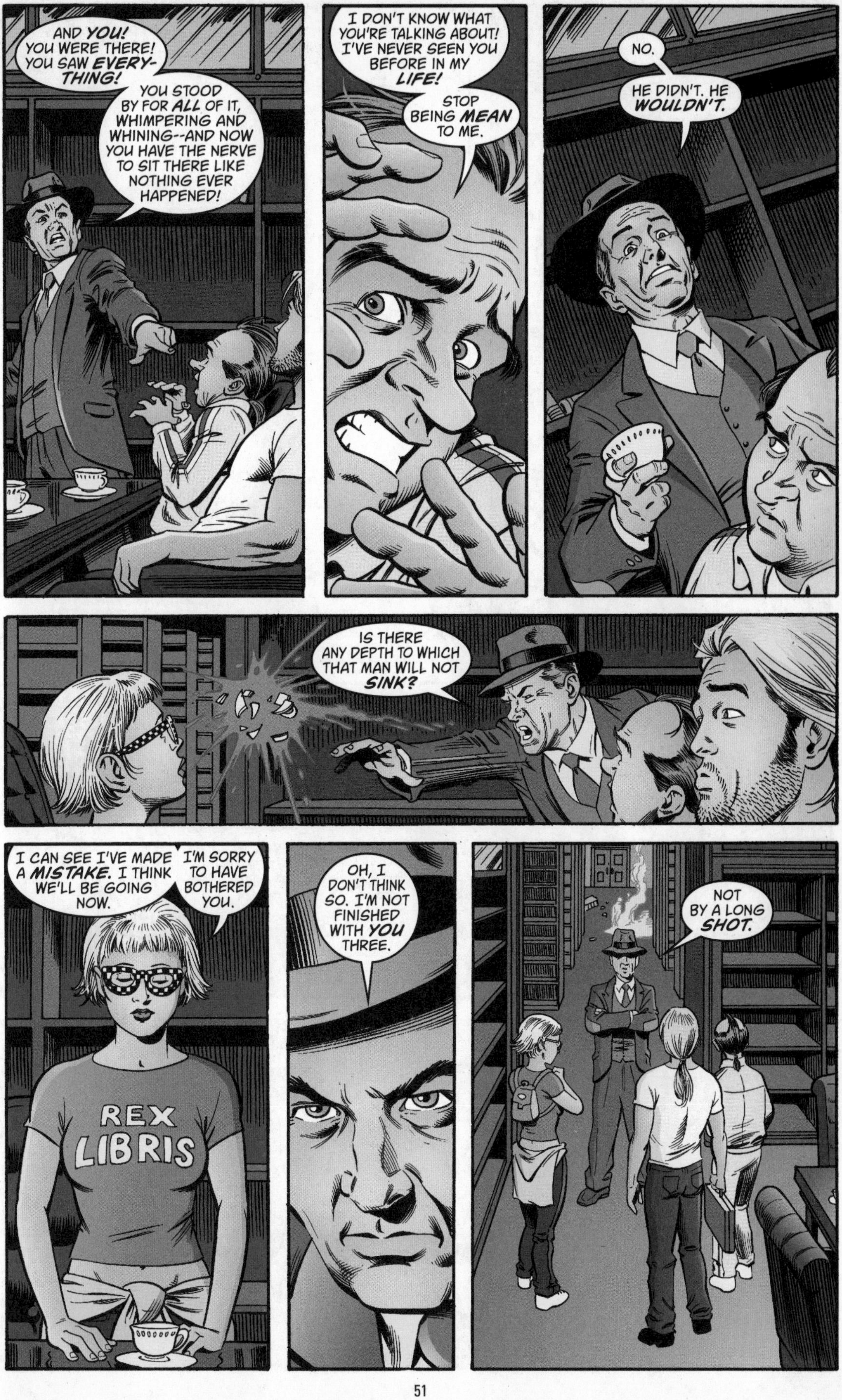

AND YOU! YOU WERE THERE! YOU SAW EVERY-THING!
YOU STOOD BY FOR ALL OF IT, WHIMPERING AND WHINING--AND NOW YOU HAVE THE NERVE TO SIT THERE LIKE NOTHING EVER HAPPENED!
I DON'T KNOW WHAT YOU'RE TALKING ABOUT! I'VE NEVER SEEN YOU BEFORE IN MY LIFE!
STOP BEING MEAN TO ME.
NO.
HE DIDN'T. HE WOULDN'T.
IS THERE ANY DEPTH TO WHICH THAT MAN WILL NOT SINK?
I CAN SEE I'VE MADE A MISTAKE. I THINK WE'LL BE GOING NOW.
I'M SORRY TO HAVE BOTHERED YOU.
REX LIBRIS
OH, I DON'T THINK SO. I'M NOT FINISHED WITH YOU THREE.
NOT BY A LONG SHOT.

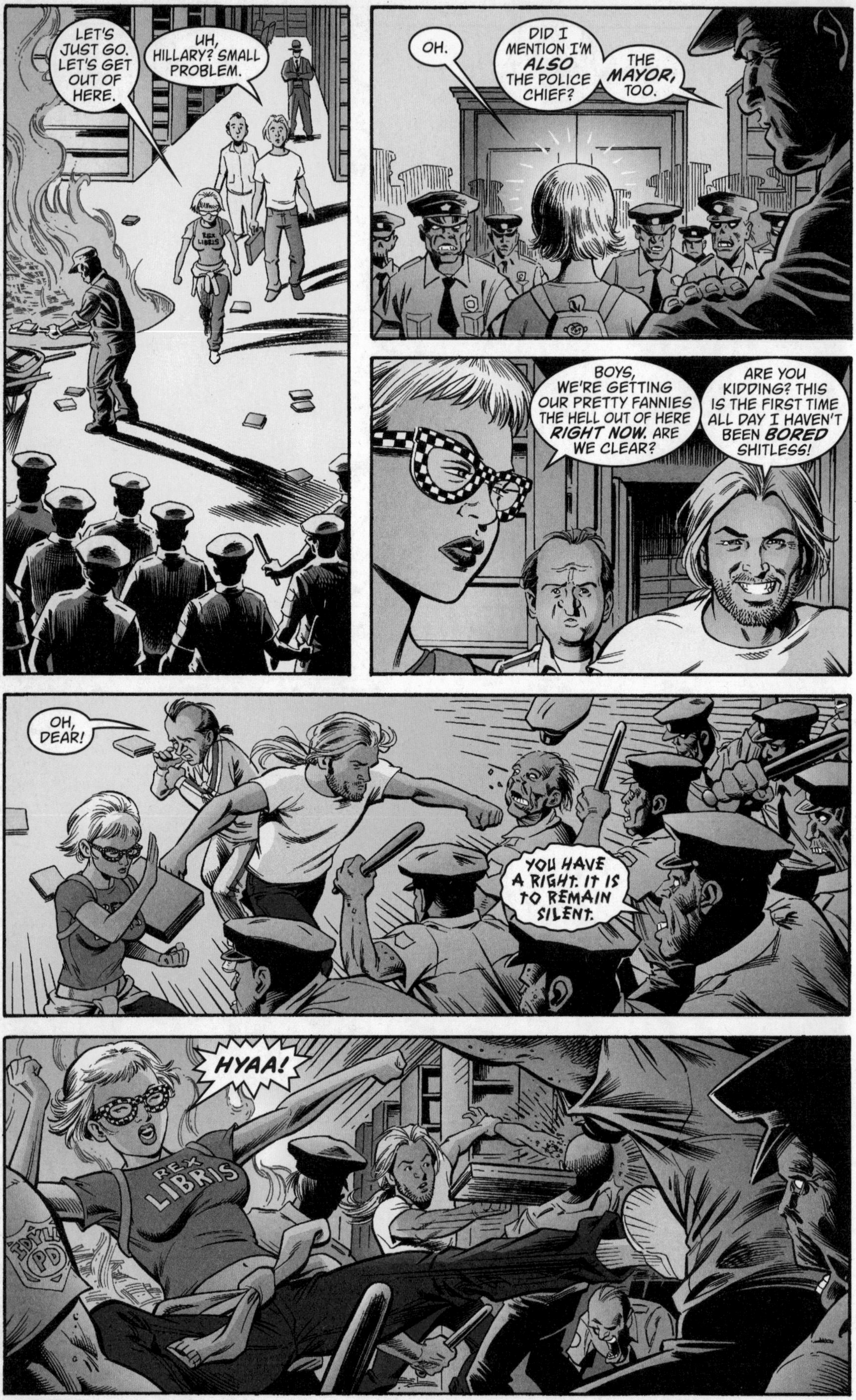
LET'S JUST GO. LET'S GET OUT OF HERE.
UH, HILLARY? SMALL PROBLEM.
OH.
DID I MENTION I'M ALSO THE POLICE CHIEF?
THE MAYOR, TOO.
BOYS, WE'RE GETTING OUR PRETTY FANNIES THE HELL OUT OF HERE RIGHT NOW. ARE WE CLEAR?
ARE YOU KIDDING? THIS IS THE FIRST TIME ALL DAY I HAVEN'T BEEN BORED SHITLESS!
OH, DEAR!
YOU HAVE A RIGHT. IT IS TO REMAIN SILENT.
HYAA!
REX LIBRIS
PD

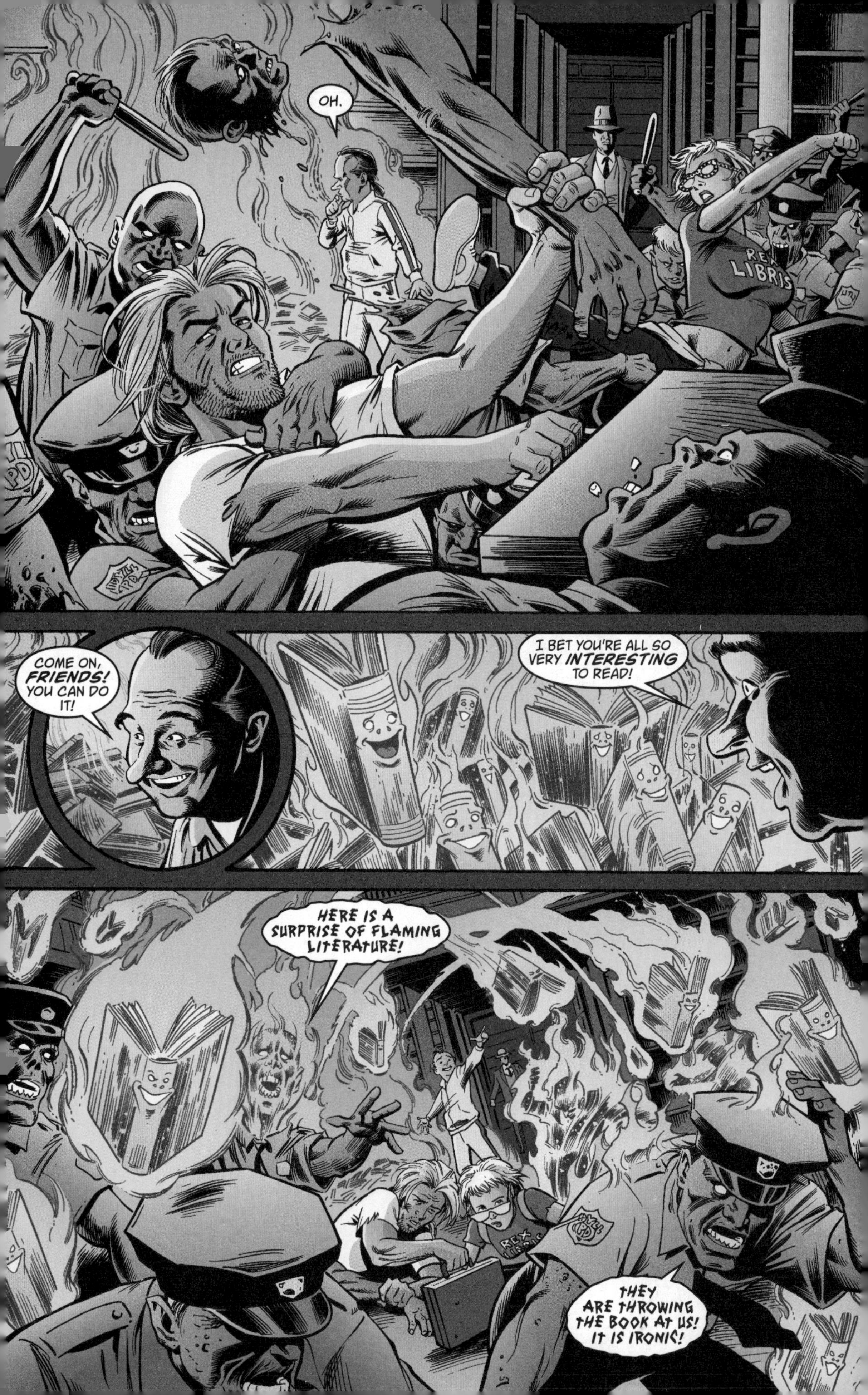
OH.
REX LIBRIS
COME ON, FRIENDS! YOU CAN DO IT!
I BET YOU'RE ALL SO VERY INTERESTING TO READ!
HERE IS A SURPRISE OF FLAMING LITERATURE!
THEY ARE THROWING THE BOOK AT US! IT IS IRONIC!

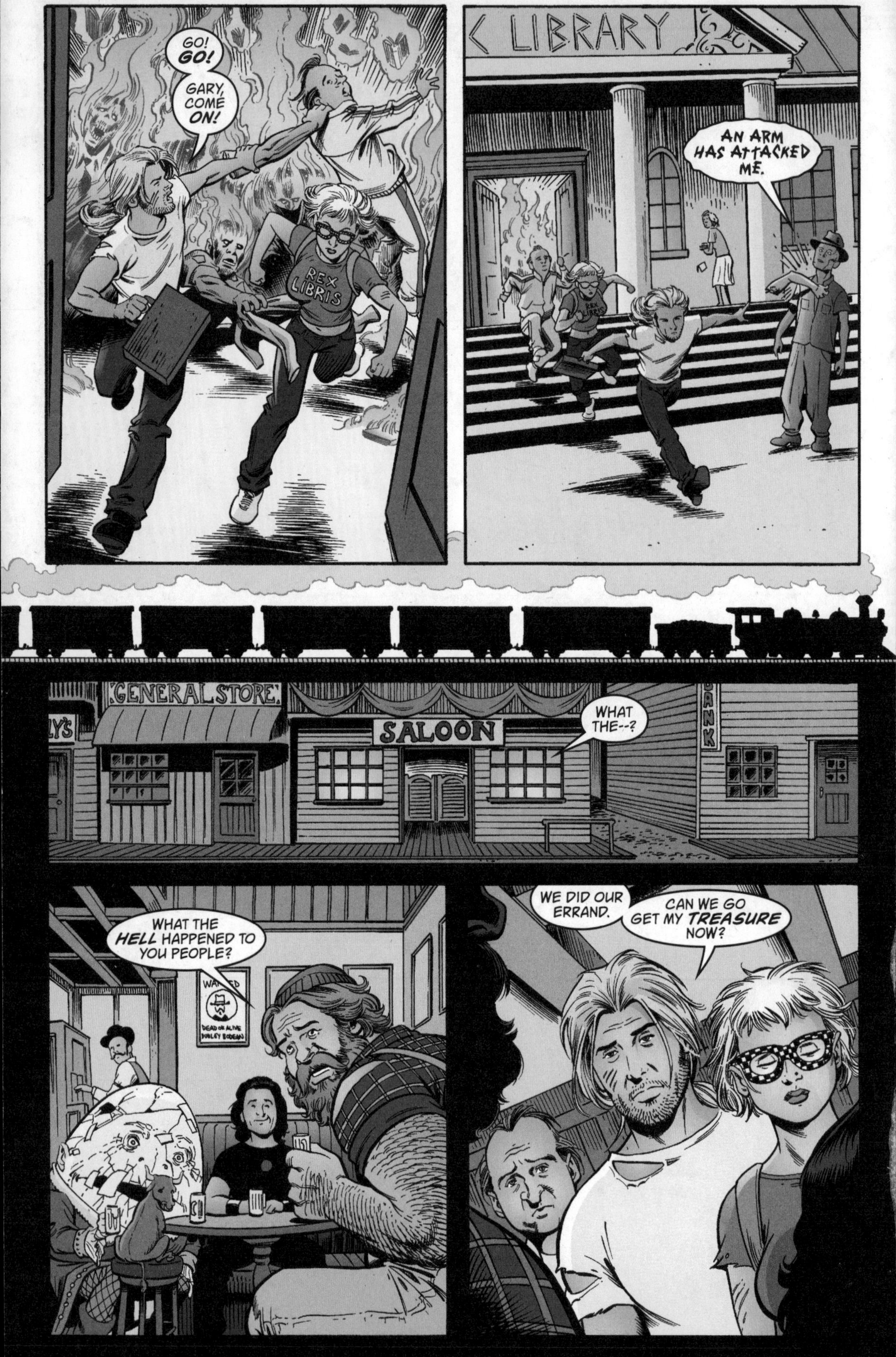
GO! GO!
GARY, COME ON!
REX LIBRIS
LIBRARY
AN ARM HAS ATTACKED ME.
GENERAL STORE
SALOON
WHAT THE--?
WHAT THE HELL HAPPENED TO YOU PEOPLE?
WE DID OUR ERRAND.
CAN WE GO GET MY TREASURE NOW?

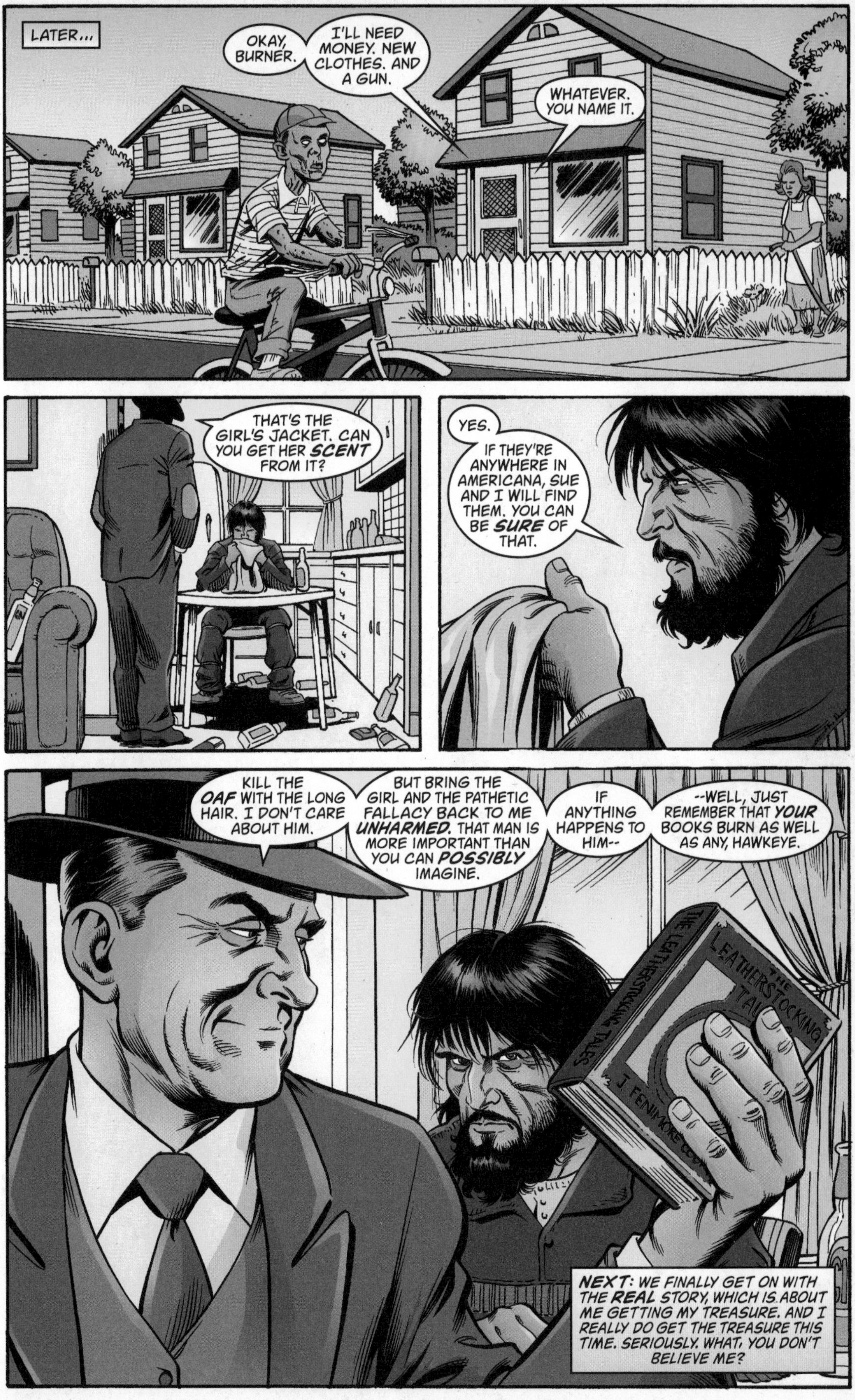
LATER...
OKAY, BURNER.
I'LL NEED MONEY. NEW CLOTHES. AND A GUN.
WHATEVER. YOU NAME IT.
THAT'S THE GIRL'S JACKET. CAN YOU GET HER SCENT FROM IT?
YES.
IF THEY'RE ANYWHERE IN AMERICANA, SUE AND I WILL FIND THEM. YOU CAN BE SURE OF THAT.
KILL THE OAF WITH THE LONG HAIR. I DON'T CARE ABOUT HIM.
BUT BRING THE GIRL AND THE PATHETIC FALLACY BACK TO ME UNHARMED. THAT MAN IS MORE IMPORTANT THAN YOU CAN POSSIBLY IMAGINE.
IF ANYTHING HAPPENS TO HIM--
--WELL, JUST REMEMBER THAT YOUR BOOKS BURN AS WELL AS ANY, HAWKEYE.
THE LEATHERSTOCKING TALES
NEXT: WE FINALLY GET ON WITH THE REAL STORY, WHICH IS ABOUT ME GETTING MY TREASURE. AND I REALLY DO GET THE TREASURE THIS TIME. SERIOUSLY. WHAT, YOU DON'T BELIEVE ME?

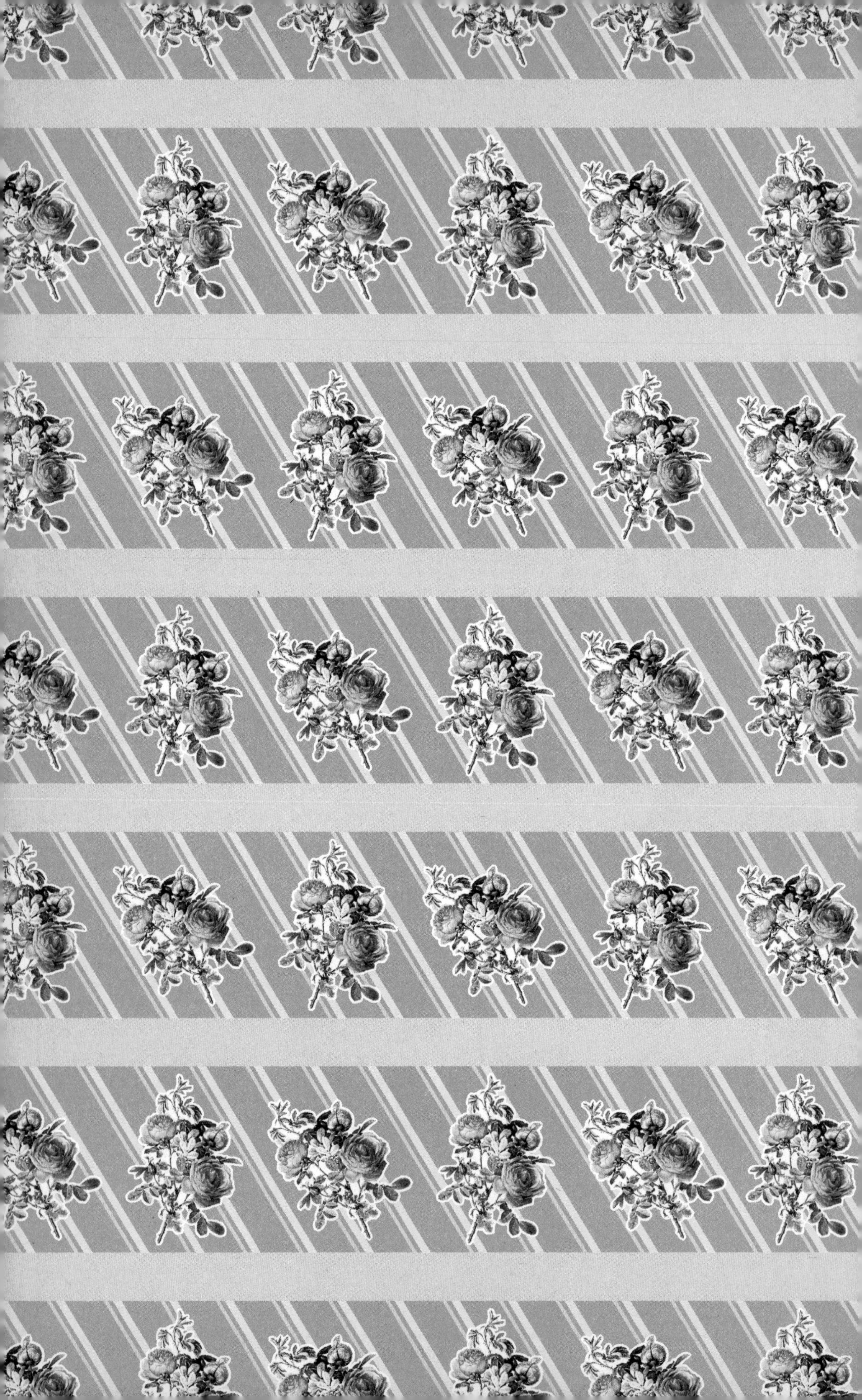

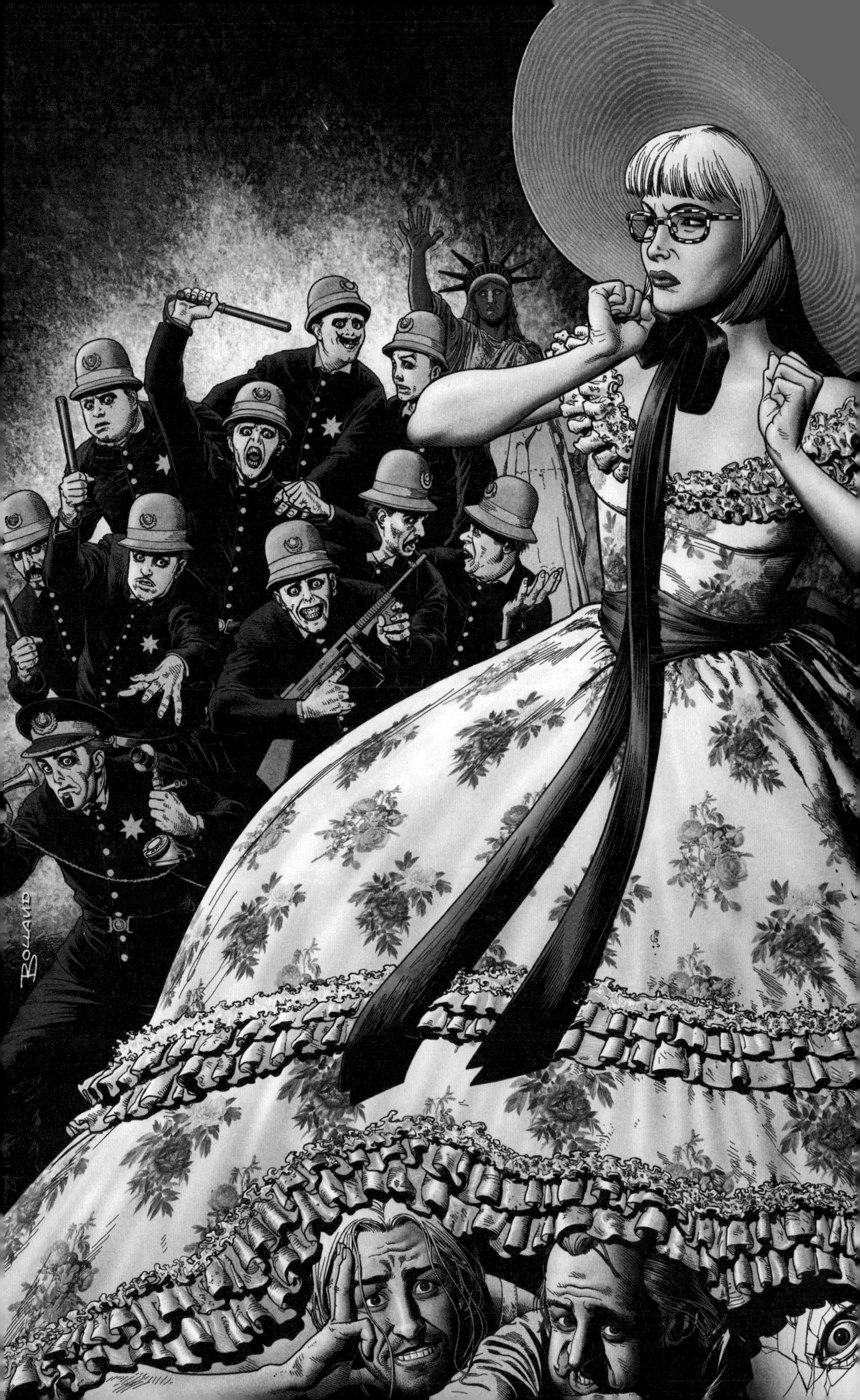
BOLLAND

*"Stop acting like a little bitch
and be a **man** for **once** in your life!"*

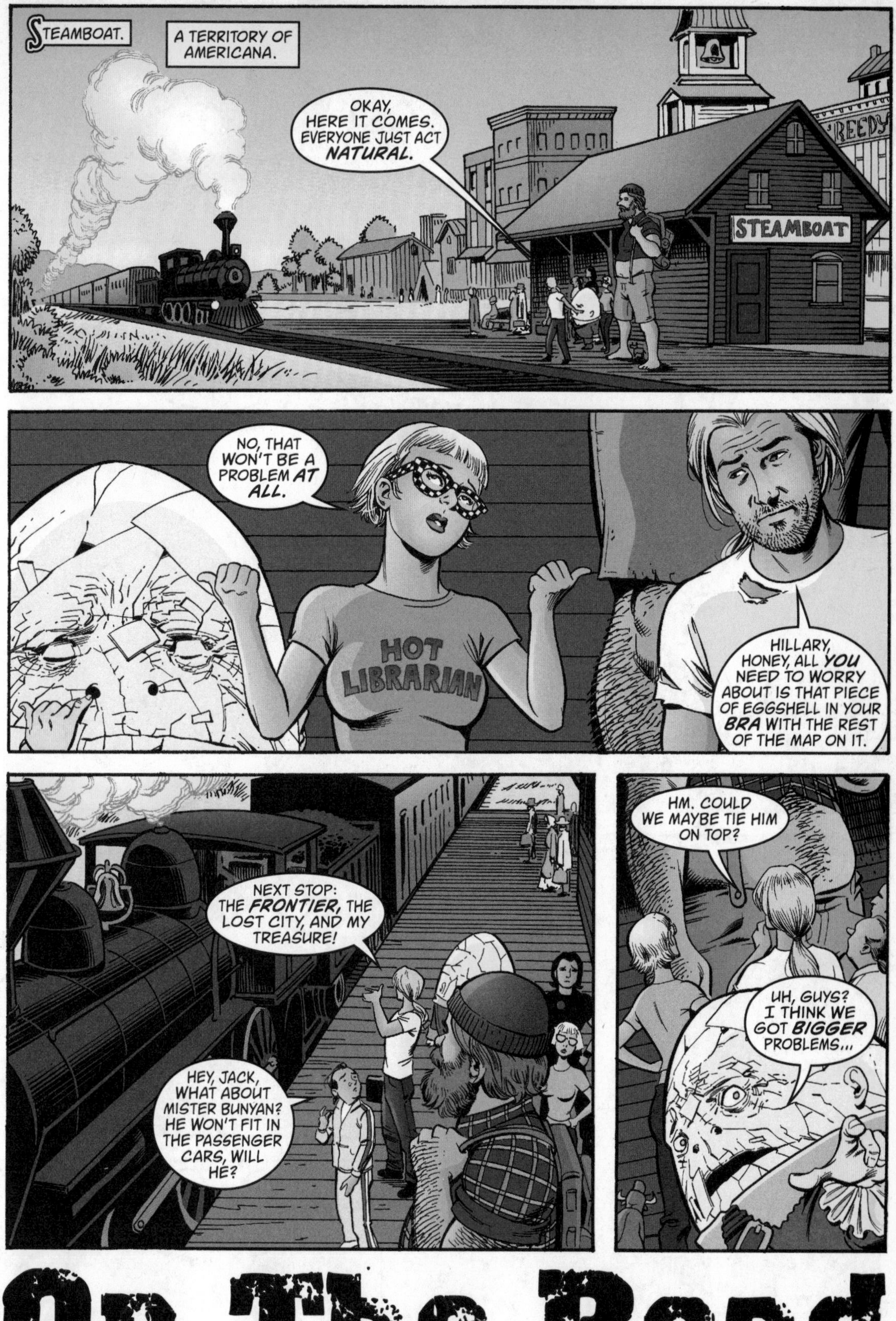
STEAMBOAT.
A TERRITORY OF AMERICANA.
OKAY, HERE IT COMES. EVERYONE JUST ACT *NATURAL.*
STEAMBOAT
NO, THAT WON'T BE A PROBLEM *AT ALL.*
HOT LIBRARIAN
HILLARY, HONEY, ALL *YOU* NEED TO WORRY ABOUT IS THAT PIECE OF EGGSHELL IN YOUR *BRA* WITH THE REST OF THE MAP ON IT.
NEXT STOP: THE *FRONTIER,* THE LOST CITY, AND MY TREASURE!
HEY, JACK, WHAT ABOUT MISTER BUNYAN? HE WON'T FIT IN THE PASSENGER CARS, WILL HE?
HM. COULD WE MAYBE TIE HIM ON TOP?
UH, GUYS? I THINK WE GOT *BIGGER* PROBLEMS...

On The Road

Part Three of AMERICANA

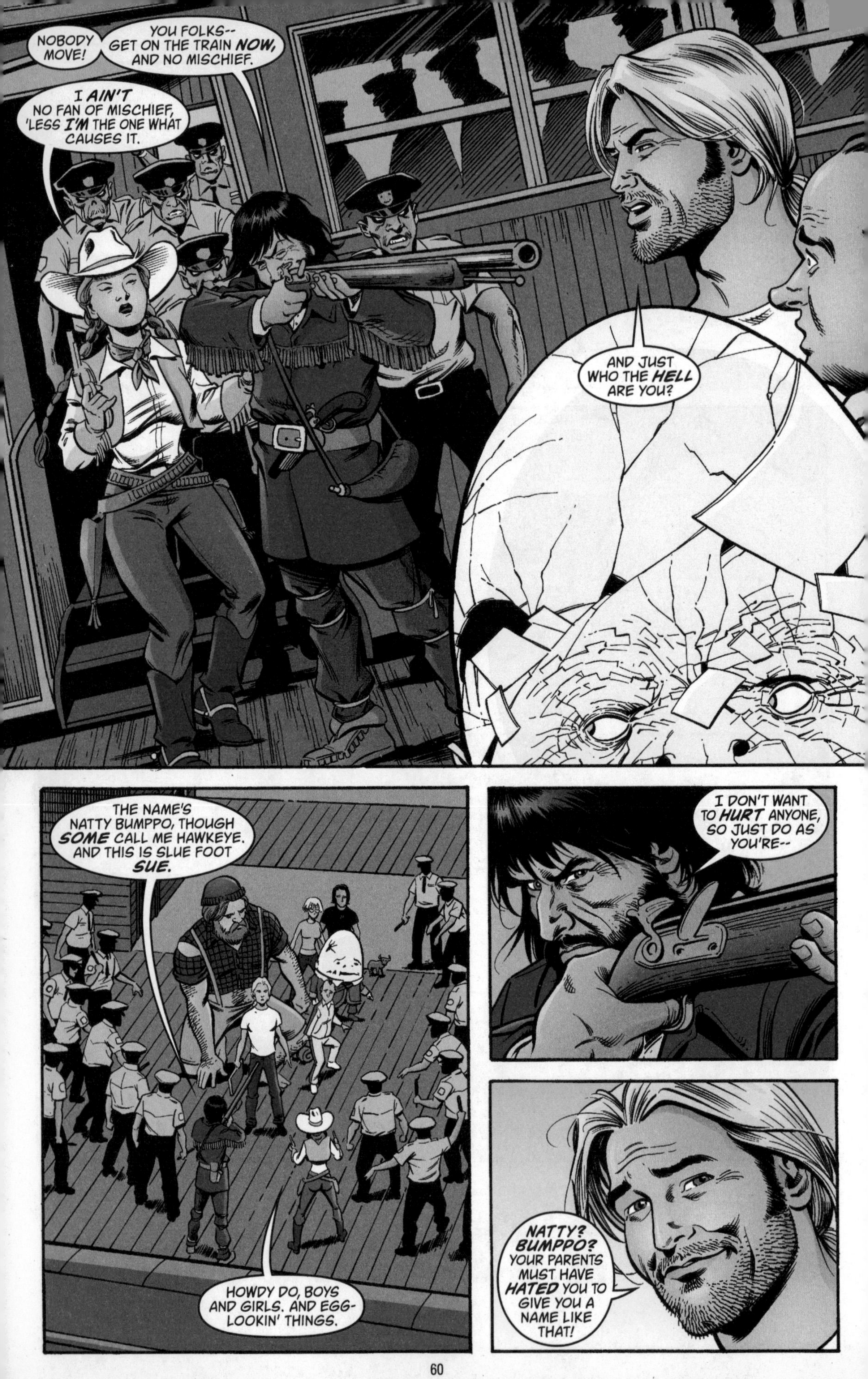

NOBODY MOVE!
YOU FOLKS-- GET ON THE TRAIN NOW, AND NO MISCHIEF.
I AIN'T NO FAN OF MISCHIEF, 'LESS I'M THE ONE WHAT CAUSES IT.
AND JUST WHO THE HELL ARE YOU?
THE NAME'S NATTY BUMPPO, THOUGH SOME CALL ME HAWKEYE. AND THIS IS SLUE FOOT SUE.
HOWDY DO, BOYS AND GIRLS. AND EGG-LOOKIN' THINGS.
I DON'T WANT TO HURT ANYONE, SO JUST DO AS YOU'RE--
NATTY? BUMPPO? YOUR PARENTS MUST HAVE HATED YOU TO GIVE YOU A NAME LIKE THAT!

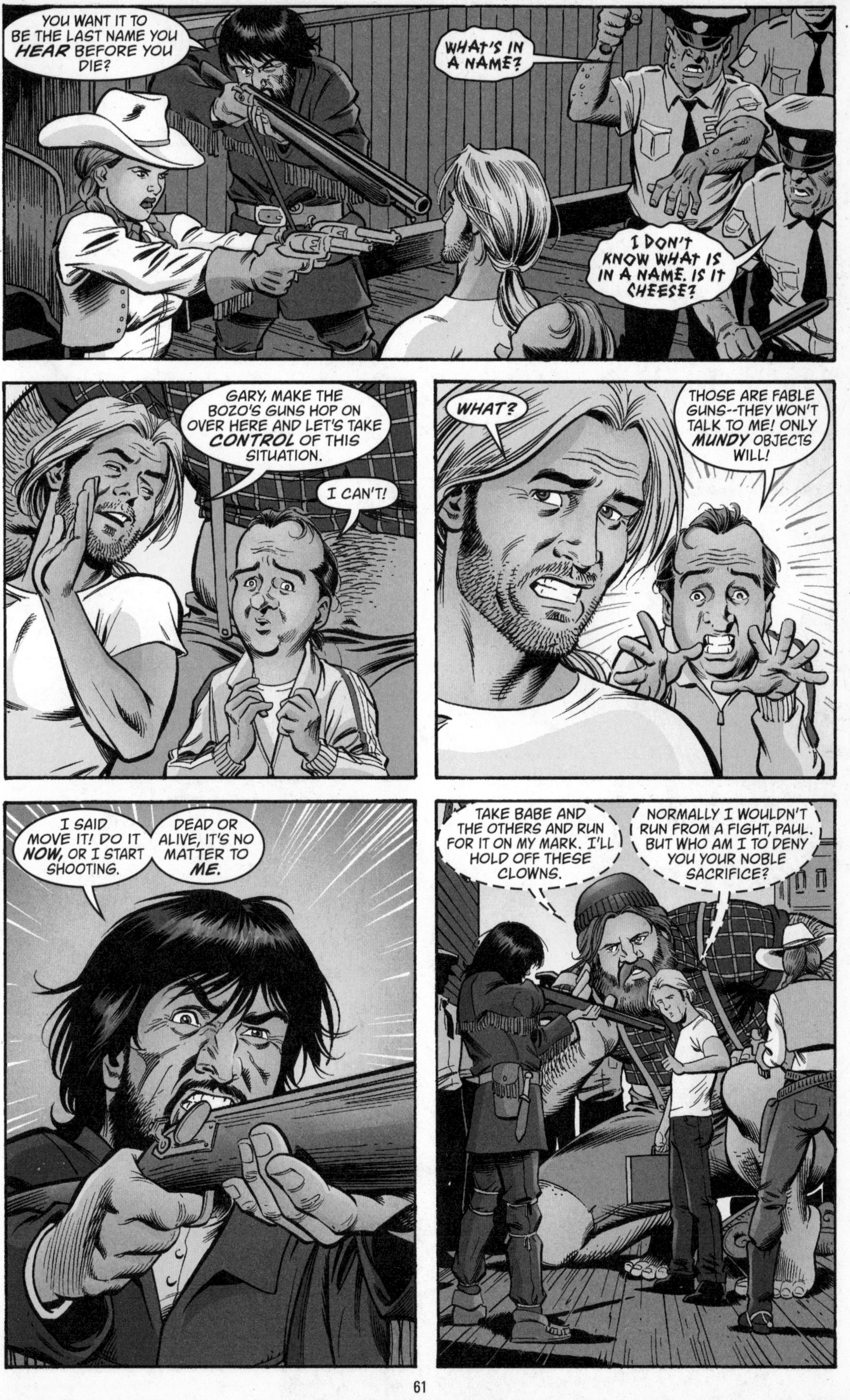
YOU WANT IT TO BE THE LAST NAME YOU HEAR BEFORE YOU DIE?
WHAT'S IN A NAME?
I DON'T KNOW WHAT IS IN A NAME. IS IT CHEESE?
GARY, MAKE THE BOZO'S GUNS HOP ON OVER HERE AND LET'S TAKE CONTROL OF THIS SITUATION.
I CAN'T!
WHAT?
THOSE ARE FABLE GUNS--THEY WON'T TALK TO ME! ONLY MUNDY OBJECTS WILL!
I SAID MOVE IT! DO IT NOW, OR I START SHOOTING.
DEAD OR ALIVE, IT'S NO MATTER TO ME.
TAKE BABE AND THE OTHERS AND RUN FOR IT ON MY MARK. I'LL HOLD OFF THESE CLOWNS.
NORMALLY I WOULDN'T RUN FROM A FIGHT, PAUL. BUT WHO AM I TO DENY YOU YOUR NOBLE SACRIFICE?

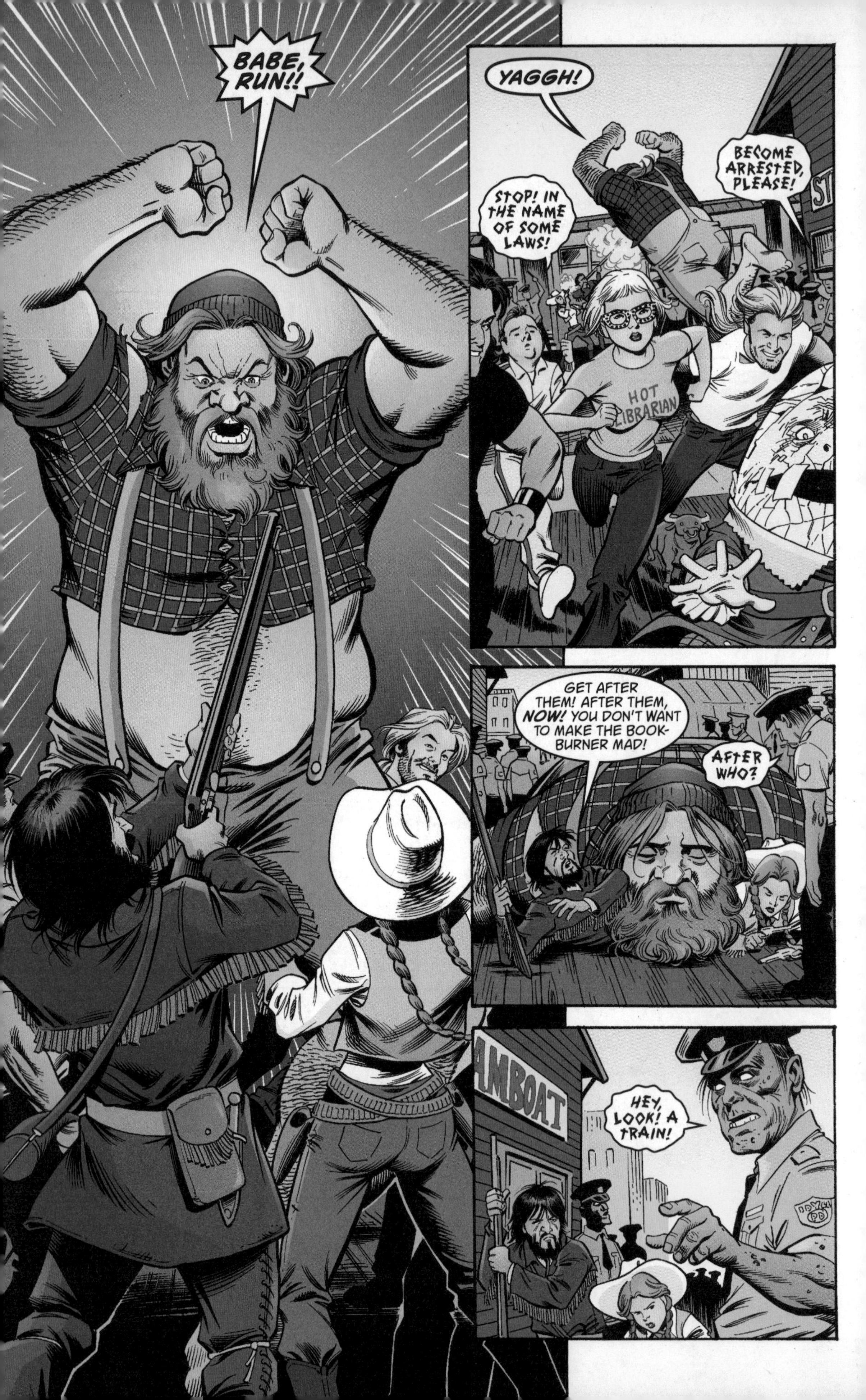
BABE, RUN!!
YAGGH!
STOP! IN THE NAME OF SOME LAWS!
BECOME ARRESTED, PLEASE!
HOT LIBRARIAN
GET AFTER THEM! AFTER THEM, NOW! YOU DON'T WANT TO MAKE THE BOOK-BURNER MAD!
AFTER WHO?
AMBOAT
HEY, LOOK! A TRAIN!

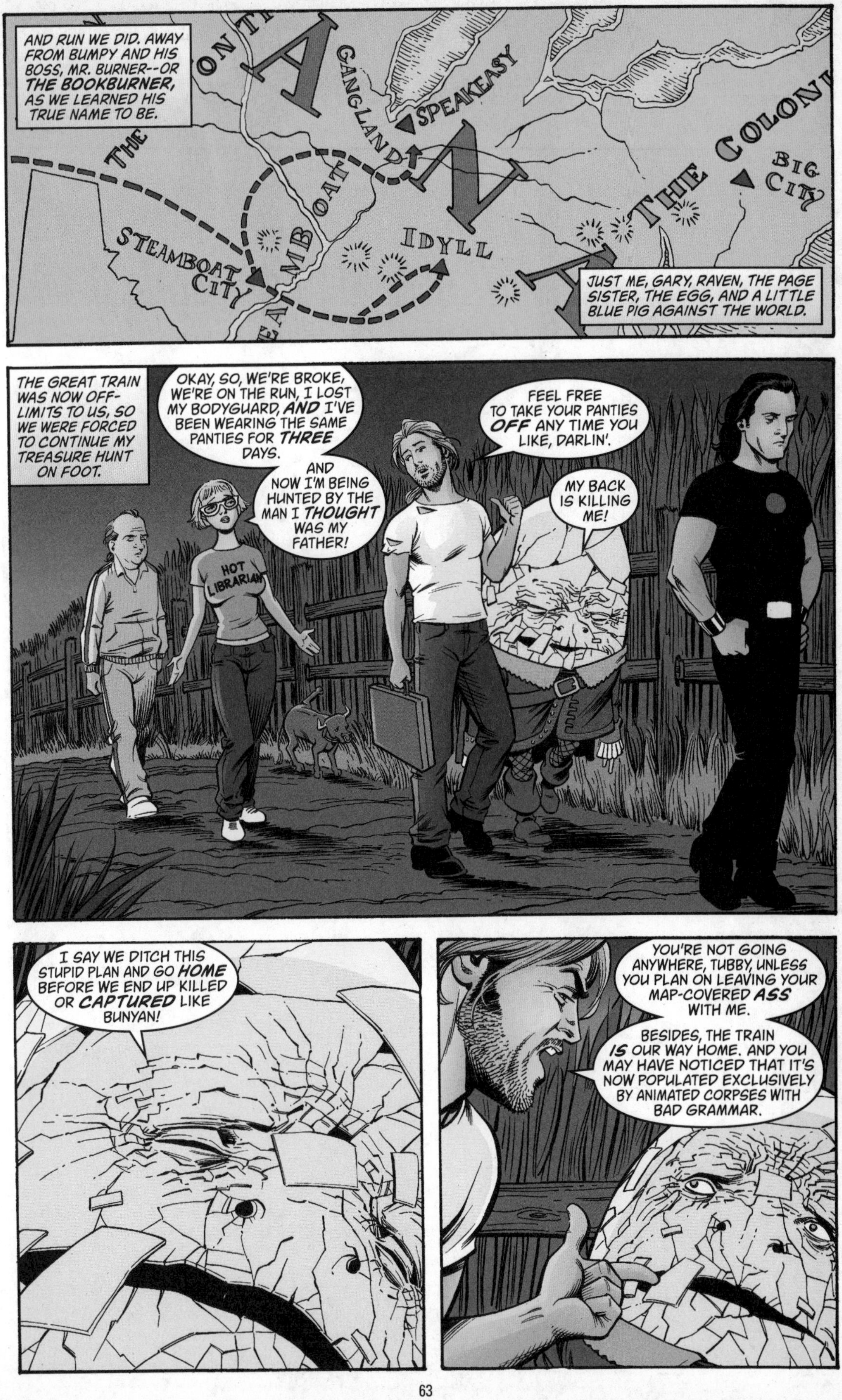
AND RUN WE DID. AWAY FROM BUMPY AND HIS BOSS, MR. BURNER--OR THE BOOKBURNER, AS WE LEARNED HIS TRUE NAME TO BE.
GANGLAND
SPEAKEASY
STEAMBOAT CITY
IDYLL
BIG CITY
JUST ME, GARY, RAVEN, THE PAGE SISTER, THE EGG, AND A LITTLE BLUE PIG AGAINST THE WORLD.
THE GREAT TRAIN WAS NOW OFF-LIMITS TO US, SO WE WERE FORCED TO CONTINUE MY TREASURE HUNT ON FOOT.
OKAY, SO, WE'RE BROKE, WE'RE ON THE RUN, I LOST MY BODYGUARD, AND I'VE BEEN WEARING THE SAME PANTIES FOR THREE DAYS.
AND NOW I'M BEING HUNTED BY THE MAN I THOUGHT WAS MY FATHER!
FEEL FREE TO TAKE YOUR PANTIES OFF ANY TIME YOU LIKE, DARLIN'.
MY BACK IS KILLING ME!
HOT LIBRARIAN
I SAY WE DITCH THIS STUPID PLAN AND GO HOME BEFORE WE END UP KILLED OR CAPTURED LIKE BUNYAN!
YOU'RE NOT GOING ANYWHERE, TUBBY, UNLESS YOU PLAN ON LEAVING YOUR MAP-COVERED ASS WITH ME.
BESIDES, THE TRAIN IS OUR WAY HOME. AND YOU MAY HAVE NOTICED THAT IT'S NOW POPULATED EXCLUSIVELY BY ANIMATED CORPSES WITH BAD GRAMMAR.

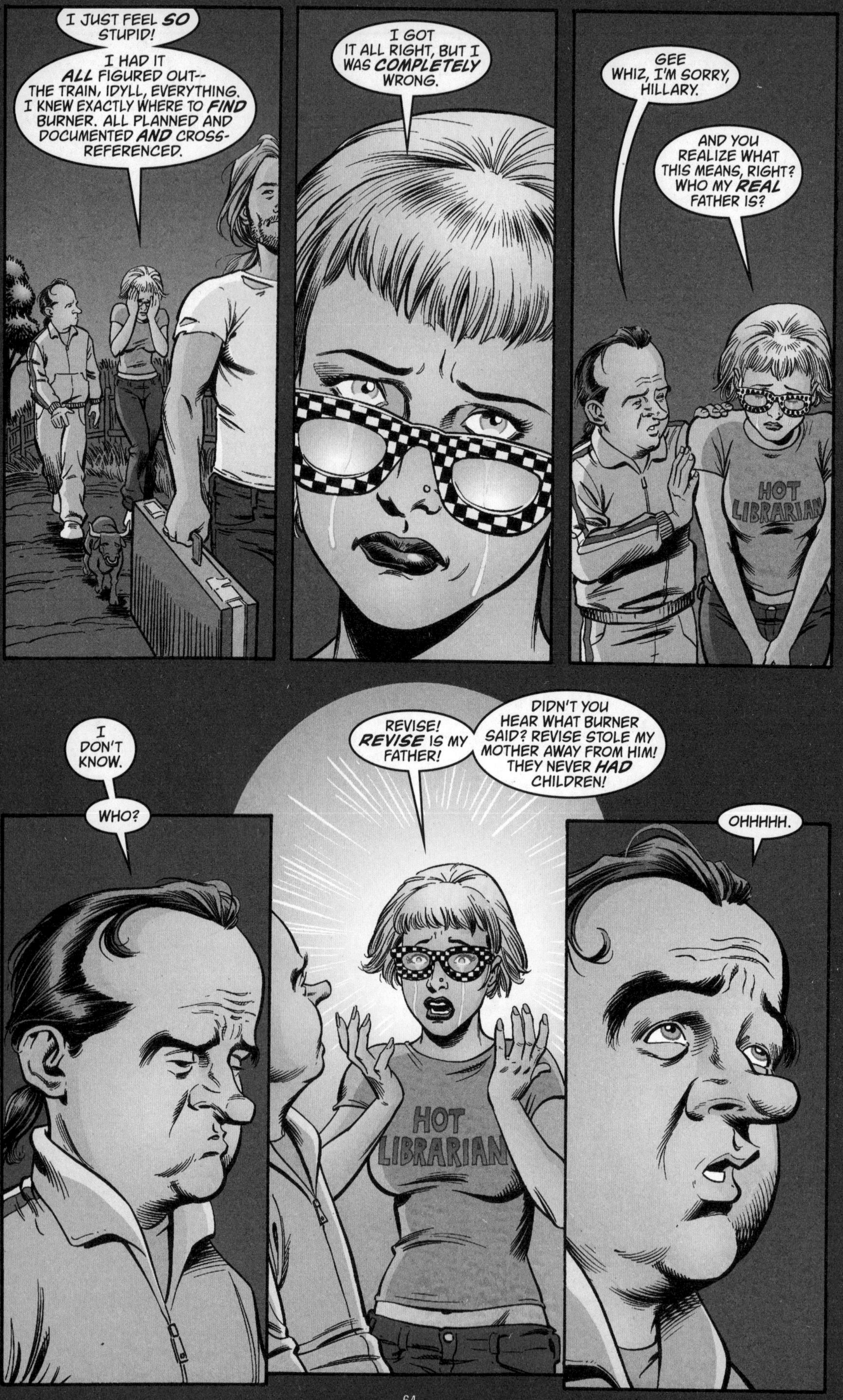
I JUST FEEL SO STUPID!
I HAD IT ALL FIGURED OUT-- THE TRAIN, IDYLL, EVERYTHING. I KNEW EXACTLY WHERE TO FIND BURNER. ALL PLANNED AND DOCUMENTED AND CROSS-REFERENCED.
I GOT IT ALL RIGHT, BUT I WAS COMPLETELY WRONG.
GEE WHIZ, I'M SORRY, HILLARY.
AND YOU REALIZE WHAT THIS MEANS, RIGHT? WHO MY REAL FATHER IS?
I DON'T KNOW.
WHO?
REVISE! REVISE IS MY FATHER!
DIDN'T YOU HEAR WHAT BURNER SAID? REVISE STOLE MY MOTHER AWAY FROM HIM! THEY NEVER HAD CHILDREN!
OHHHHH.

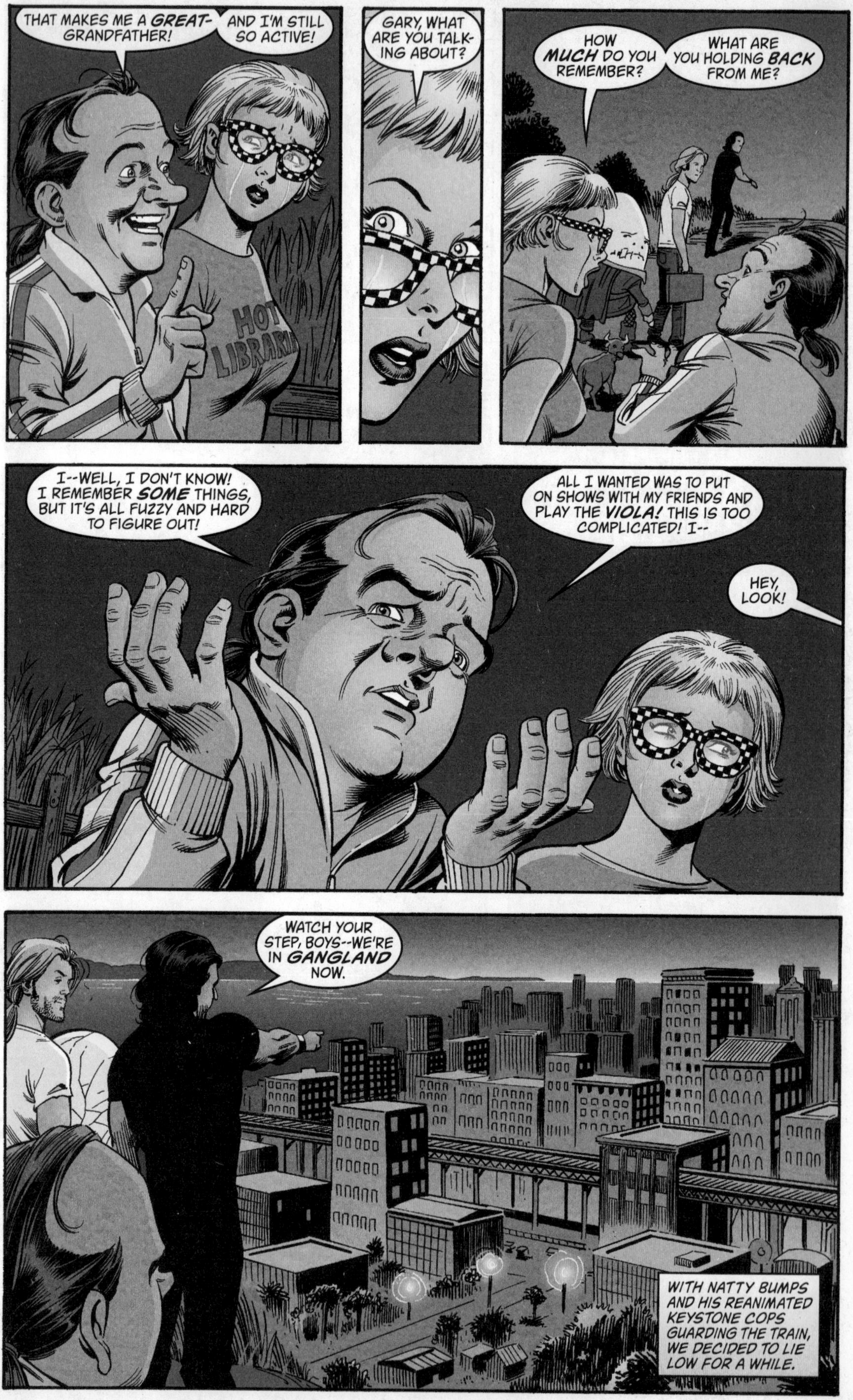

THAT MAKES ME A GREAT-GRANDFATHER!
AND I'M STILL SO ACTIVE!
GARY, WHAT ARE YOU TALKING ABOUT?
HOT LIBRARI
HOW MUCH DO YOU REMEMBER?
WHAT ARE YOU HOLDING BACK FROM ME?
I--WELL, I DON'T KNOW! I REMEMBER SOME THINGS, BUT IT'S ALL FUZZY AND HARD TO FIGURE OUT!
ALL I WANTED WAS TO PUT ON SHOWS WITH MY FRIENDS AND PLAY THE VIOLA! THIS IS TOO COMPLICATED! I--
HEY, LOOK!
WATCH YOUR STEP, BOYS--WE'RE IN GANGLAND NOW.
WITH NATTY BUMPS AND HIS REANIMATED KEYSTONE COPS GUARDING THE TRAIN, WE DECIDED TO LIE LOW FOR A WHILE.

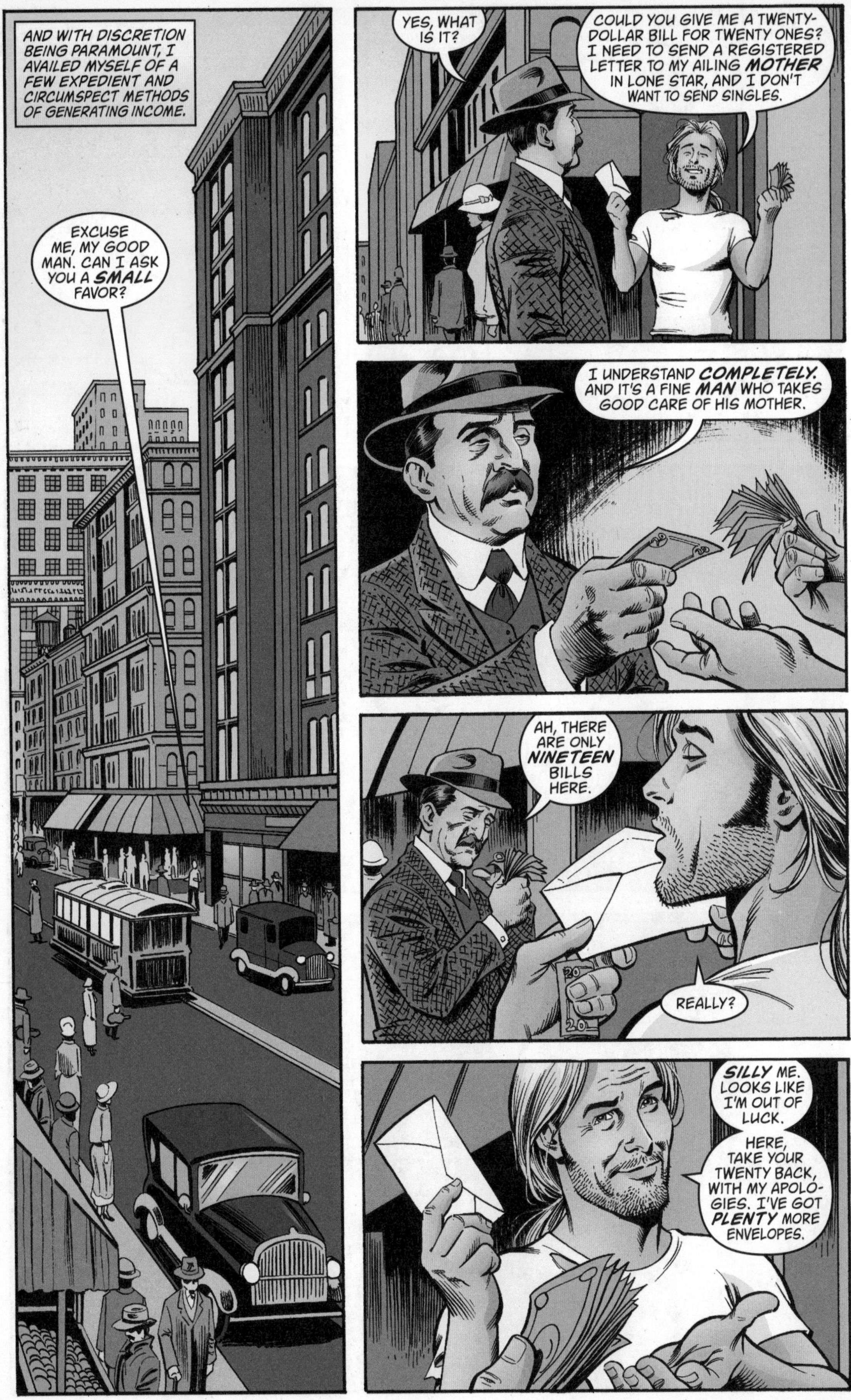
AND WITH DISCRETION BEING PARAMOUNT, I AVAILED MYSELF OF A FEW EXPEDIENT AND CIRCUMSPECT METHODS OF GENERATING INCOME.
EXCUSE ME, MY GOOD MAN. CAN I ASK YOU A SMALL FAVOR?
YES, WHAT IS IT?
COULD YOU GIVE ME A TWENTY-DOLLAR BILL FOR TWENTY ONES? I NEED TO SEND A REGISTERED LETTER TO MY AILING MOTHER IN LONE STAR, AND I DON'T WANT TO SEND SINGLES.
I UNDERSTAND COMPLETELY. AND IT'S A FINE MAN WHO TAKES GOOD CARE OF HIS MOTHER.
AH, THERE ARE ONLY NINETEEN BILLS HERE.
REALLY?
SILLY ME. LOOKS LIKE I'M OUT OF LUCK.
HERE, TAKE YOUR TWENTY BACK, WITH MY APOLOGIES. I'VE GOT PLENTY MORE ENVELOPES.

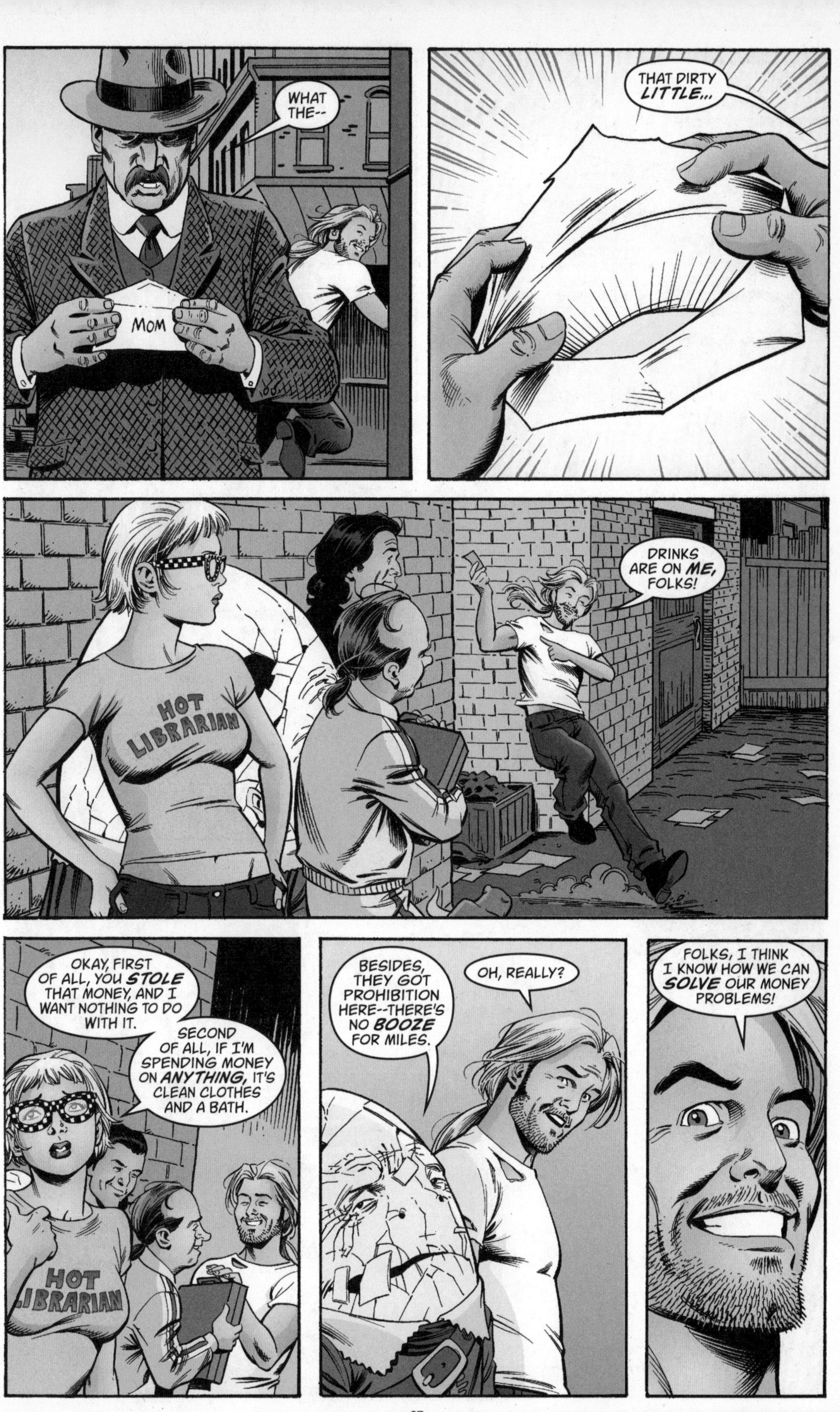

WHAT THE--
MOM
THAT DIRTY LITTLE...
DRINKS ARE ON ME, FOLKS!
HOT LIBRARIAN
OKAY, FIRST OF ALL, YOU STOLE THAT MONEY, AND I WANT NOTHING TO DO WITH IT.
SECOND OF ALL, IF I'M SPENDING MONEY ON ANYTHING, IT'S CLEAN CLOTHES AND A BATH.
HOT LIBRARIAN
BESIDES, THEY GOT PROHIBITION HERE--THERE'S NO BOOZE FOR MILES.
OH, REALLY?
FOLKS, I THINK I KNOW HOW WE CAN SOLVE OUR MONEY PROBLEMS!

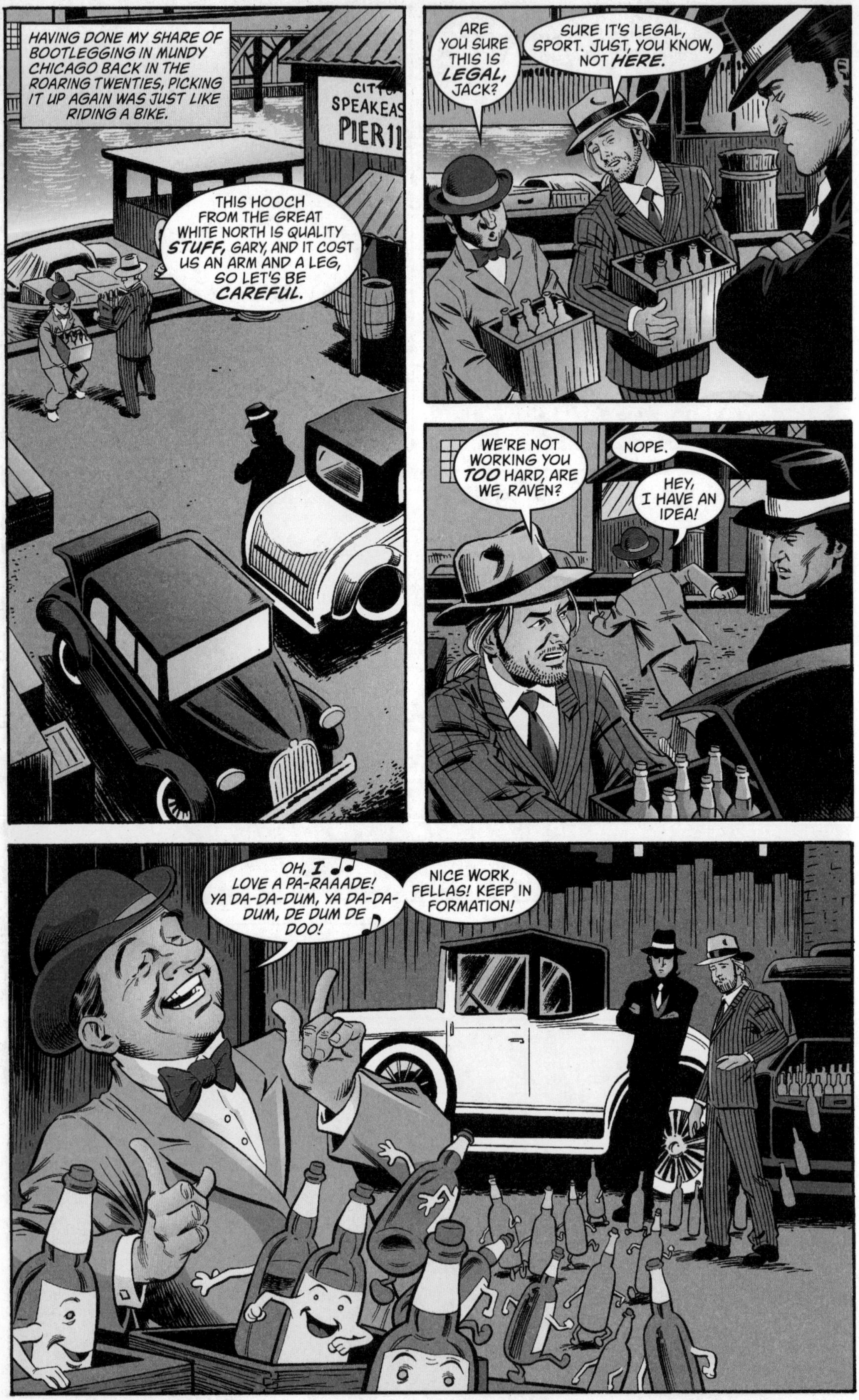

HAVING DONE MY SHARE OF BOOTLEGGING IN MUNDY CHICAGO BACK IN THE ROARING TWENTIES, PICKING IT UP AGAIN WAS JUST LIKE RIDING A BIKE.
SPEAKEAS
PIER 11
THIS HOOCH FROM THE GREAT WHITE NORTH IS QUALITY STUFF, GARY, AND IT COST US AN ARM AND A LEG, SO LET'S BE CAREFUL.
ARE YOU SURE THIS IS LEGAL, JACK?
SURE IT'S LEGAL, SPORT. JUST, YOU KNOW, NOT HERE.
WE'RE NOT WORKING YOU TOO HARD, ARE WE, RAVEN?
NOPE.
HEY, I HAVE AN IDEA!
OH, I LOVE A PA-RAAADE! YA DA-DA-DUM, YA DA-DA-DUM, DE DUM DE DOO!
NICE WORK, FELLAS! KEEP IN FORMATION!

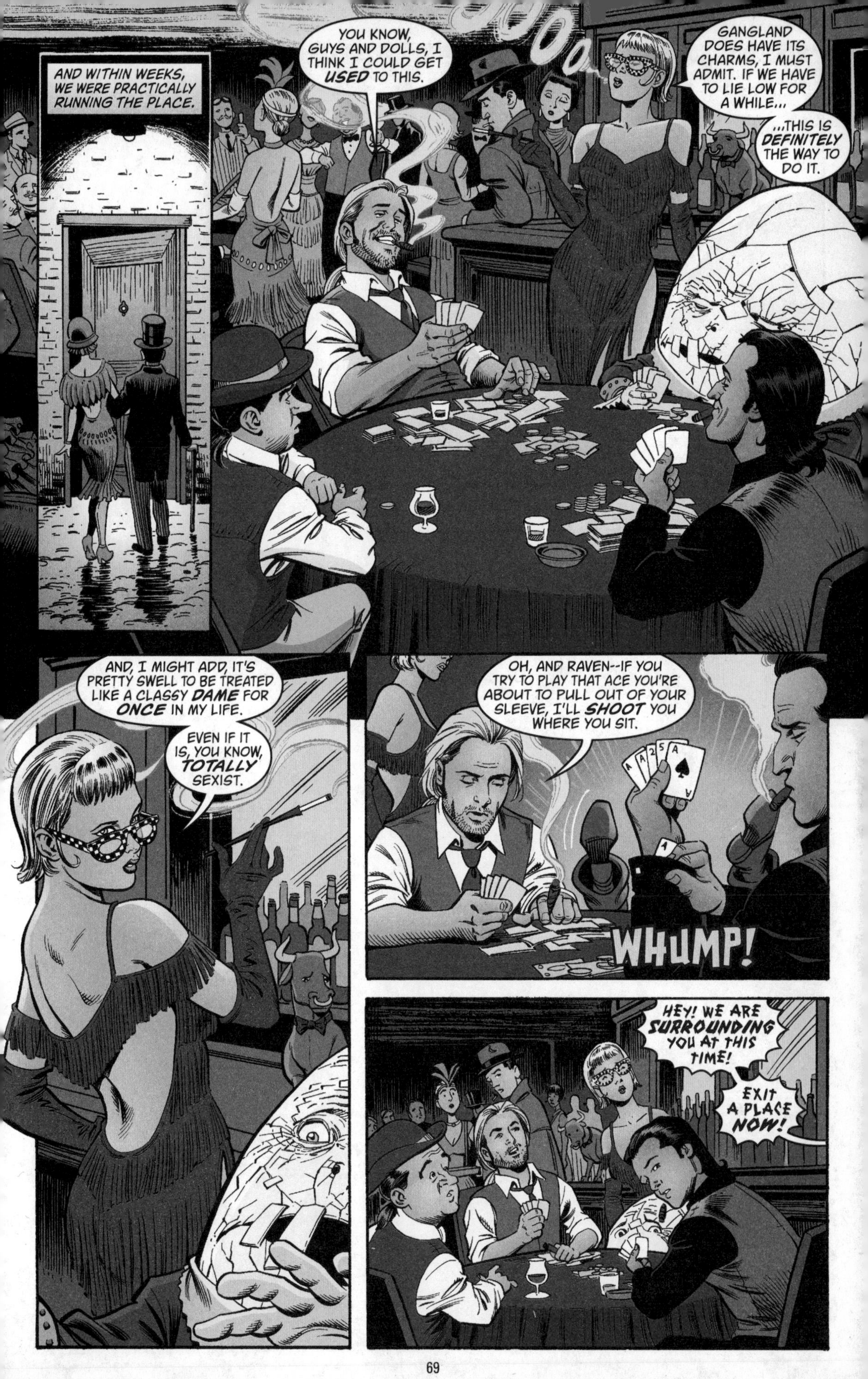
AND WITHIN WEEKS, WE WERE PRACTICALLY RUNNING THE PLACE.
YOU KNOW, GUYS AND DOLLS, I THINK I COULD GET USED TO THIS.
GANGLAND DOES HAVE ITS CHARMS, I MUST ADMIT. IF WE HAVE TO LIE LOW FOR A WHILE...
...THIS IS DEFINITELY THE WAY TO DO IT.
AND, I MIGHT ADD, IT'S PRETTY SWELL TO BE TREATED LIKE A CLASSY DAME FOR ONCE IN MY LIFE.
EVEN IF IT IS, YOU KNOW, TOTALLY SEXIST.
OH, AND RAVEN--IF YOU TRY TO PLAY THAT ACE YOU'RE ABOUT TO PULL OUT OF YOUR SLEEVE, I'LL SHOOT YOU WHERE YOU SIT.
WHUMP!
HEY! WE ARE SURROUNDING YOU AT THIS TIME!
EXIT A PLACE NOW!

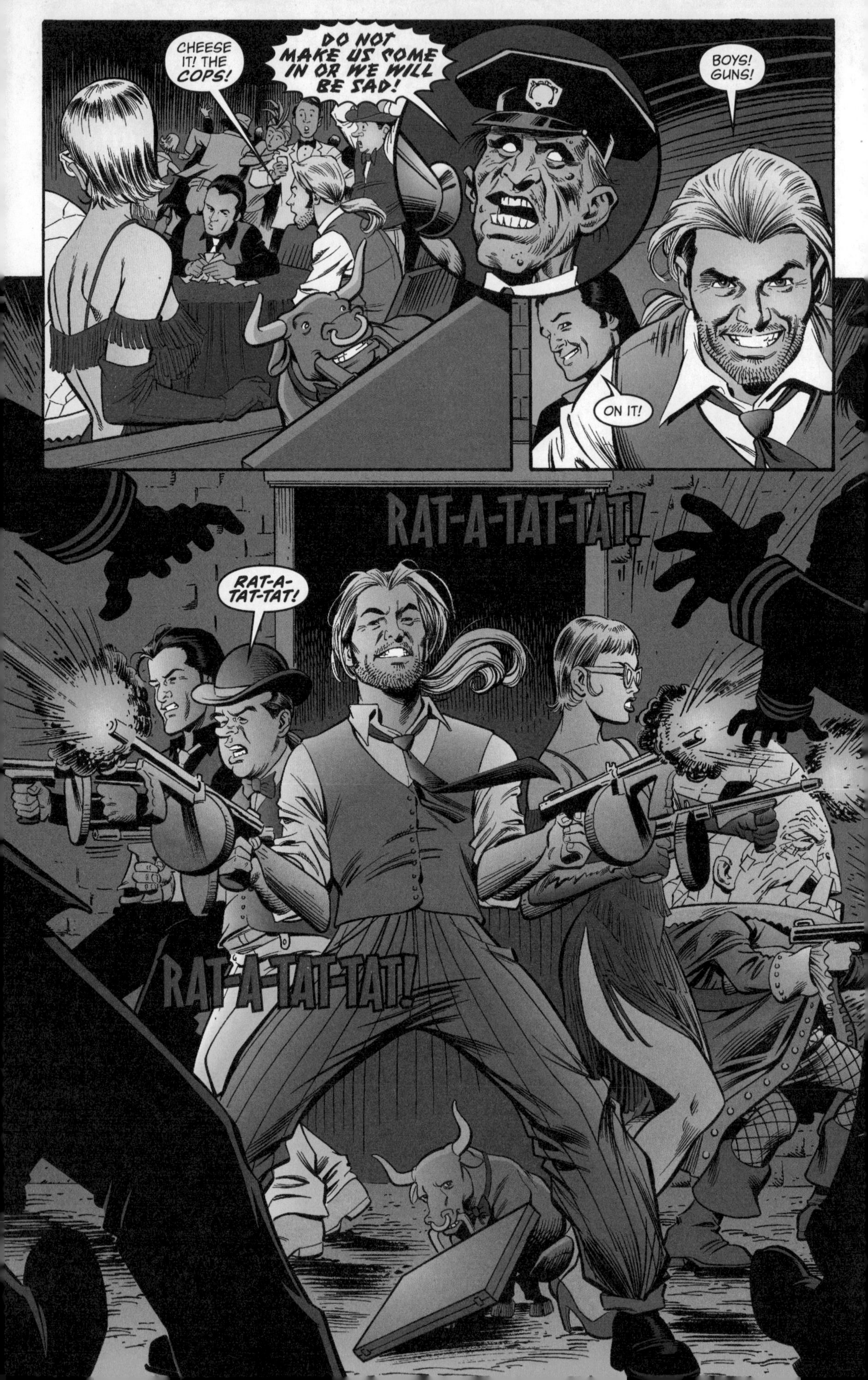
CHEESE IT! THE COPS!
DO NOT MAKE US COME IN OR WE WILL BE SAD!
BOYS! GUNS!
ON IT!
RAT-A-TAT-TAT!
RAT-A-TAT-TAT!
RAT-A-TAT-TAT!

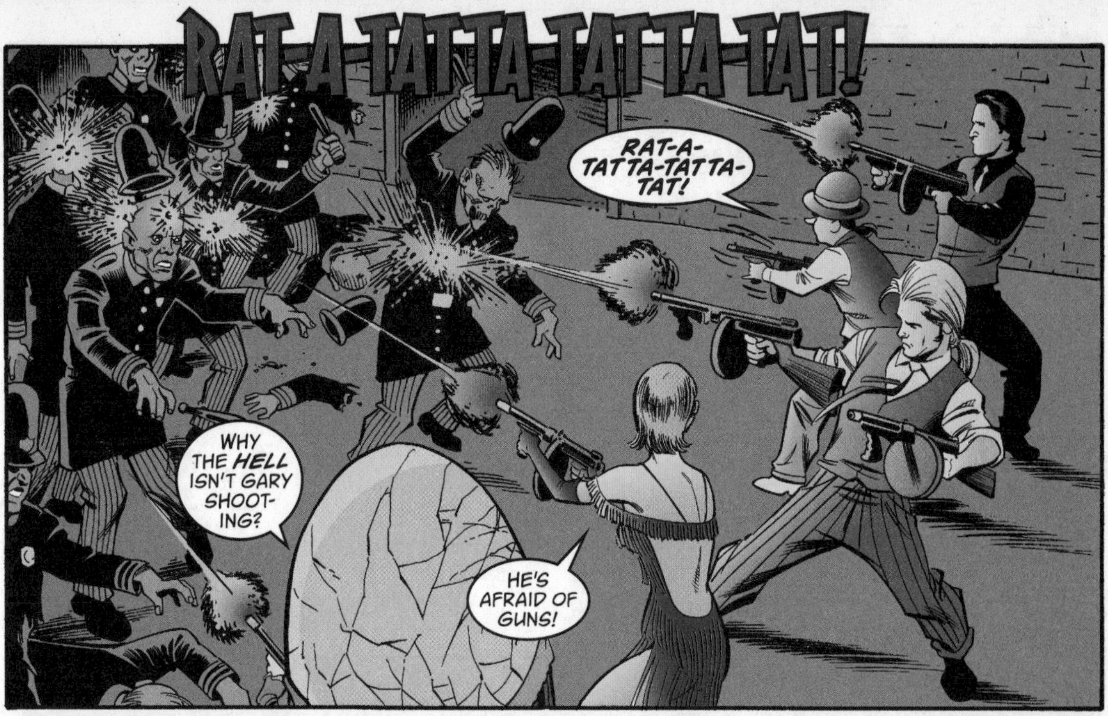
RAT-A-TATTA-TATTA-TAT!
RAT-A-TATTA-TATTA-TAT!
WHY THE HELL ISN'T GARY SHOOTING?
HE'S AFRAID OF GUNS!

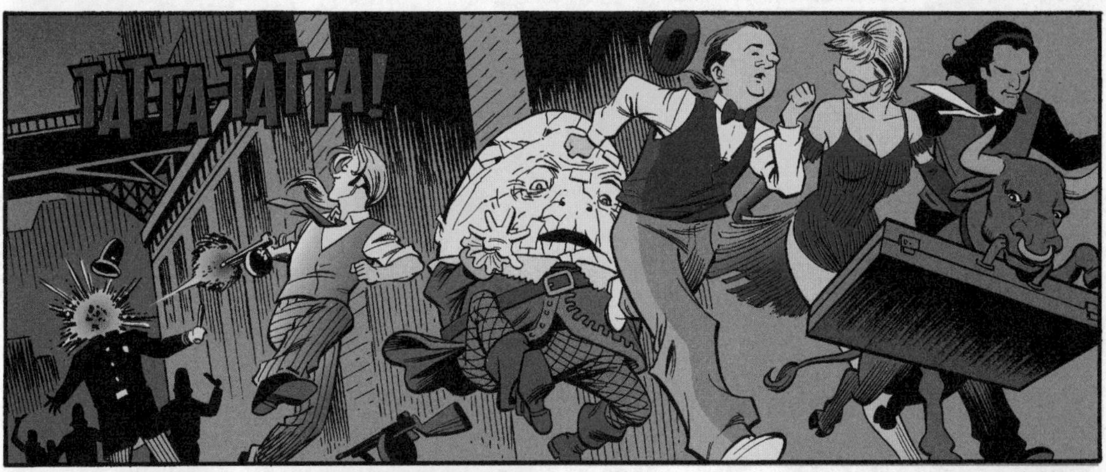
TAT-TA-TATTA!

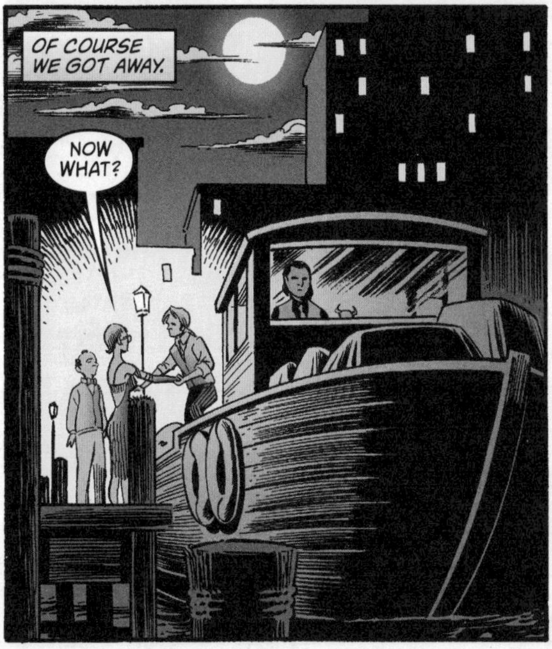
OF COURSE WE GOT AWAY.
NOW WHAT?

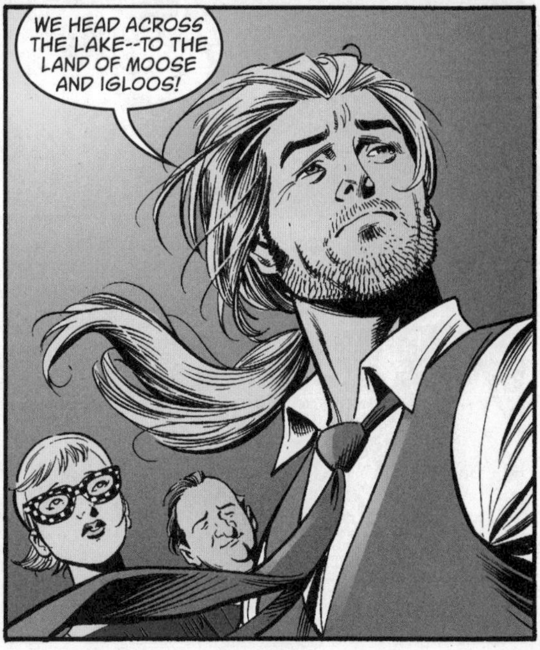
WE HEAD ACROSS THE LAKE--TO THE LAND OF MOOSE AND IGLOOS!

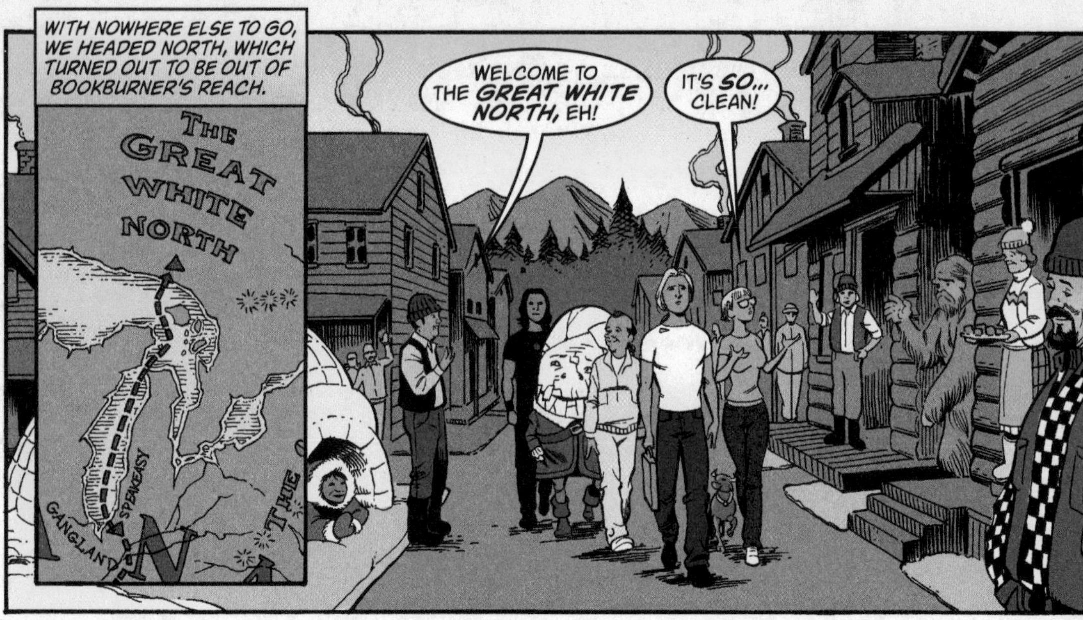
WITH NOWHERE ELSE TO GO, WE HEADED NORTH, WHICH TURNED OUT TO BE OUT OF BOOKBURNER'S REACH.
THE GREAT WHITE NORTH
SPEAKEASY
GANGLAND
THE
WELCOME TO THE GREAT WHITE NORTH, EH!
IT'S SO... CLEAN!

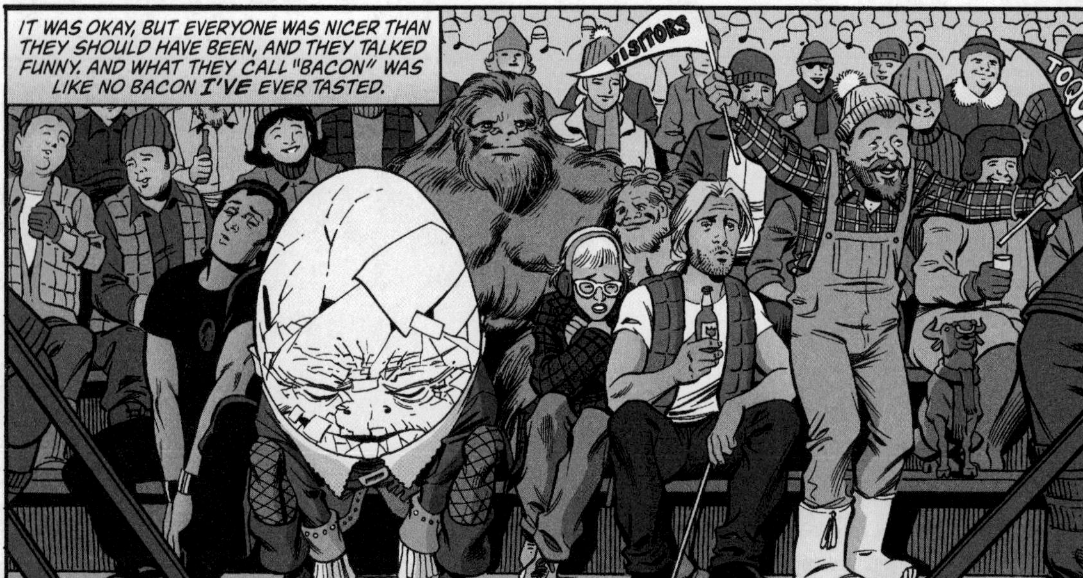
IT WAS OKAY, BUT EVERYONE WAS NICER THAN THEY SHOULD HAVE BEEN, AND THEY TALKED FUNNY. AND WHAT THEY CALL "BACON" WAS LIKE NO BACON I'VE EVER TASTED.
VISITORS
TOQUES

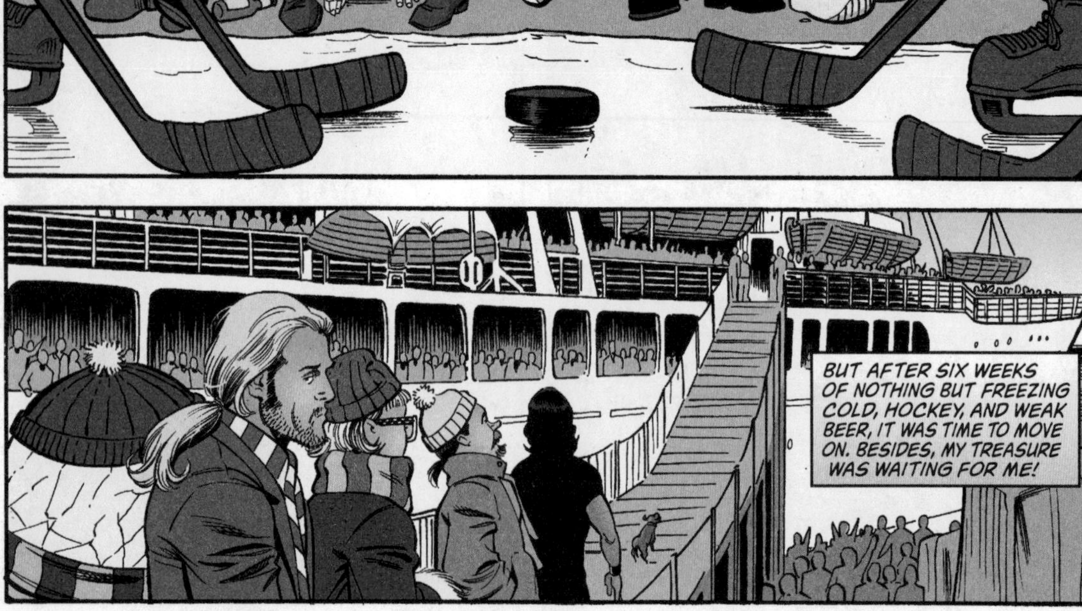
BUT AFTER SIX WEEKS OF NOTHING BUT FREEZING COLD, HOCKEY, AND WEAK BEER, IT WAS TIME TO MOVE ON. BESIDES, MY TREASURE WAS WAITING FOR ME!

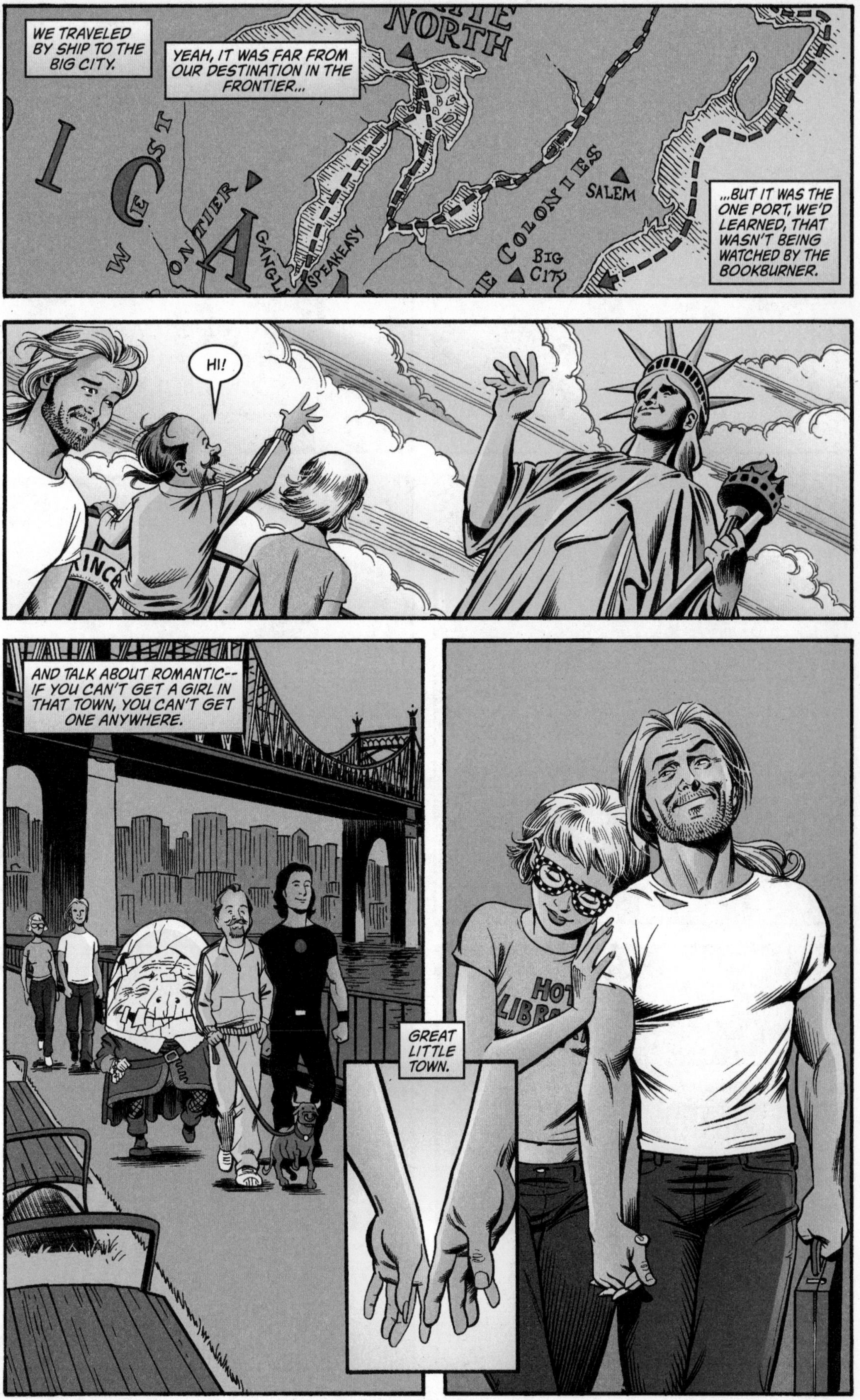
WE TRAVELED BY SHIP TO THE BIG CITY.
YEAH, IT WAS FAR FROM OUR DESTINATION IN THE FRONTIER...
NORTH
SALEM
SPEAKEASY
BIG CITY
...BUT IT WAS THE ONE PORT, WE'D LEARNED, THAT WASN'T BEING WATCHED BY THE BOOKBURNER.
HI!
AND TALK ABOUT ROMANTIC-- IF YOU CAN'T GET A GIRL IN THAT TOWN, YOU CAN'T GET ONE ANYWHERE.
GREAT LITTLE TOWN.

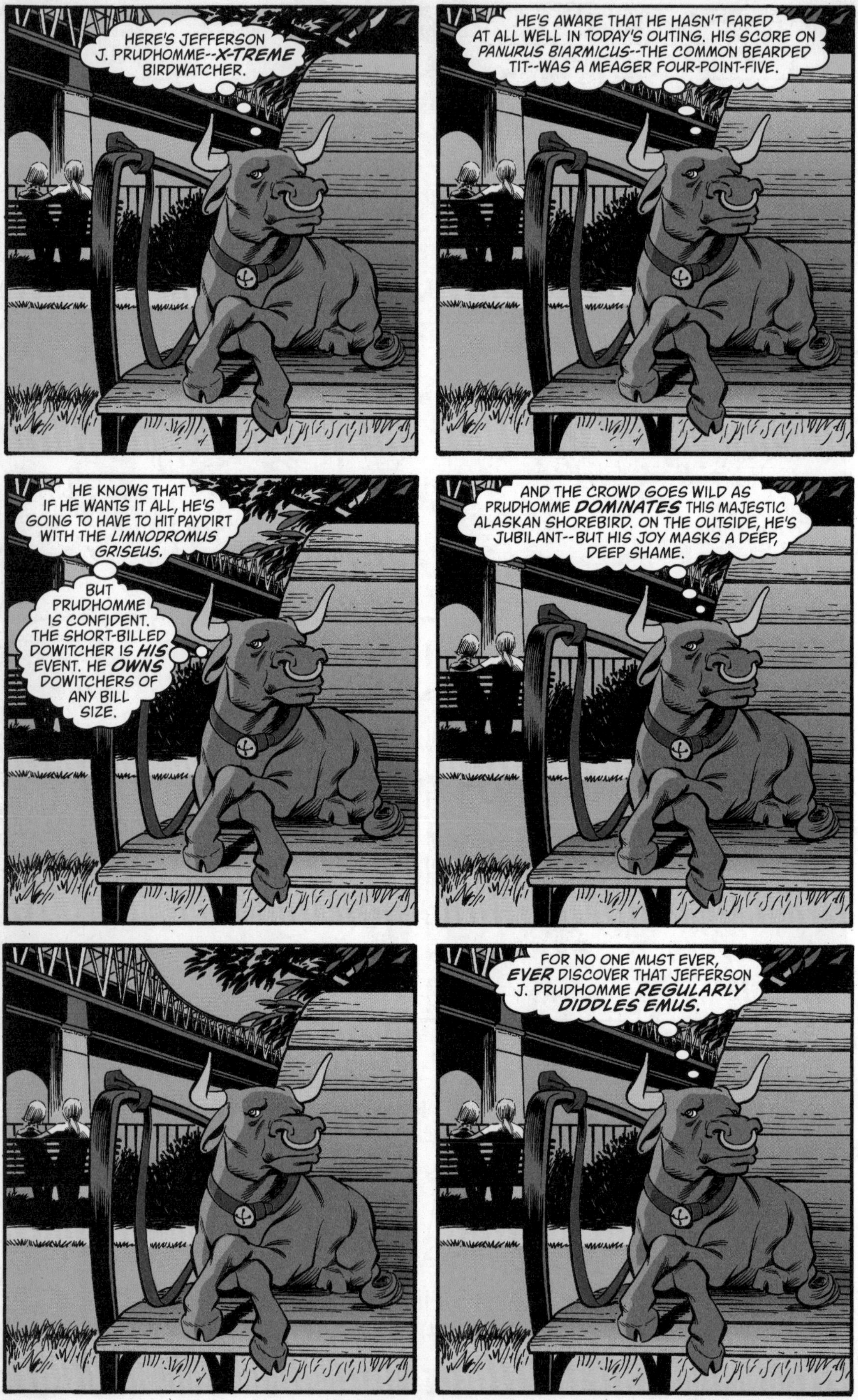
HERE'S JEFFERSON J. PRUDHOMME--X-TREME BIRDWATCHER.
HE'S AWARE THAT HE HASN'T FARED AT ALL WELL IN TODAY'S OUTING. HIS SCORE ON PANURUS BIARMICUS--THE COMMON BEARDED TIT--WAS A MEAGER FOUR-POINT-FIVE.
HE KNOWS THAT IF HE WANTS IT ALL, HE'S GOING TO HAVE TO HIT PAYDIRT WITH THE LIMNODROMUS GRISEUS.
BUT PRUDHOMME IS CONFIDENT. THE SHORT-BILLED DOWITCHER IS HIS EVENT. HE OWNS DOWITCHERS OF ANY BILL SIZE.
AND THE CROWD GOES WILD AS PRUDHOMME DOMINATES THIS MAJESTIC ALASKAN SHOREBIRD. ON THE OUTSIDE, HE'S JUBILANT--BUT HIS JOY MASKS A DEEP, DEEP SHAME.
FOR NO ONE MUST EVER, EVER DISCOVER THAT JEFFERSON J. PRUDHOMME REGULARLY DIDDLES EMUS.

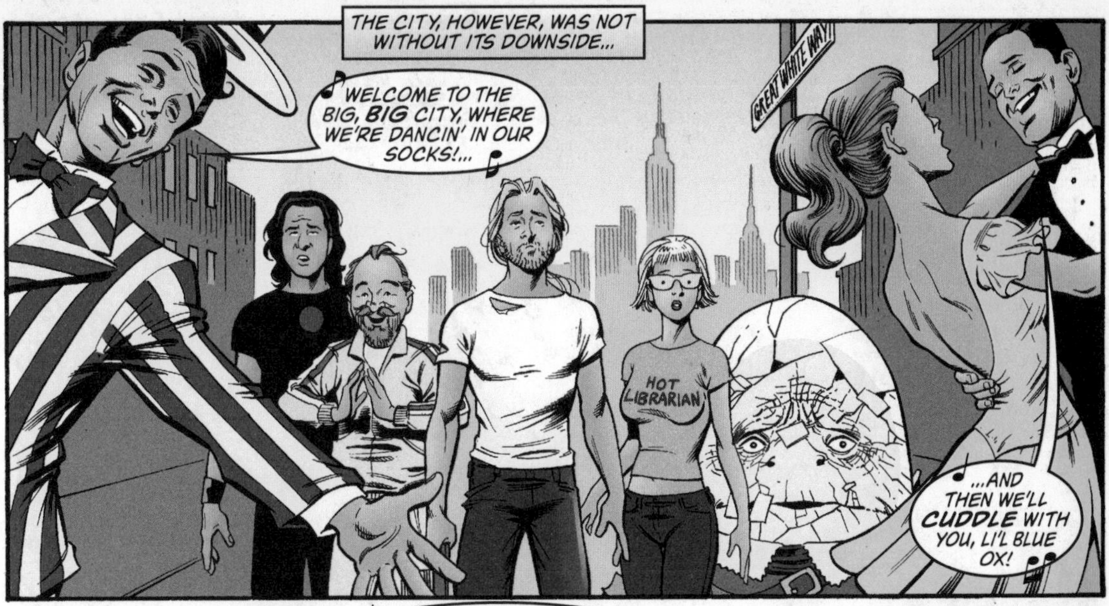
THE CITY, HOWEVER, WAS NOT WITHOUT ITS DOWNSIDE...
WELCOME TO THE BIG, BIG CITY, WHERE WE'RE DANCIN' IN OUR SOCKS!...
GREAT WHITE WAY
HOT LIBRARIAN
...AND THEN WE'LL CUDDLE WITH YOU, LI'L BLUE OX!

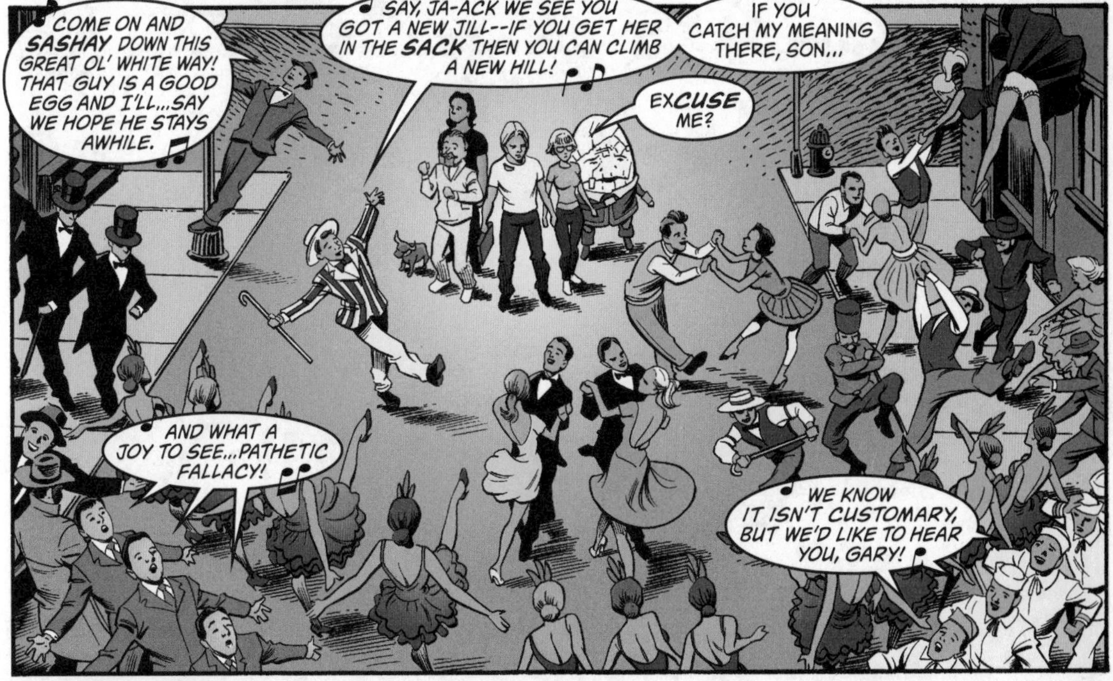
COME ON AND SASHAY DOWN THIS GREAT OL' WHITE WAY! THAT GUY IS A GOOD EGG AND I'LL...SAY WE HOPE HE STAYS AWHILE.
SAY, JA-ACK WE SEE YOU GOT A NEW JILL--IF YOU GET HER IN THE SACK THEN YOU CAN CLIMB A NEW HILL!
IF YOU CATCH MY MEANING THERE, SON...
EXCUSE ME?
AND WHAT A JOY TO SEE...PATHETIC FALLACY!
WE KNOW IT ISN'T CUSTOMARY, BUT WE'D LIKE TO HEAR YOU, GARY!

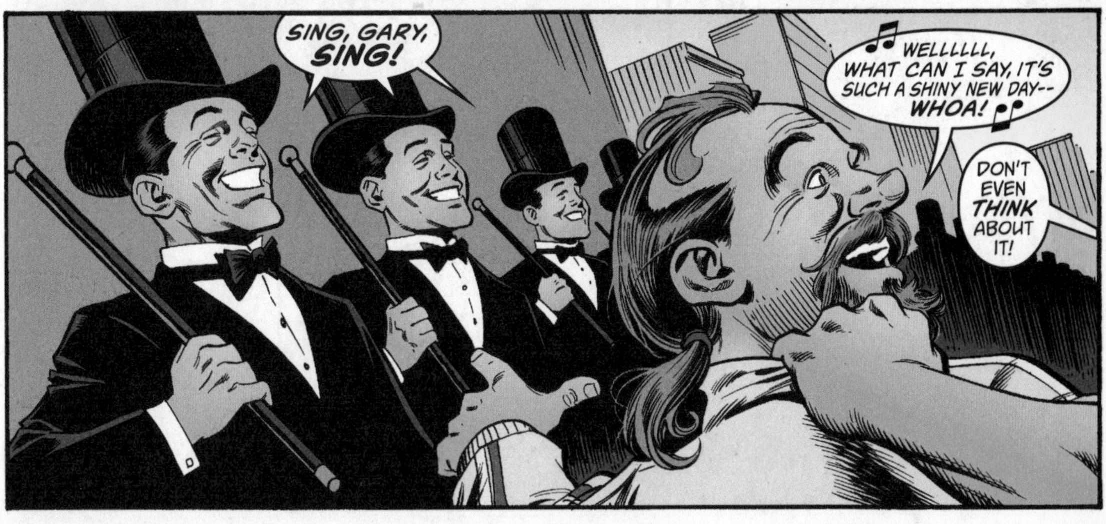
SING, GARY, SING!
WELLLLLL, WHAT CAN I SAY, IT'S SUCH A SHINY NEW DAY--WHOA!
DON'T EVEN THINK ABOUT IT!

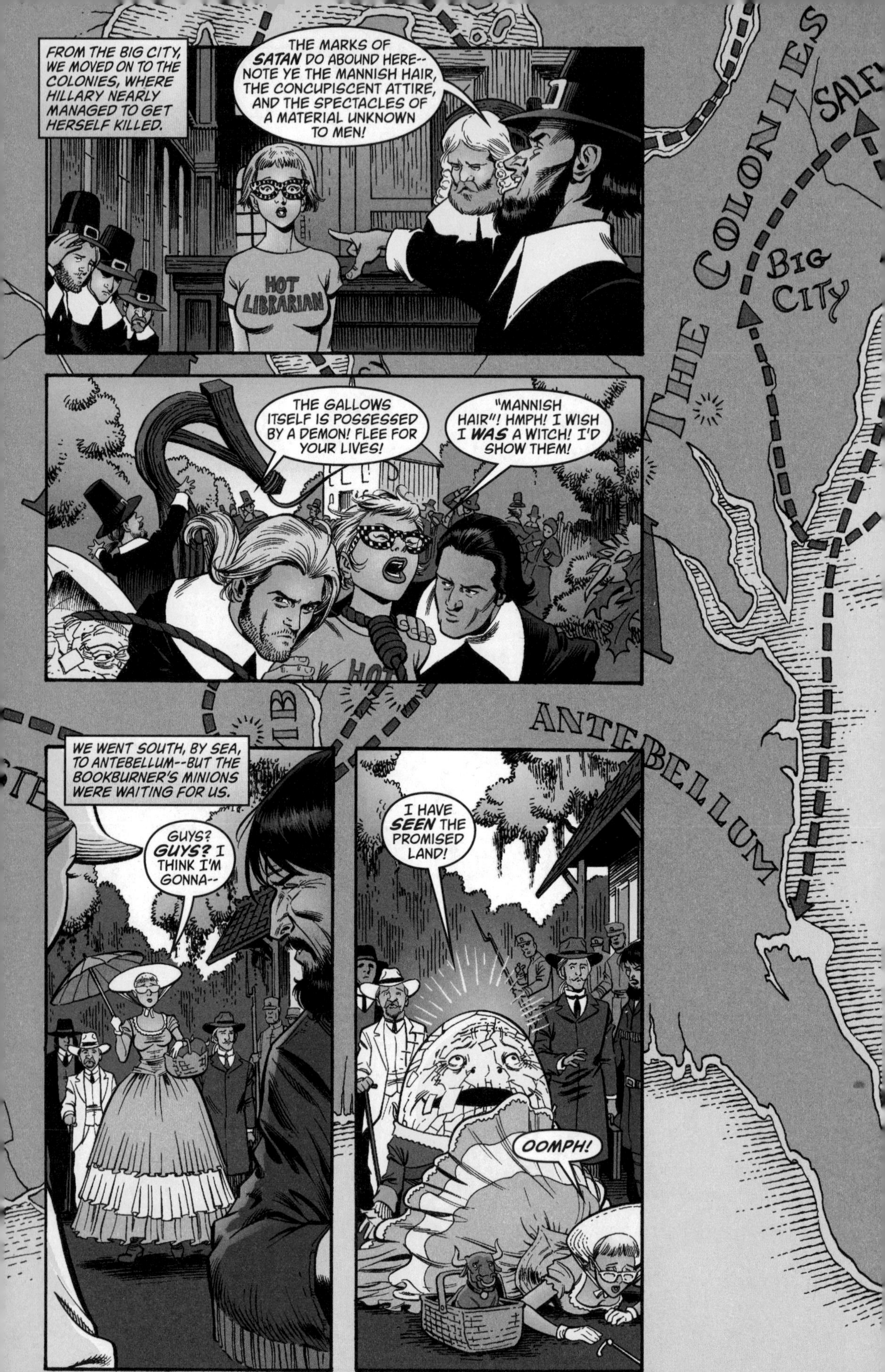
FROM THE BIG CITY, WE MOVED ON TO THE COLONIES, WHERE HILLARY NEARLY MANAGED TO GET HERSELF KILLED.
THE MARKS OF SATAN DO ABOUND HERE-- NOTE YE THE MANNISH HAIR, THE CONCUPISCENT ATTIRE, AND THE SPECTACLES OF A MATERIAL UNKNOWN TO MEN!
HOT LIBRARIAN
THE GALLOWS ITSELF IS POSSESSED BY A DEMON! FLEE FOR YOUR LIVES!
"MANNISH HAIR"! HMPH! I WISH I WAS A WITCH! I'D SHOW THEM!
WE WENT SOUTH, BY SEA, TO ANTEBELLUM--BUT THE BOOKBURNER'S MINIONS WERE WAITING FOR US.
GUYS? GUYS? I THINK I'M GONNA--
I HAVE SEEN THE PROMISED LAND!
OOMPH!
THE COLONIES
SALEM
BIG CITY
ANTEBELLUM

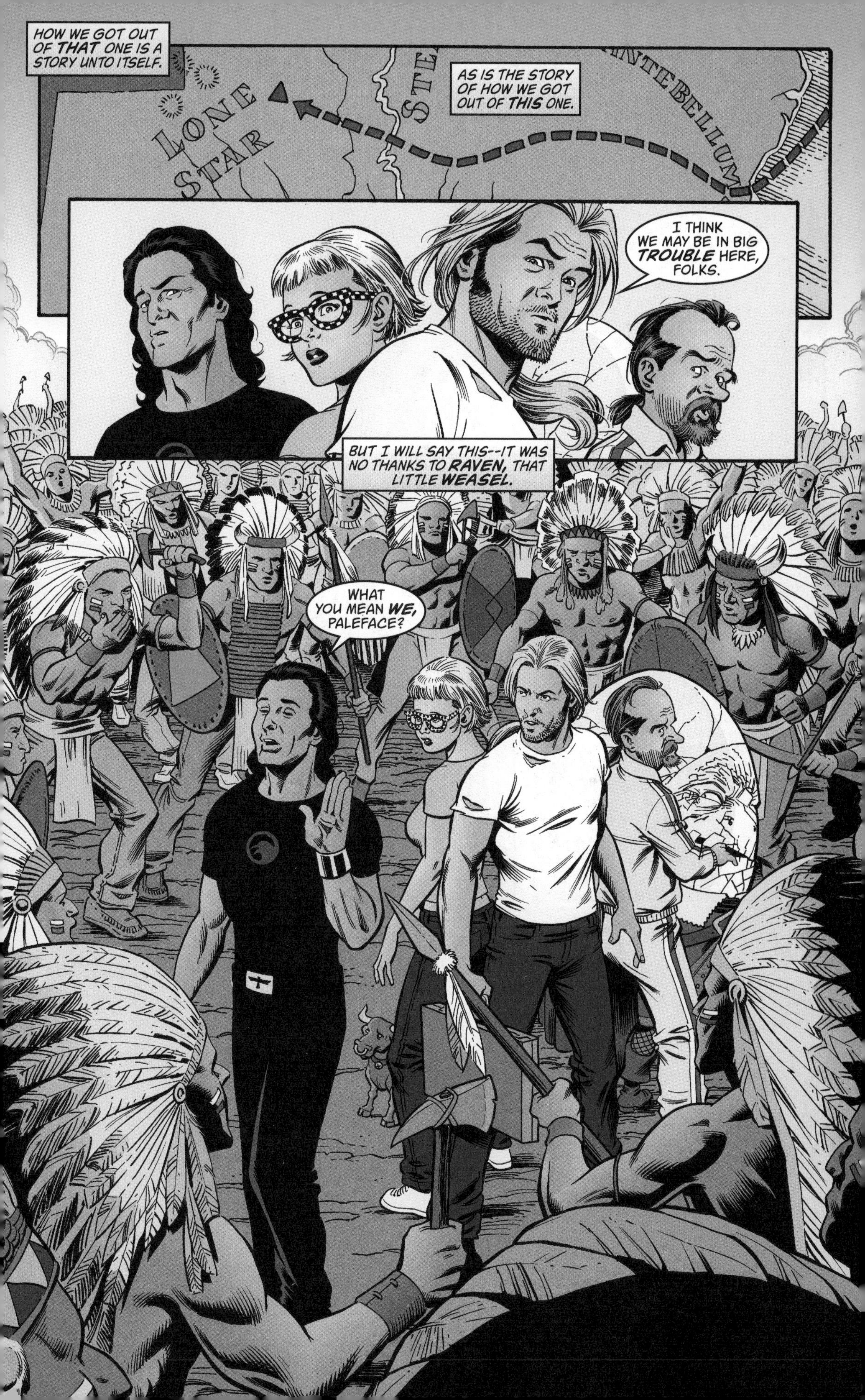
HOW WE GOT OUT OF THAT ONE IS A STORY UNTO ITSELF.
LONE STAR
STE
ANTEBELLUM
AS IS THE STORY OF HOW WE GOT OUT OF THIS ONE.
I THINK WE MAY BE IN BIG TROUBLE HERE, FOLKS.
BUT I WILL SAY THIS--IT WAS NO THANKS TO RAVEN, THAT LITTLE WEASEL.
WHAT YOU MEAN WE, PALEFACE?

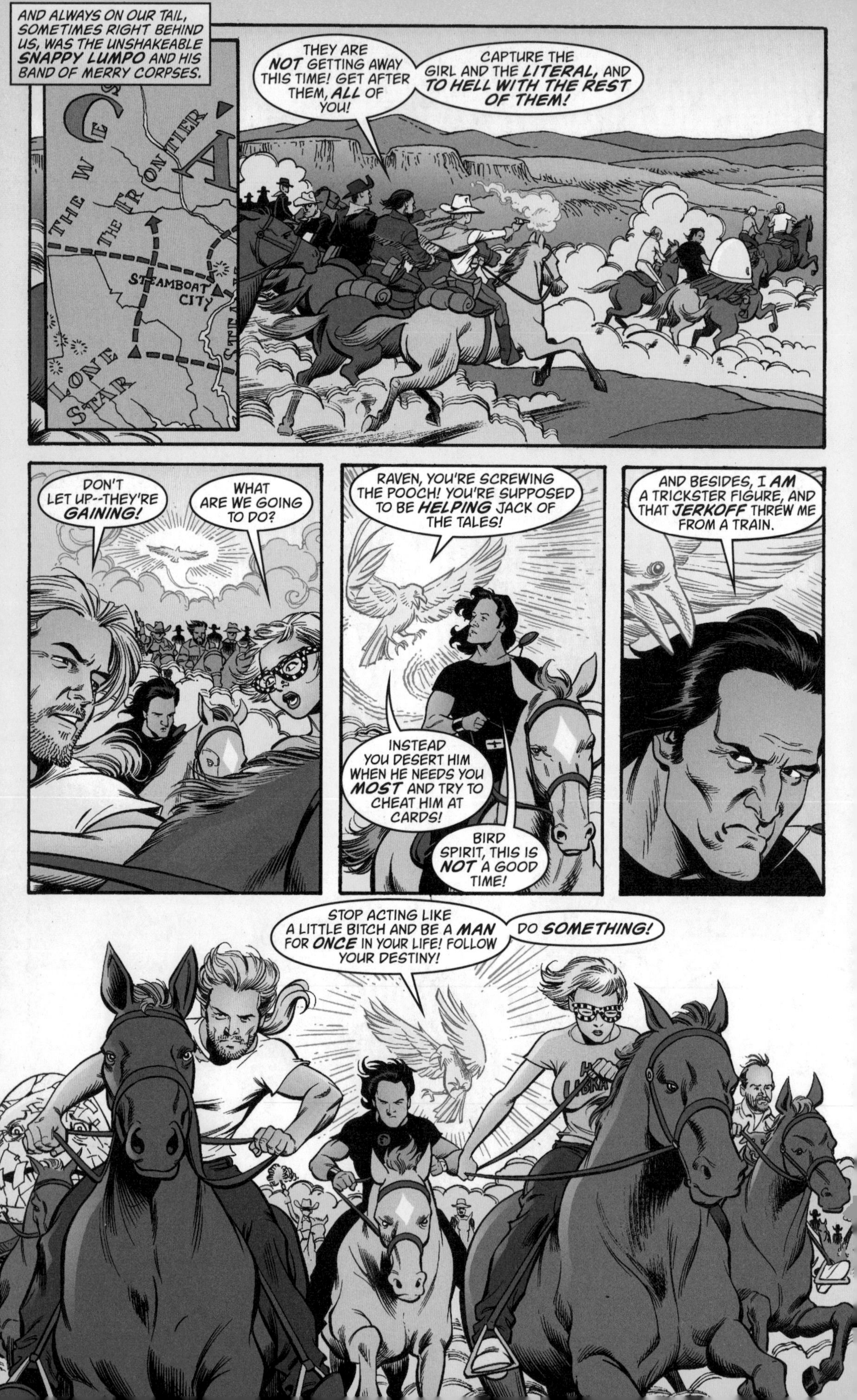
AND ALWAYS ON OUR TAIL, SOMETIMES RIGHT BEHIND US, WAS THE UNSHAKEABLE SNAPPY LUMPO AND HIS BAND OF MERRY CORPSES.
THE WEST
THE FRONTIER
STEAMBOAT CITY
LONE STAR
THEY ARE NOT GETTING AWAY THIS TIME! GET AFTER THEM, ALL OF YOU!
CAPTURE THE GIRL AND THE LITERAL, AND TO HELL WITH THE REST OF THEM!
DON'T LET UP--THEY'RE GAINING!
WHAT ARE WE GOING TO DO?
RAVEN, YOU'RE SCREWING THE POOCH! YOU'RE SUPPOSED TO BE HELPING JACK OF THE TALES!
INSTEAD YOU DESERT HIM WHEN HE NEEDS YOU MOST AND TRY TO CHEAT HIM AT CARDS!
BIRD SPIRIT, THIS IS NOT A GOOD TIME!
AND BESIDES, I AM A TRICKSTER FIGURE, AND THAT JERKOFF THREW ME FROM A TRAIN.
STOP ACTING LIKE A LITTLE BITCH AND BE A MAN FOR ONCE IN YOUR LIFE! FOLLOW YOUR DESTINY!
DO SOMETHING!

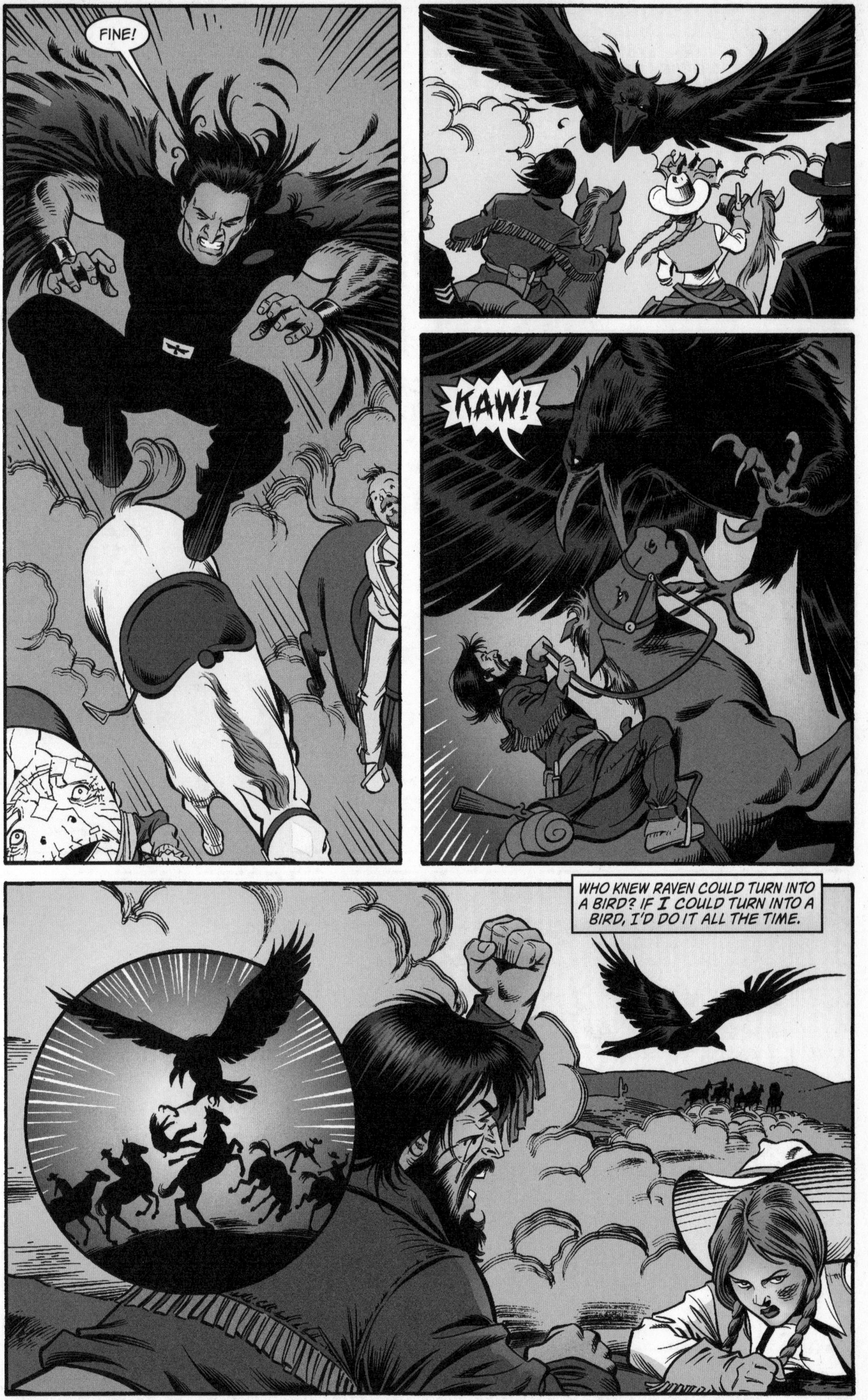
FINE!
KAW!
WHO KNEW RAVEN COULD TURN INTO A BIRD? IF I COULD TURN INTO A BIRD, I'D DO IT ALL THE TIME.

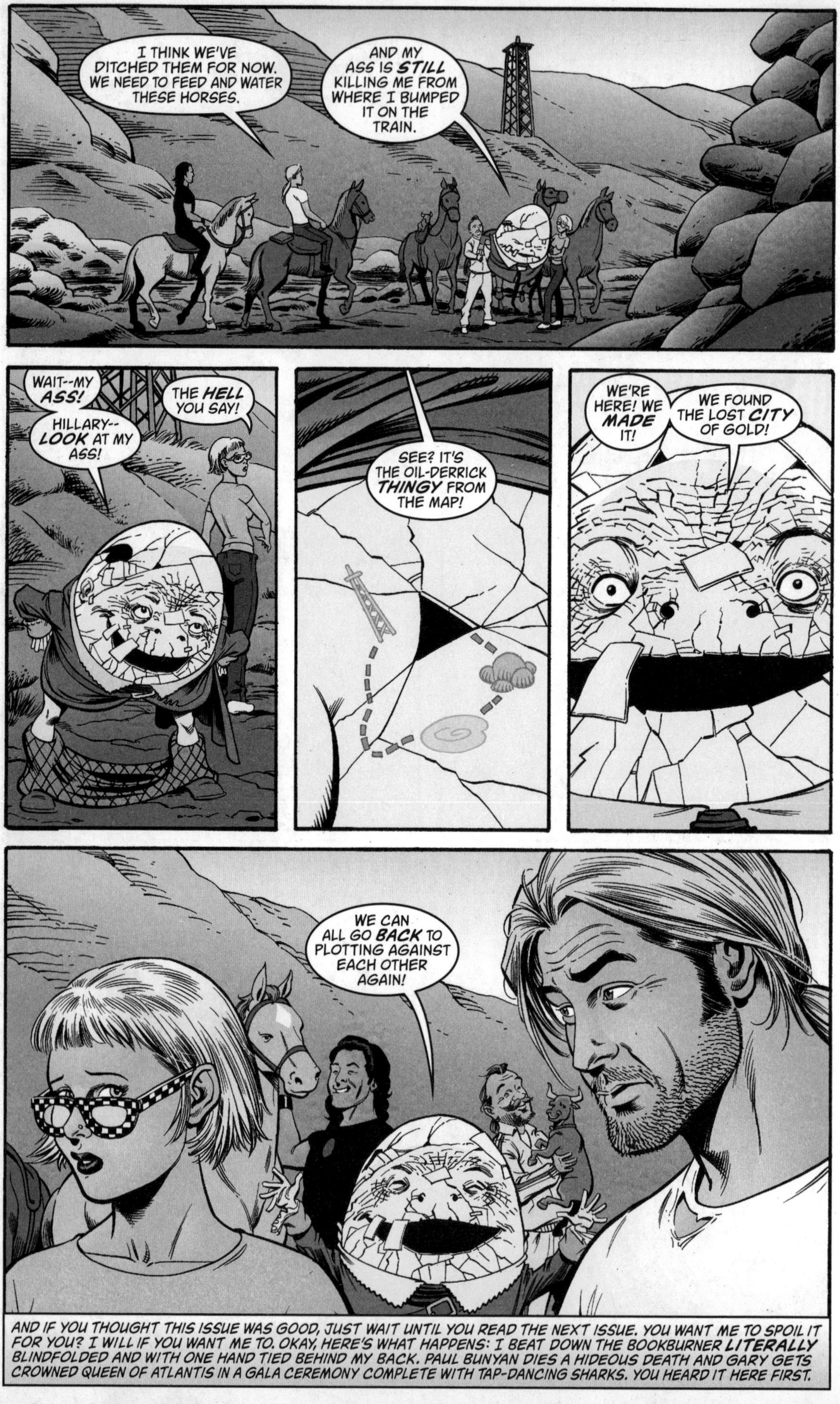
I THINK WE'VE DITCHED THEM FOR NOW. WE NEED TO FEED AND WATER THESE HORSES.
AND MY ASS IS STILL KILLING ME FROM WHERE I BUMPED IT ON THE TRAIN.
WAIT--MY ASS!
HILLARY--LOOK AT MY ASS!
THE HELL YOU SAY!
SEE? IT'S THE OIL-DERRICK THINGY FROM THE MAP!
WE'RE HERE! WE MADE IT!
WE FOUND THE LOST CITY OF GOLD!
WE CAN ALL GO BACK TO PLOTTING AGAINST EACH OTHER AGAIN!
AND IF YOU THOUGHT THIS ISSUE WAS GOOD, JUST WAIT UNTIL YOU READ THE NEXT ISSUE. YOU WANT ME TO SPOIL IT FOR YOU? I WILL IF YOU WANT ME TO. OKAY, HERE'S WHAT HAPPENS: I BEAT DOWN THE BOOKBURNER LITERALLY BLINDFOLDED AND WITH ONE HAND TIED BEHIND MY BACK. PAUL BUNYAN DIES A HIDEOUS DEATH AND GARY GETS CROWNED QUEEN OF ATLANTIS IN A GALA CEREMONY COMPLETE WITH TAP-DANCING SHARKS. YOU HEARD IT HERE FIRST.

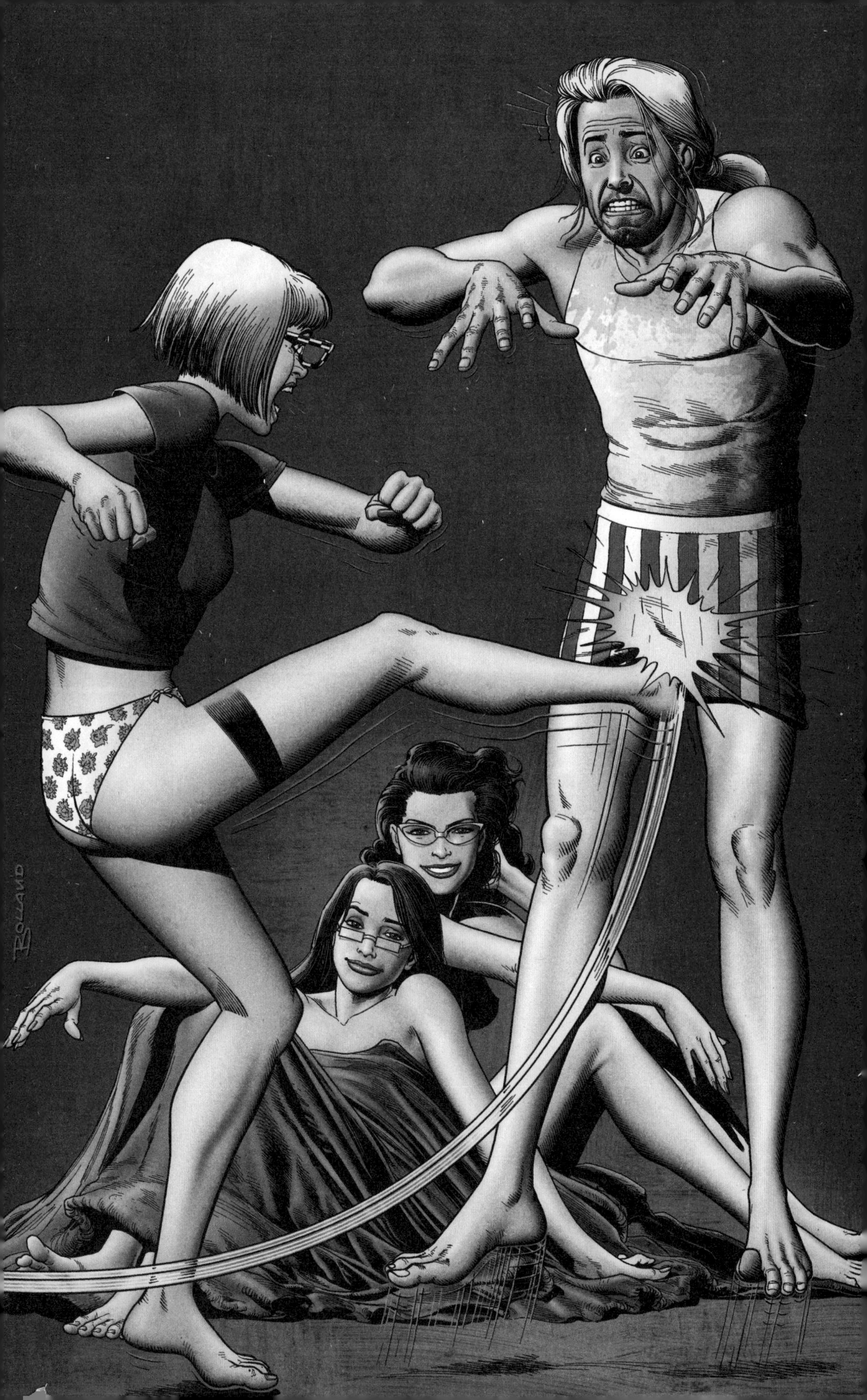
BOLLAND

"Finally! My treasure!
Nothing can **possibly** go wrong **now!**"

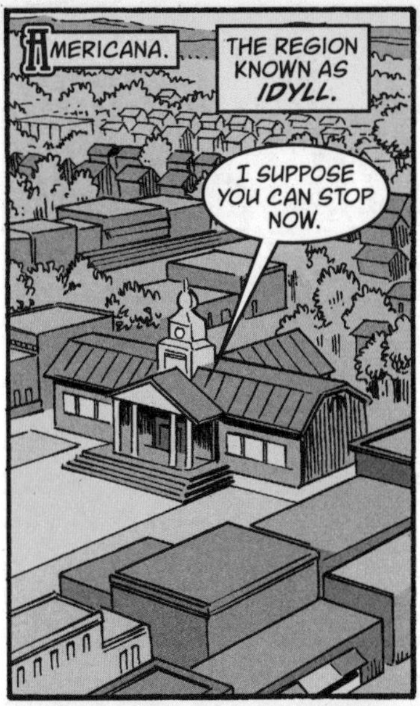
AMERICANA.
THE REGION KNOWN AS IDYLL.
I SUPPOSE YOU CAN STOP NOW.

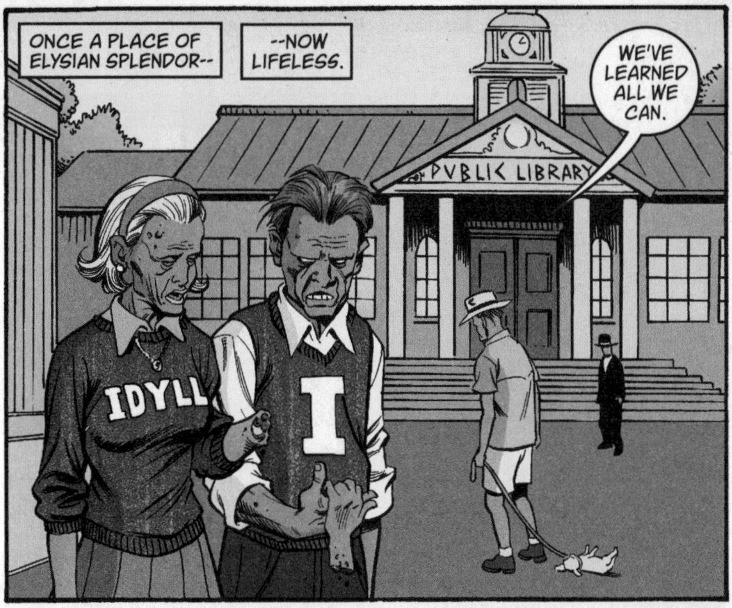
ONCE A PLACE OF ELYSIAN SPLENDOR--
--NOW LIFELESS.
PVBLIC LIBRARY
WE'VE LEARNED ALL WE CAN.
IDYLL

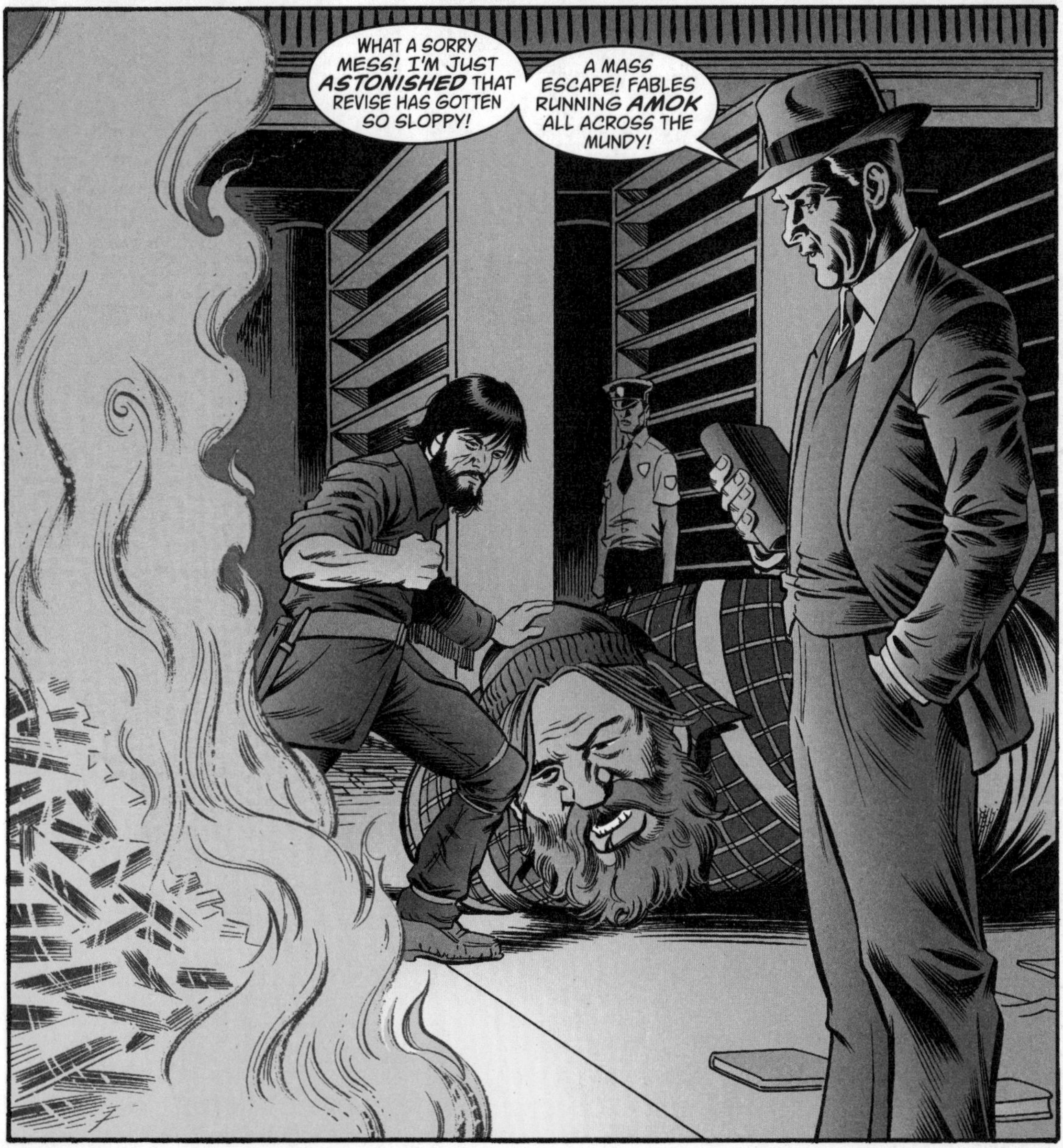
WHAT A SORRY MESS! I'M JUST ASTONISHED THAT REVISE HAS GOTTEN SO SLOPPY!
A MASS ESCAPE! FABLES RUNNING AMOK ALL ACROSS THE MUNDY!

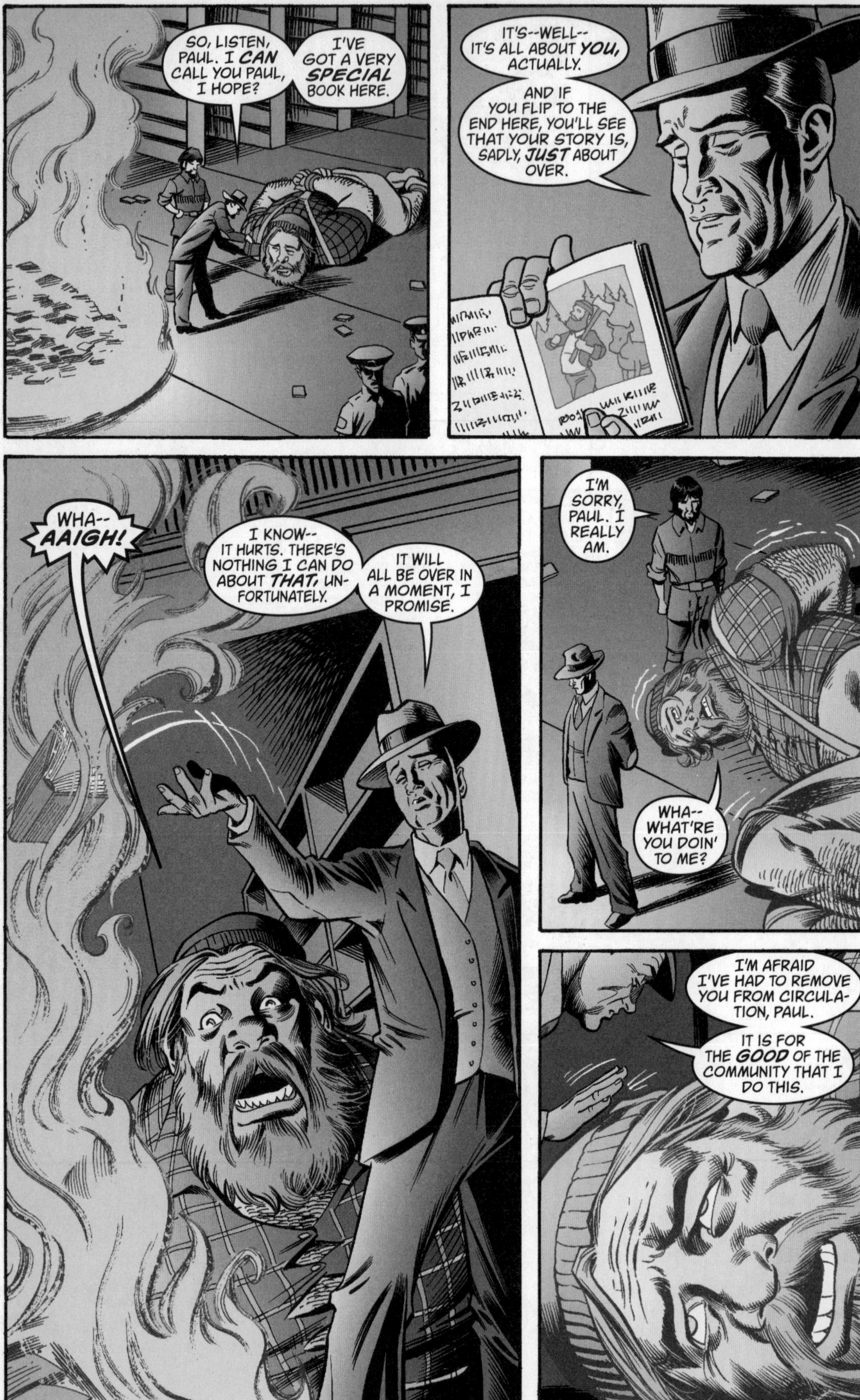

SO, LISTEN, PAUL. I CAN CALL YOU PAUL, I HOPE?
I'VE GOT A VERY SPECIAL BOOK HERE.
IT'S--WELL-- IT'S ALL ABOUT YOU, ACTUALLY.
AND IF YOU FLIP TO THE END HERE, YOU'LL SEE THAT YOUR STORY IS, SADLY, JUST ABOUT OVER.
WHA-- AAIGH!
I KNOW-- IT HURTS. THERE'S NOTHING I CAN DO ABOUT THAT, UNFORTUNATELY.
IT WILL ALL BE OVER IN A MOMENT, I PROMISE.
I'M SORRY, PAUL. I REALLY AM.
WHA-- WHAT'RE YOU DOIN' TO ME?
I'M AFRAID I'VE HAD TO REMOVE YOU FROM CIRCULATION, PAUL.
IT IS FOR THE GOOD OF THE COMMUNITY THAT I DO THIS.

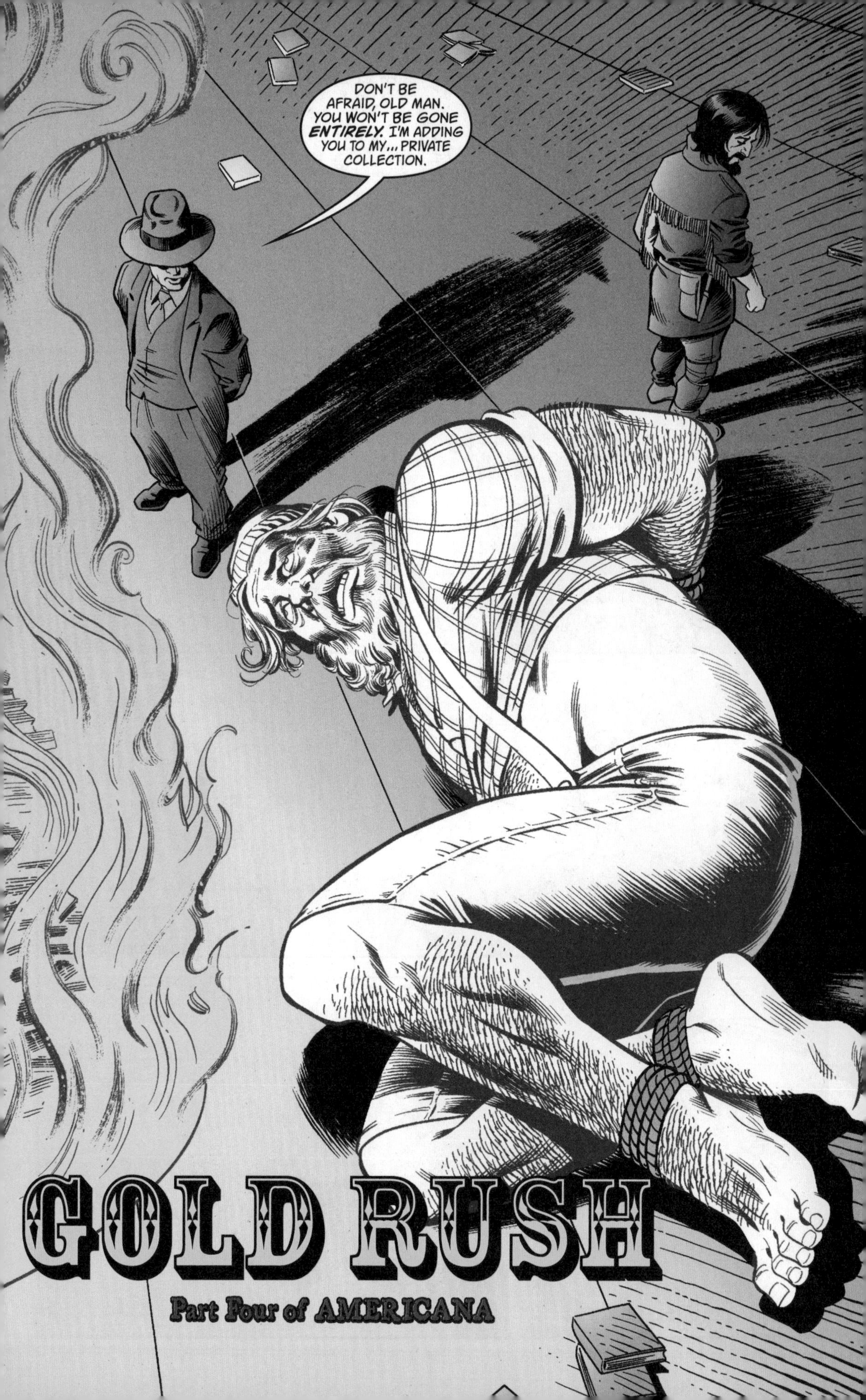
DON'T BE AFRAID, OLD MAN. YOU WON'T BE GONE ENTIRELY. I'M ADDING YOU TO MY... PRIVATE COLLECTION.
GOLD RUSH
Part Four of AMERICANA

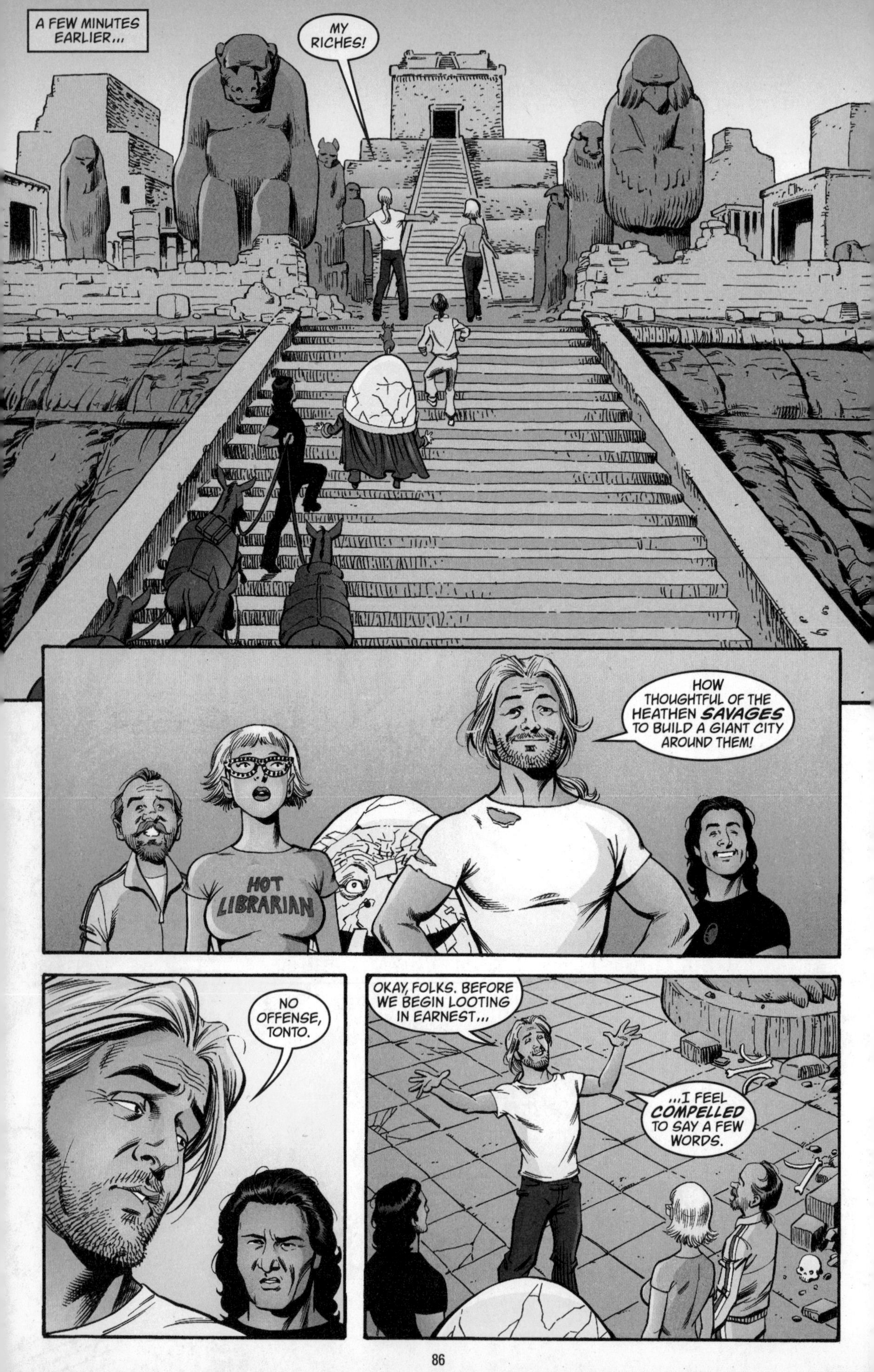
A FEW MINUTES EARLIER...
MY RICHES!
HOW THOUGHTFUL OF THE HEATHEN SAVAGES TO BUILD A GIANT CITY AROUND THEM!
HOT LIBRARIAN
NO OFFENSE, TONTO.
OKAY, FOLKS. BEFORE WE BEGIN LOOTING IN EARNEST...
...I FEEL COMPELLED TO SAY A FEW WORDS.

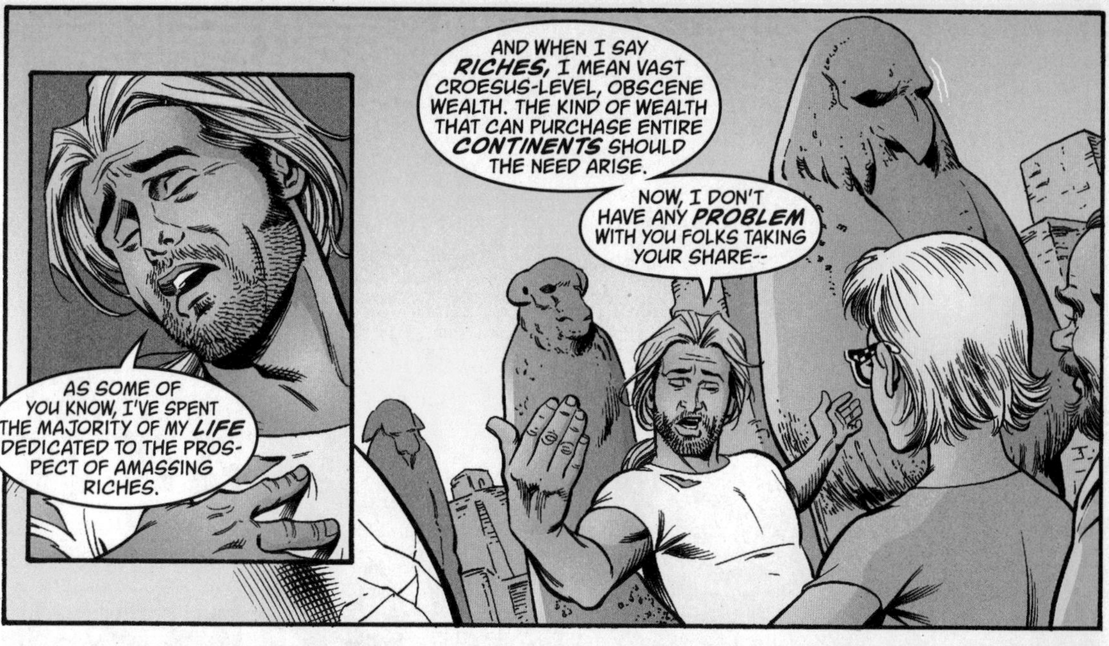
AS SOME OF YOU KNOW, I'VE SPENT THE MAJORITY OF MY LIFE DEDICATED TO THE PROSPECT OF AMASSING RICHES.
AND WHEN I SAY RICHES, I MEAN VAST CROESUS-LEVEL, OBSCENE WEALTH. THE KIND OF WEALTH THAT CAN PURCHASE ENTIRE CONTINENTS SHOULD THE NEED ARISE.
NOW, I DON'T HAVE ANY PROBLEM WITH YOU FOLKS TAKING YOUR SHARE--

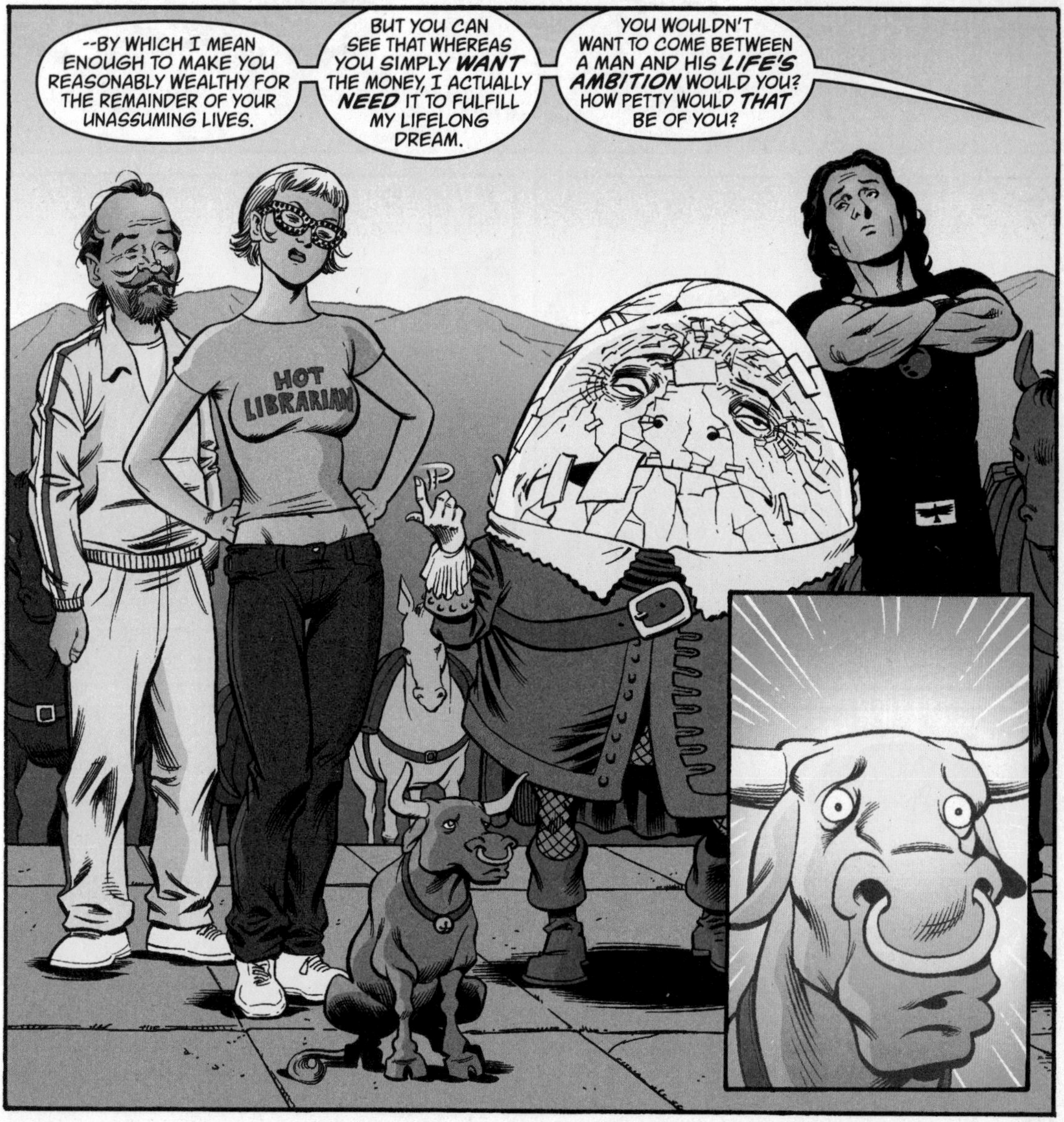
--BY WHICH I MEAN ENOUGH TO MAKE YOU REASONABLY WEALTHY FOR THE REMAINDER OF YOUR UNASSUMING LIVES.
BUT YOU CAN SEE THAT WHEREAS YOU SIMPLY WANT THE MONEY, I ACTUALLY NEED IT TO FULFILL MY LIFELONG DREAM.
YOU WOULDN'T WANT TO COME BETWEEN A MAN AND HIS LIFE'S AMBITION WOULD YOU? HOW PETTY WOULD THAT BE OF YOU?
HOT LIBRARIAN

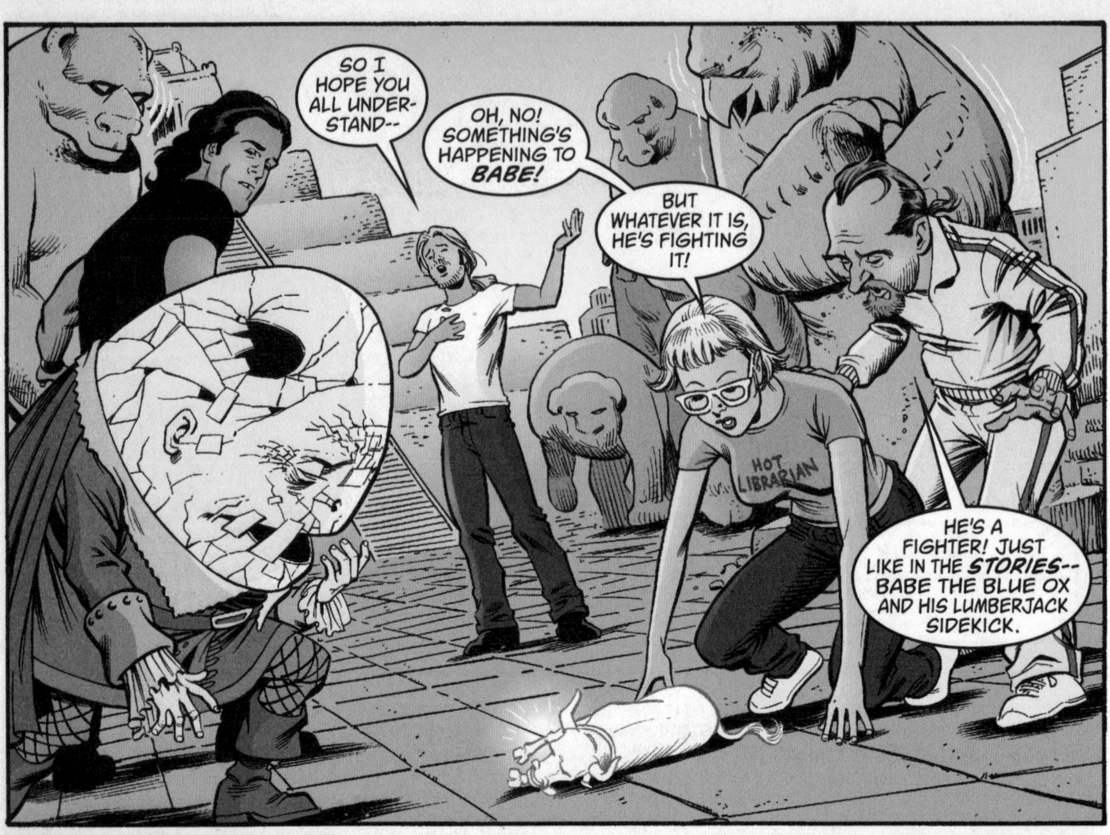
SO I HOPE YOU ALL UNDER-STAND--
OH, NO! SOMETHING'S HAPPENING TO BABE!
BUT WHATEVER IT IS, HE'S FIGHTING IT!
HE'S A FIGHTER! JUST LIKE IN THE STORIES-- BABE THE BLUE OX AND HIS LUMBERJACK SIDEKICK.
HOT LIBRARIAN
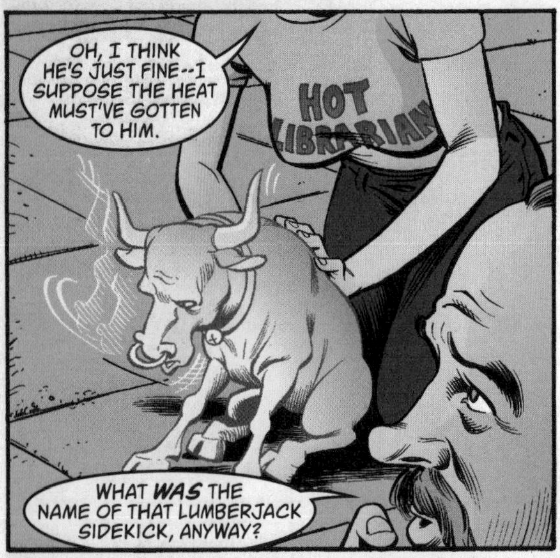
OH, I THINK HE'S JUST FINE--I SUPPOSE THE HEAT MUST'VE GOTTEN TO HIM.
HOT LIBRARIAN
WHAT WAS THE NAME OF THAT LUMBERJACK SIDEKICK, ANYWAY?
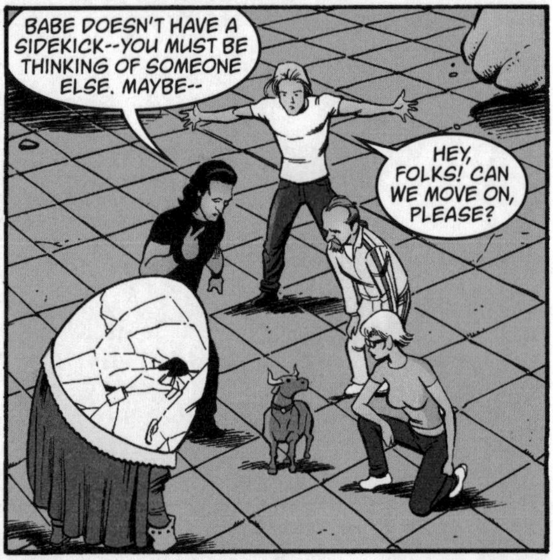
BABE DOESN'T HAVE A SIDEKICK--YOU MUST BE THINKING OF SOMEONE ELSE. MAYBE--
HEY, FOLKS! CAN WE MOVE ON, PLEASE?
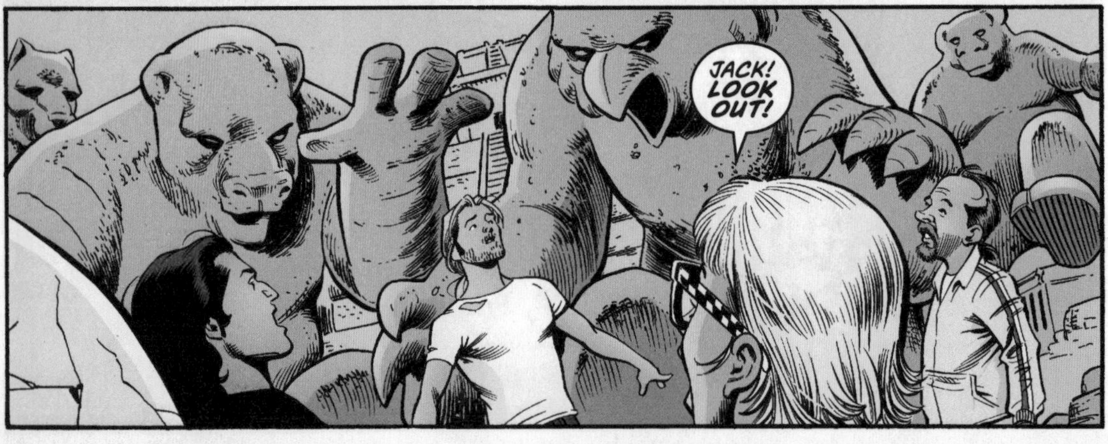
JACK! LOOK OUT!

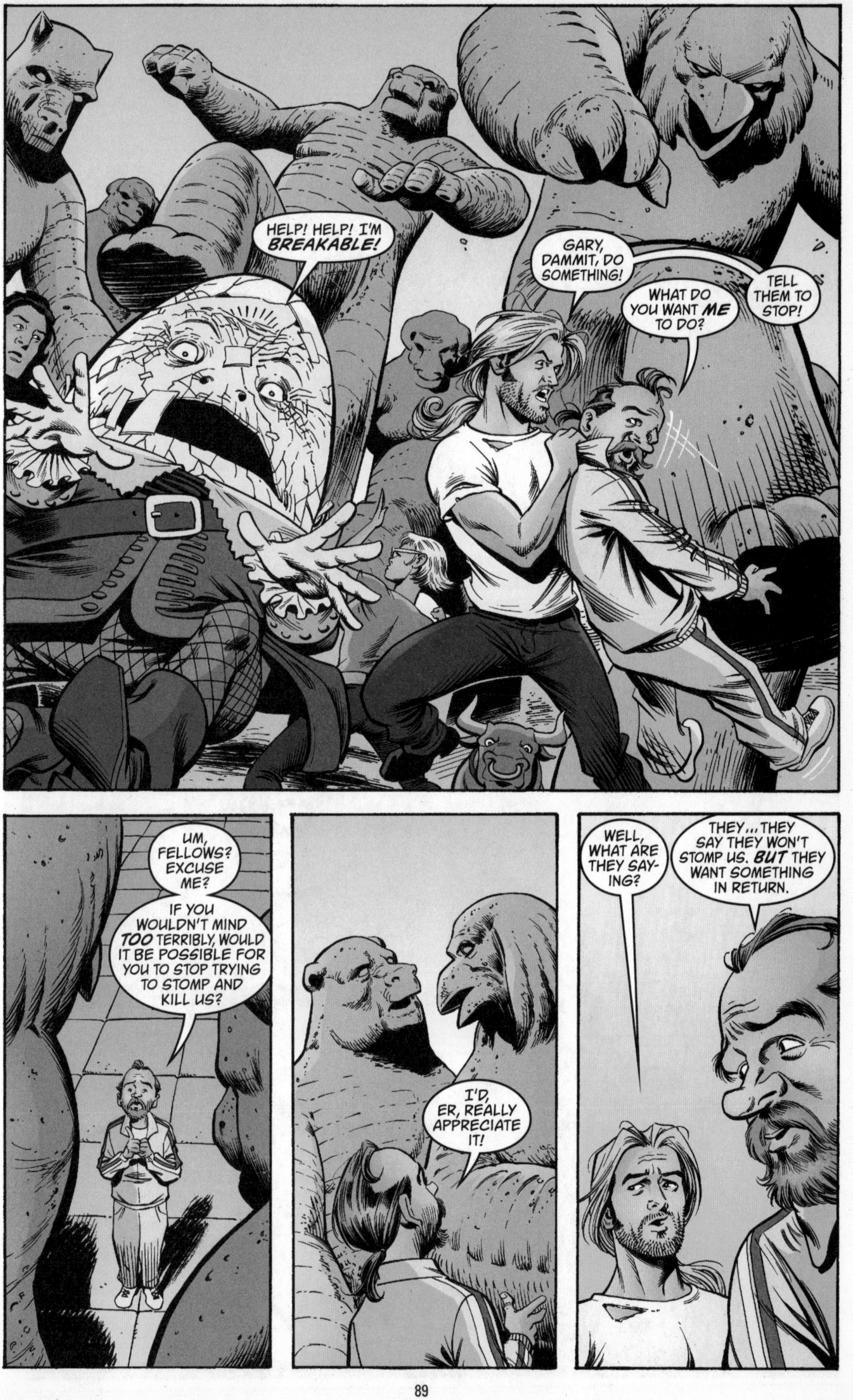
HELP! HELP! I'M ***BREAKABLE!***
GARY, DAMMIT, DO SOMETHING!
WHAT DO YOU WANT ***ME*** TO DO?
TELL THEM TO STOP!
UM, FELLOWS? EXCUSE ME?
IF YOU WOULDN'T MIND ***TOO*** TERRIBLY, WOULD IT BE POSSIBLE FOR YOU TO STOP TRYING TO STOMP AND KILL US?
I'D, ER, REALLY APPRECIATE IT!
WELL, WHAT ARE THEY SAY-ING?
THEY... THEY SAY THEY WON'T STOMP US. ***BUT*** THEY WANT SOMETHING IN RETURN.

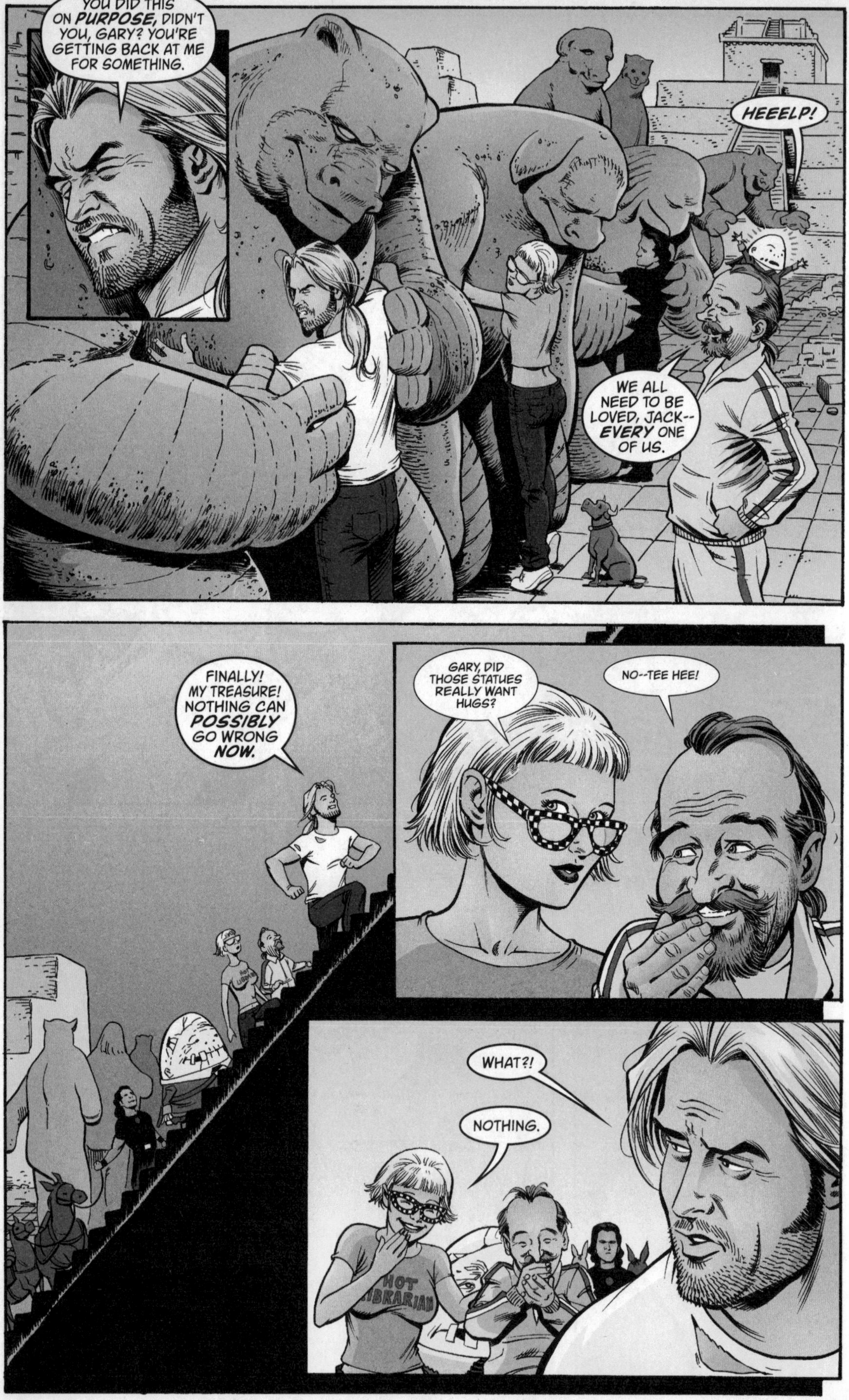
YOU DID THIS ON PURPOSE, DIDN'T YOU, GARY? YOU'RE GETTING BACK AT ME FOR SOMETHING.
HEEELP!
WE ALL NEED TO BE LOVED, JACK-- EVERY ONE OF US.
FINALLY! MY TREASURE! NOTHING CAN POSSIBLY GO WRONG NOW.
GARY, DID THOSE STATUES REALLY WANT HUGS?
NO--TEE HEE!
WHAT?!
NOTHING.
HOT LIBRARIAN

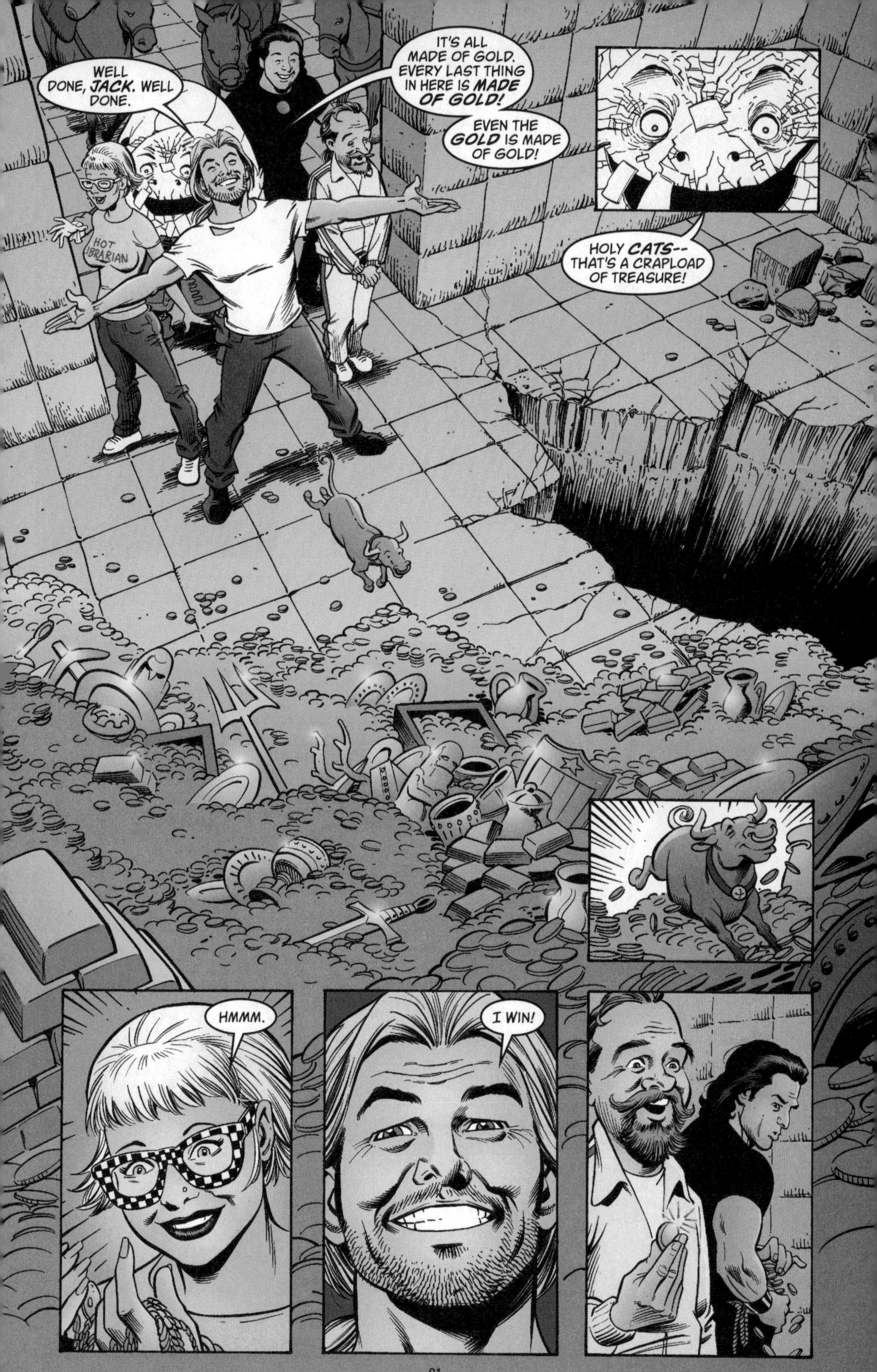
WELL DONE, JACK. WELL DONE.
IT'S ALL MADE OF GOLD. EVERY LAST THING IN HERE IS MADE OF GOLD!
EVEN THE GOLD IS MADE OF GOLD!
HOT LIBRARIAN
HOLY CATS-- THAT'S A CRAPLOAD OF TREASURE!
HMMM.
I WIN!

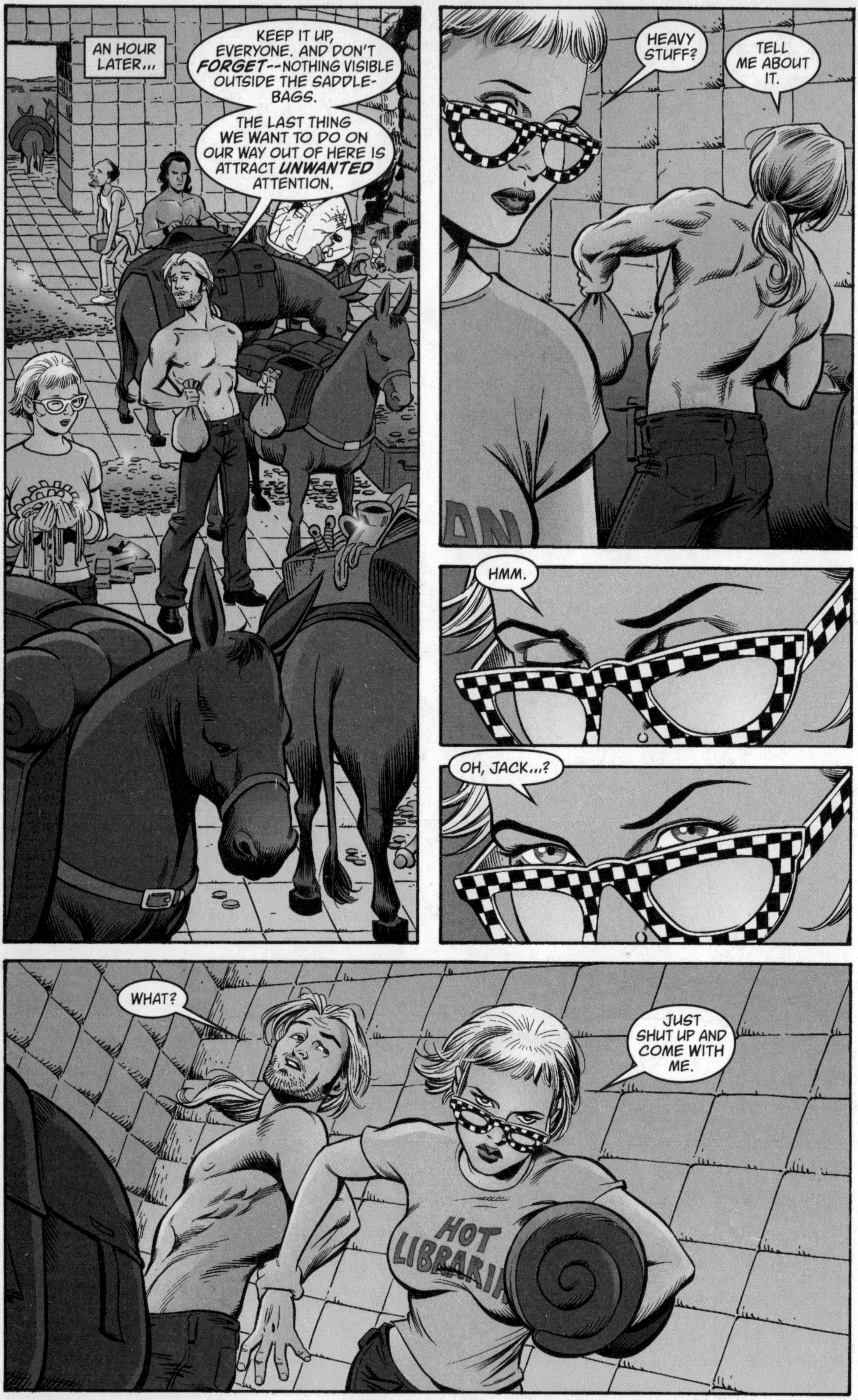
AN HOUR LATER...
KEEP IT UP, EVERYONE. AND DON'T FORGET--NOTHING VISIBLE OUTSIDE THE SADDLE-BAGS.
THE LAST THING WE WANT TO DO ON OUR WAY OUT OF HERE IS ATTRACT UNWANTED ATTENTION.
HEAVY STUFF?
TELL ME ABOUT IT.
HMM.
OH, JACK...?
WHAT?
JUST SHUT UP AND COME WITH ME.
HOT LIBRARI

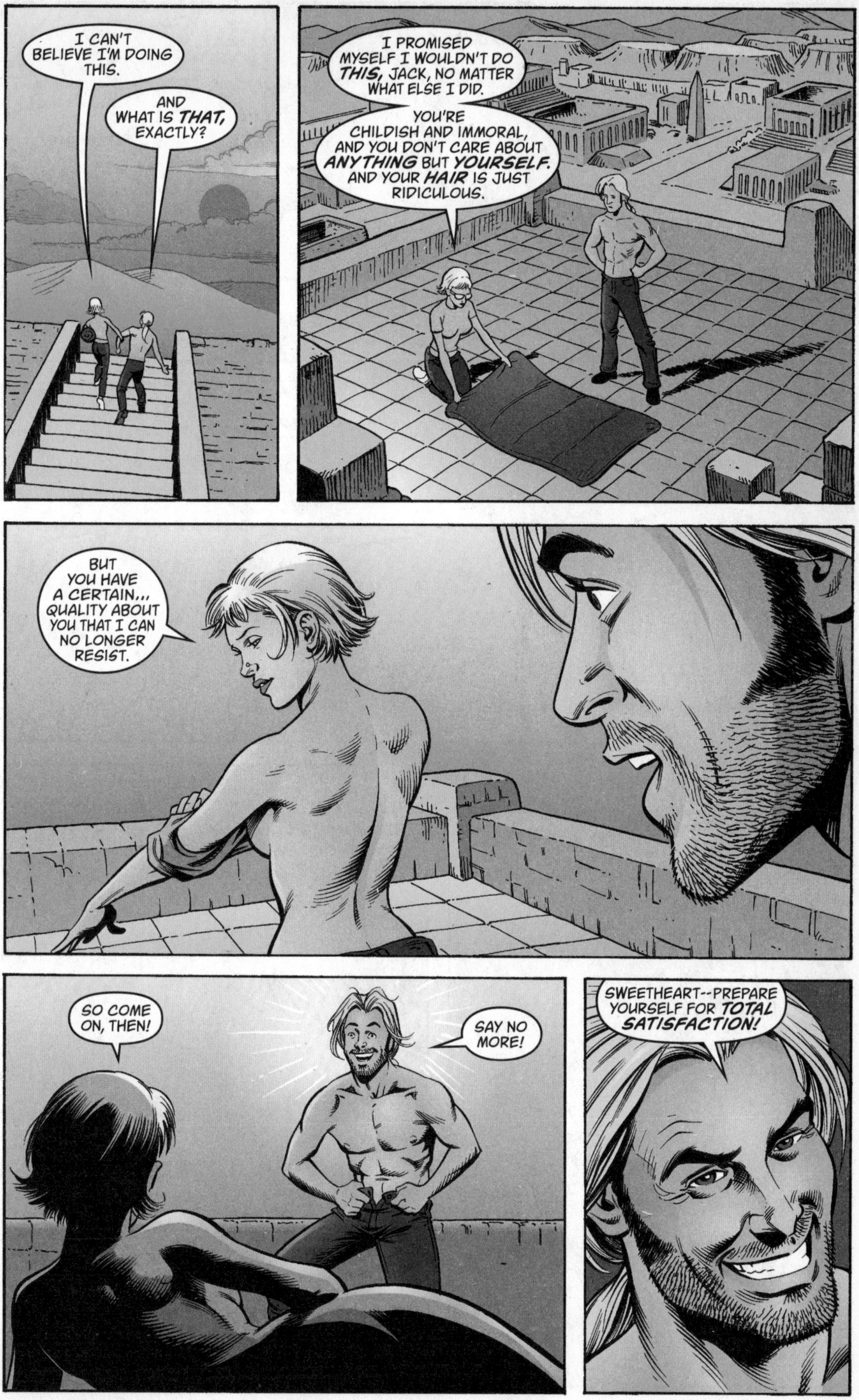
I CAN'T BELIEVE I'M DOING THIS.
AND WHAT IS THAT, EXACTLY?
I PROMISED MYSELF I WOULDN'T DO THIS, JACK, NO MATTER WHAT ELSE I DID.
YOU'RE CHILDISH AND IMMORAL, AND YOU DON'T CARE ABOUT ANYTHING BUT YOURSELF. AND YOUR HAIR IS JUST RIDICULOUS.
BUT YOU HAVE A CERTAIN... QUALITY ABOUT YOU THAT I CAN NO LONGER RESIST.
SO COME ON, THEN!
SAY NO MORE!
SWEETHEART--PREPARE YOURSELF FOR TOTAL SATISFACTION!

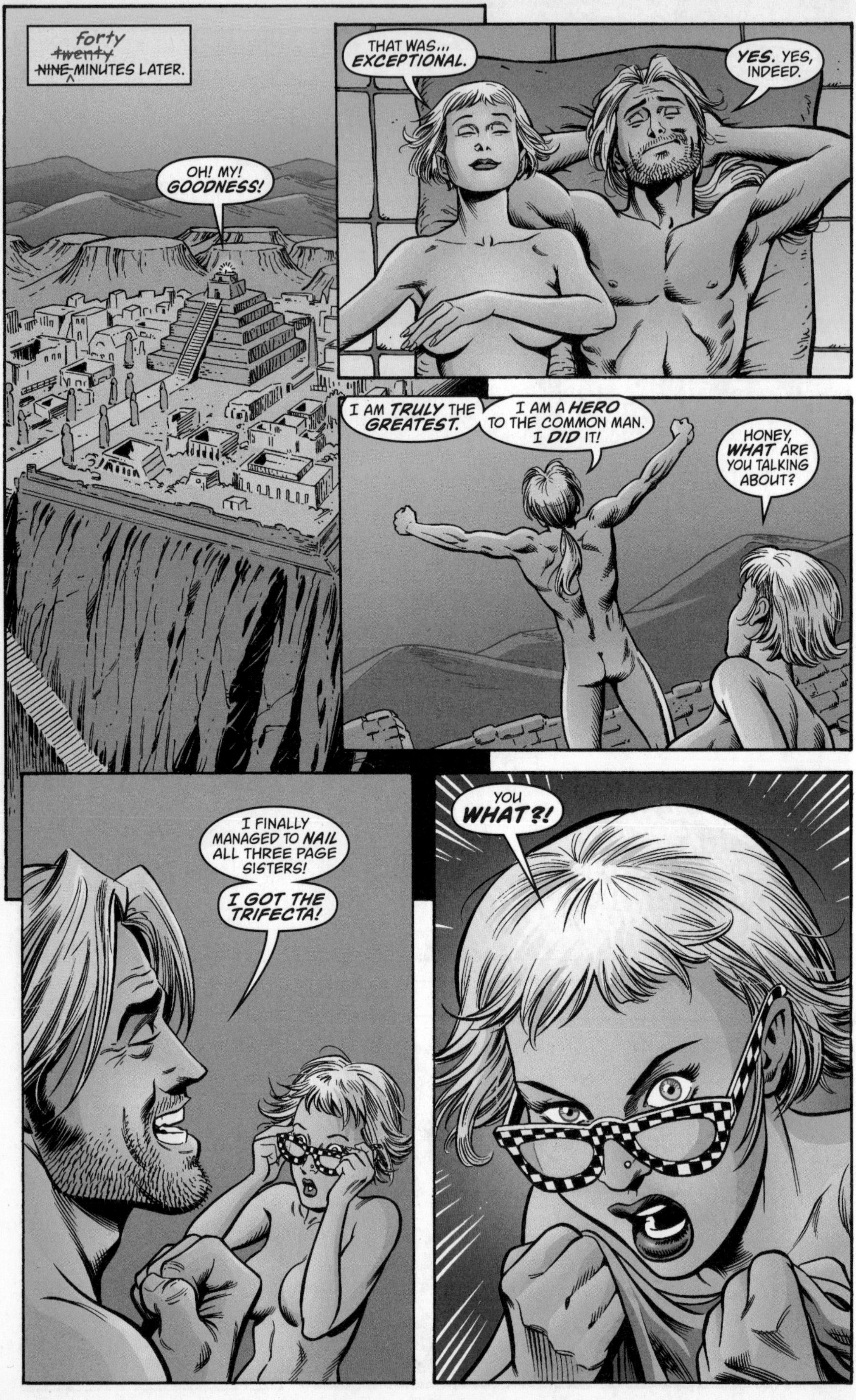
Forty
~~twenty~~
~~NINE~~ MINUTES LATER.
OH! MY! GOODNESS!
THAT WAS... EXCEPTIONAL.
YES. YES, INDEED.
I AM TRULY THE GREATEST.
I AM A HERO TO THE COMMON MAN. I DID IT!
HONEY, WHAT ARE YOU TALKING ABOUT?
I FINALLY MANAGED TO NAIL ALL THREE PAGE SISTERS!
I GOT THE TRIFECTA!
YOU WHAT?!

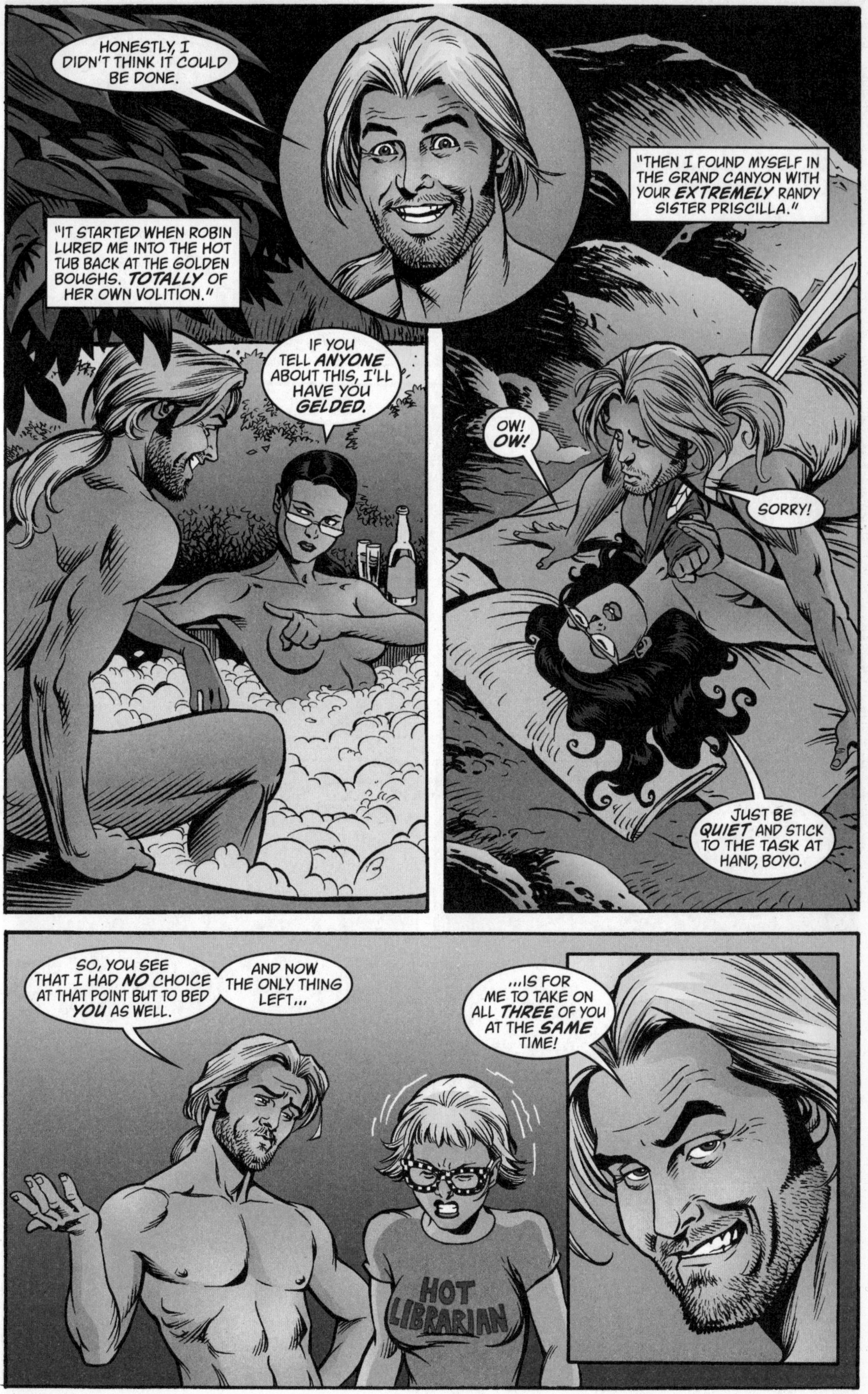
HONESTLY, I DIDN'T THINK IT COULD BE DONE.
"IT STARTED WHEN ROBIN LURED ME INTO THE HOT TUB BACK AT THE GOLDEN BOUGHS. *TOTALLY* OF HER OWN VOLITION."
"THEN I FOUND MYSELF IN THE GRAND CANYON WITH YOUR *EXTREMELY* RANDY SISTER PRISCILLA."
IF YOU TELL *ANYONE* ABOUT THIS, I'LL HAVE YOU *GELDED*.
OW! *OW!*
SORRY!
JUST BE *QUIET* AND STICK TO THE TASK AT HAND, BOYO.
SO, YOU SEE THAT I HAD *NO* CHOICE AT THAT POINT BUT TO BED *YOU* AS WELL.
AND NOW THE ONLY THING LEFT...
...IS FOR ME TO TAKE ON ALL *THREE* OF YOU AT THE *SAME* TIME!
HOT LIBRARIAN

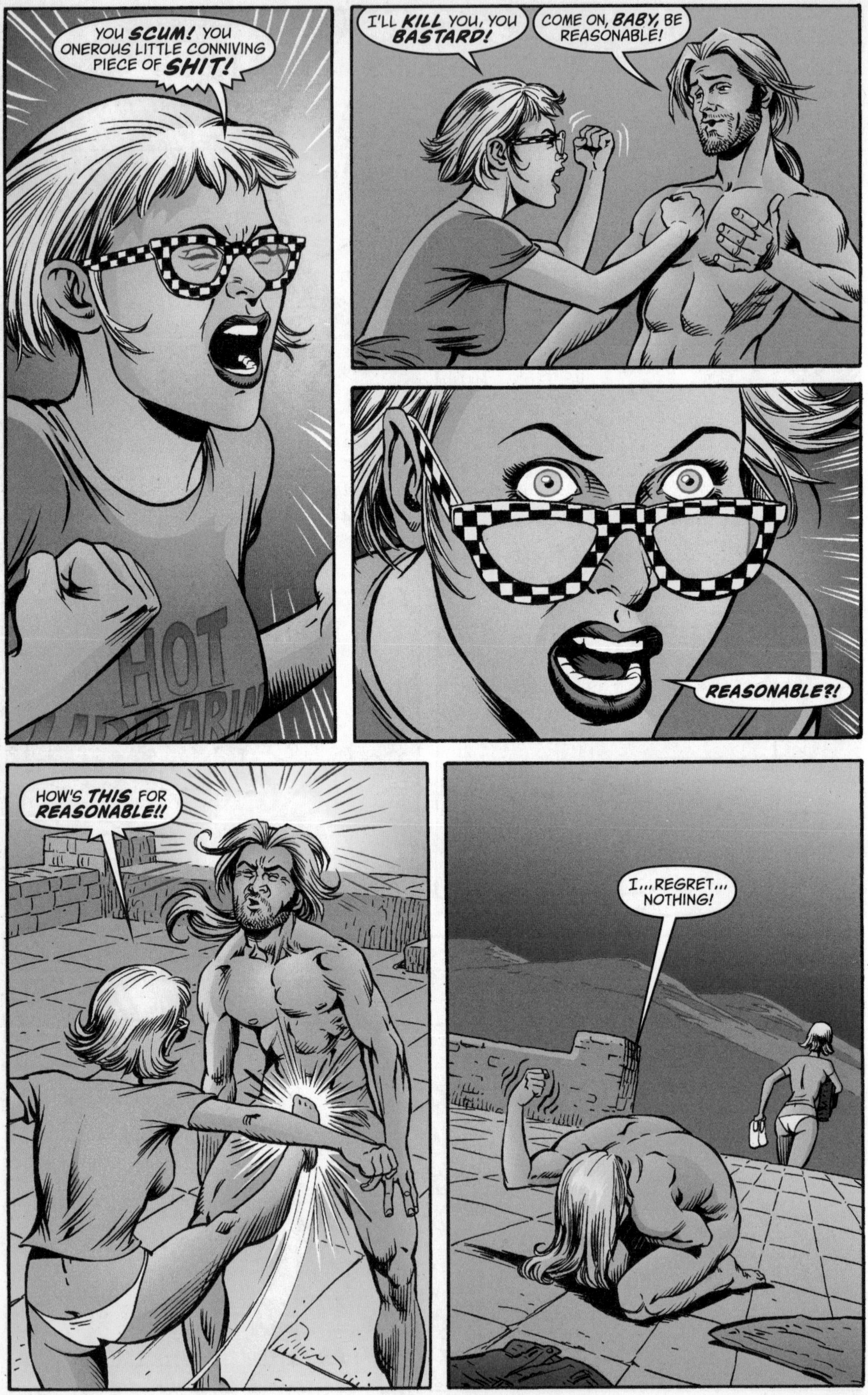
YOU SCUM! YOU ONEROUS LITTLE CONNIVING PIECE OF SHIT!
HOT
I'LL KILL YOU, YOU BASTARD!
COME ON, BABY, BE REASONABLE!
REASONABLE?!
HOW'S THIS FOR REASONABLE!!
I...REGRET... NOTHING!

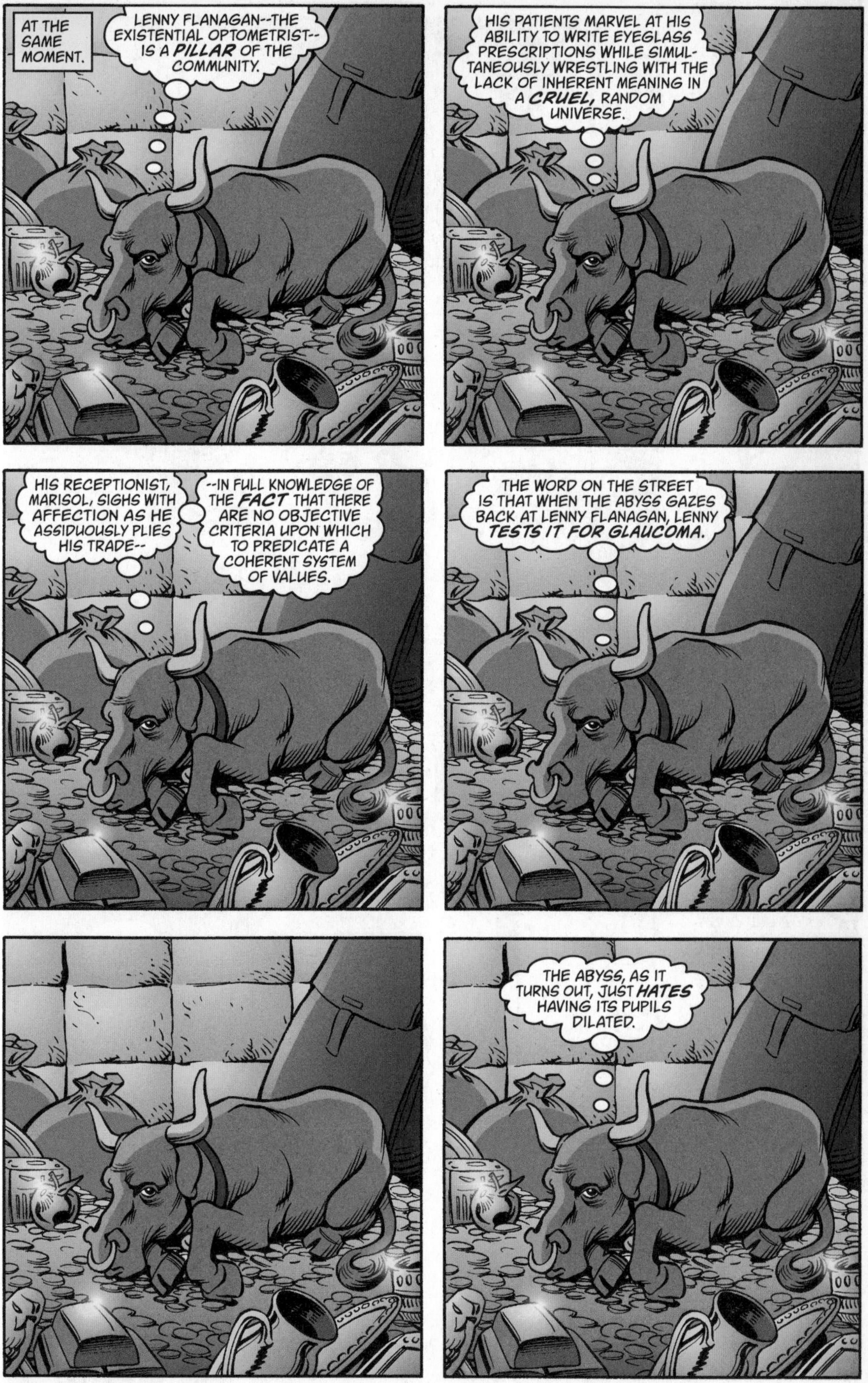
AT THE SAME MOMENT.
LENNY FLANAGAN--THE EXISTENTIAL OPTOMETRIST--IS A PILLAR OF THE COMMUNITY.
HIS PATIENTS MARVEL AT HIS ABILITY TO WRITE EYEGLASS PRESCRIPTIONS WHILE SIMUL-TANEOUSLY WRESTLING WITH THE LACK OF INHERENT MEANING IN A CRUEL, RANDOM UNIVERSE.
HIS RECEPTIONIST, MARISOL, SIGHS WITH AFFECTION AS HE ASSIDUOUSLY PLIES HIS TRADE--
--IN FULL KNOWLEDGE OF THE FACT THAT THERE ARE NO OBJECTIVE CRITERIA UPON WHICH TO PREDICATE A COHERENT SYSTEM OF VALUES.
THE WORD ON THE STREET IS THAT WHEN THE ABYSS GAZES BACK AT LENNY FLANAGAN, LENNY TESTS IT FOR GLAUCOMA.
THE ABYSS, AS IT TURNS OUT, JUST HATES HAVING ITS PUPILS DILATED.

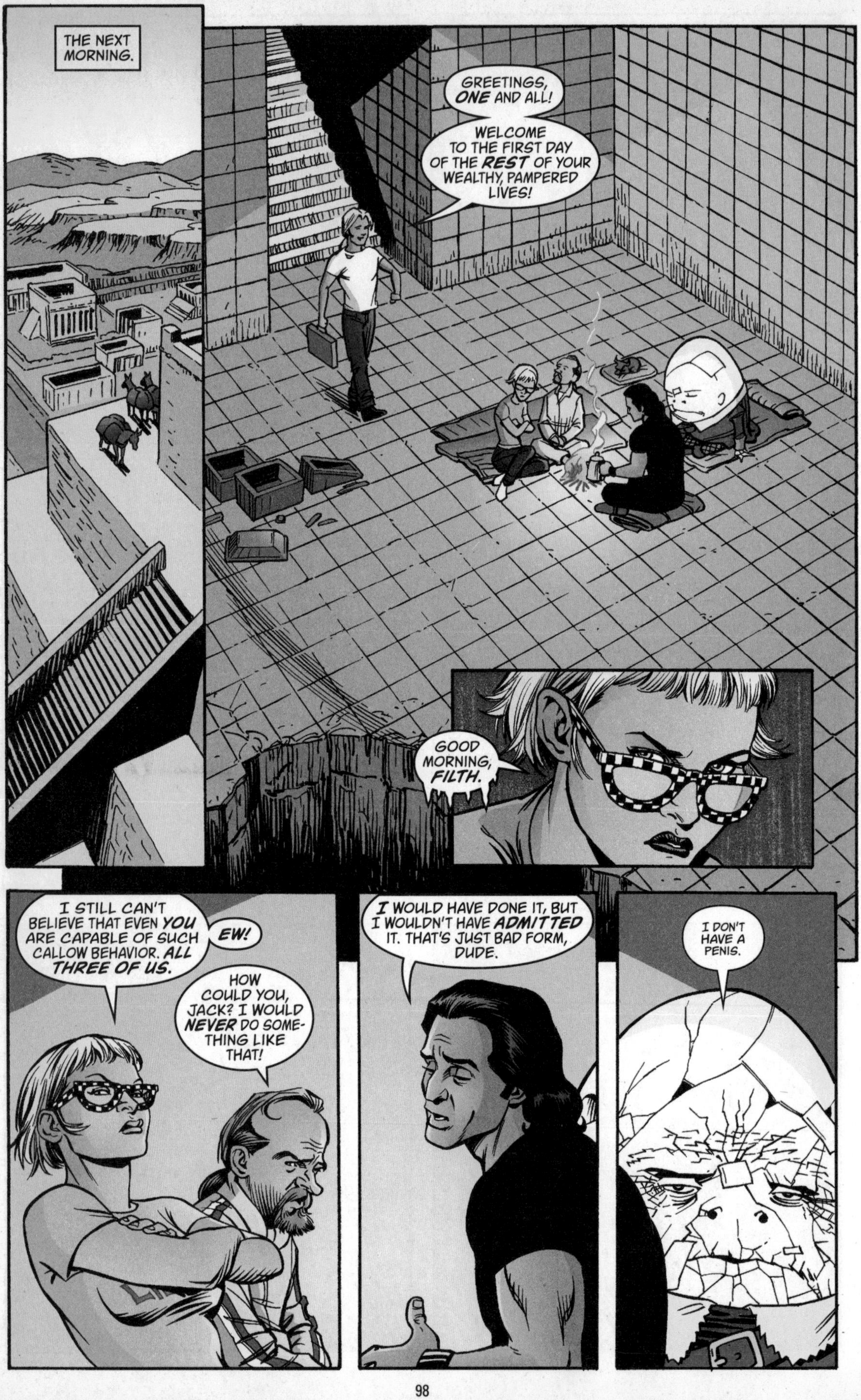
THE NEXT MORNING.
GREETINGS, ONE AND ALL!
WELCOME TO THE FIRST DAY OF THE REST OF YOUR WEALTHY, PAMPERED LIVES!
GOOD MORNING, FILTH.
I STILL CAN'T BELIEVE THAT EVEN YOU ARE CAPABLE OF SUCH CALLOW BEHAVIOR. ALL THREE OF US.
EW!
HOW COULD YOU, JACK? I WOULD NEVER DO SOMETHING LIKE THAT!
I WOULD HAVE DONE IT, BUT I WOULDN'T HAVE ADMITTED IT. THAT'S JUST BAD FORM, DUDE.
I DON'T HAVE A PENIS.

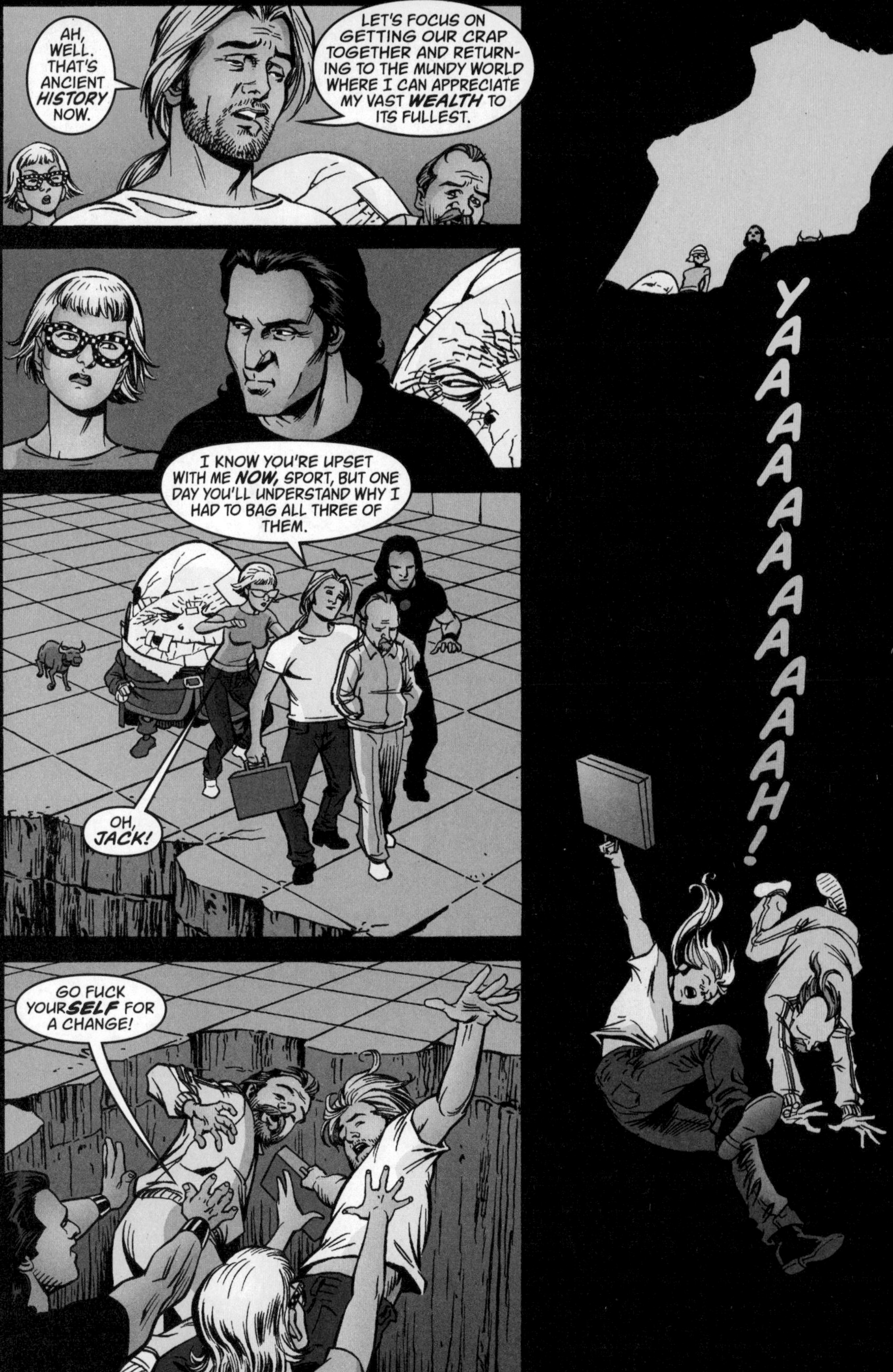
AH, WELL. THAT'S ANCIENT HISTORY NOW.
LET'S FOCUS ON GETTING OUR CRAP TOGETHER AND RETURNING TO THE MUNDY WORLD WHERE I CAN APPRECIATE MY VAST WEALTH TO ITS FULLEST.
I KNOW YOU'RE UPSET WITH ME NOW, SPORT, BUT ONE DAY YOU'LL UNDERSTAND WHY I HAD TO BAG ALL THREE OF THEM.
OH, JACK!
GO FUCK YOURSELF FOR A CHANGE!
YAAAAAAAAAAAAH!

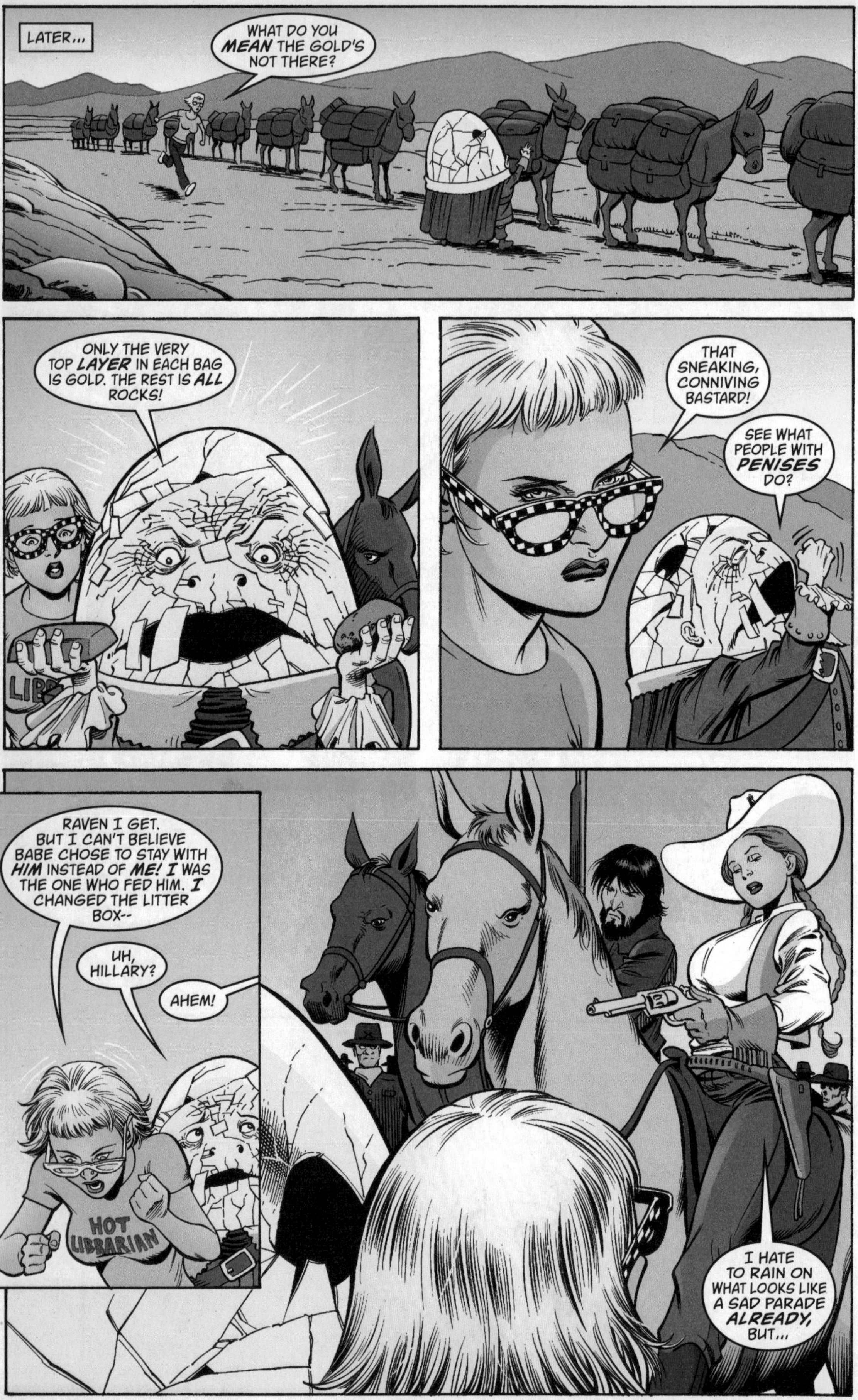
LATER...
WHAT DO YOU MEAN THE GOLD'S NOT THERE?
ONLY THE VERY TOP LAYER IN EACH BAG IS GOLD. THE REST IS ALL ROCKS!
THAT SNEAKING, CONNIVING BASTARD!
SEE WHAT PEOPLE WITH PENISES DO?
RAVEN I GET. BUT I CAN'T BELIEVE BABE CHOSE TO STAY WITH HIM INSTEAD OF ME! I WAS THE ONE WHO FED HIM. I CHANGED THE LITTER BOX--
UH, HILLARY?
AHEM!
HOT LIBRARIAN
I HATE TO RAIN ON WHAT LOOKS LIKE A SAD PARADE ALREADY, BUT...

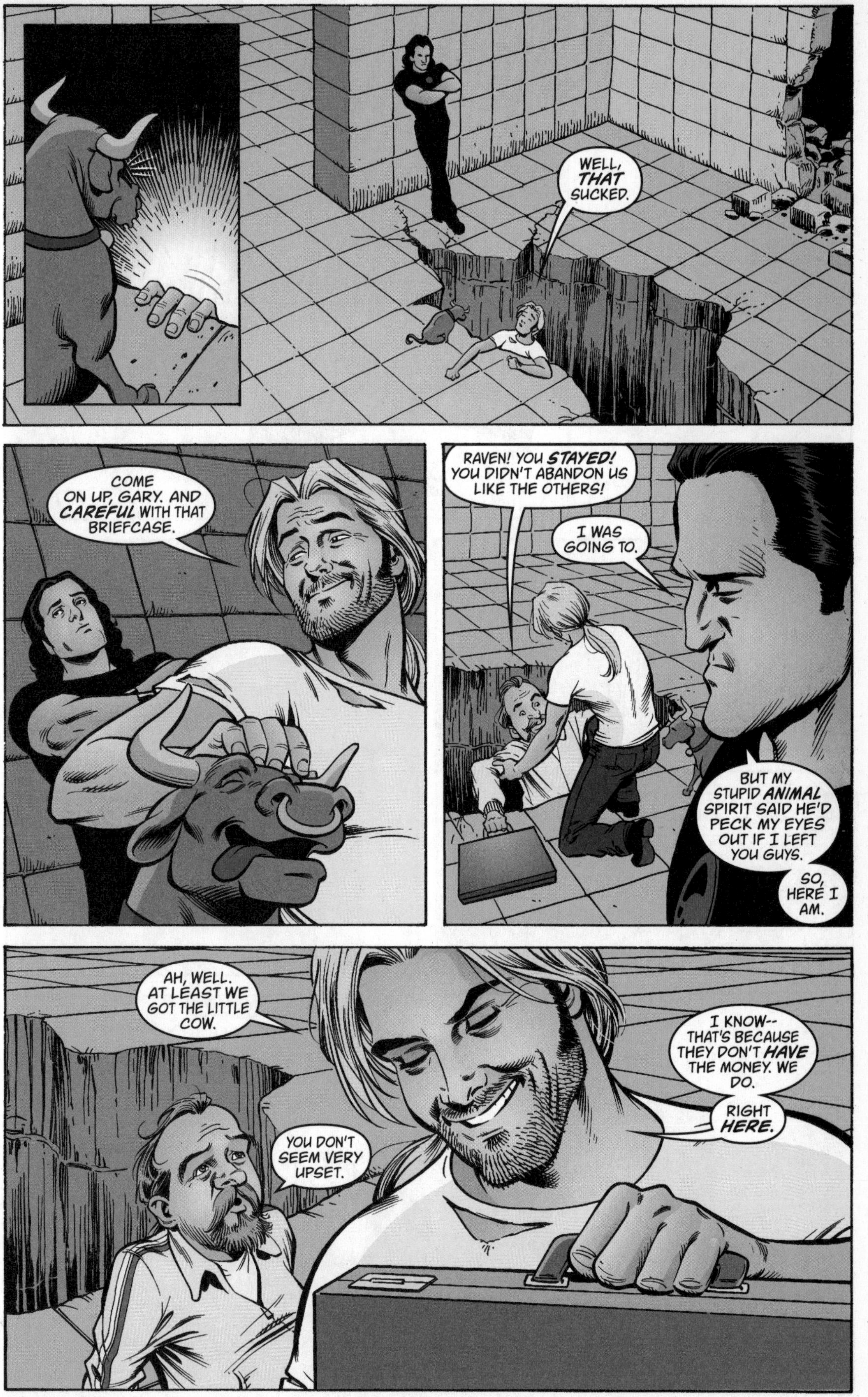

WELL, THAT SUCKED.
COME ON UP, GARY. AND CAREFUL WITH THAT BRIEFCASE.
RAVEN! YOU STAYED! YOU DIDN'T ABANDON US LIKE THE OTHERS!
I WAS GOING TO.
BUT MY STUPID ANIMAL SPIRIT SAID HE'D PECK MY EYES OUT IF I LEFT YOU GUYS.
SO, HERE I AM.
AH, WELL. AT LEAST WE GOT THE LITTLE COW.
YOU DON'T SEEM VERY UPSET.
I KNOW-- THAT'S BECAUSE THEY DON'T HAVE THE MONEY. WE DO.
RIGHT HERE.

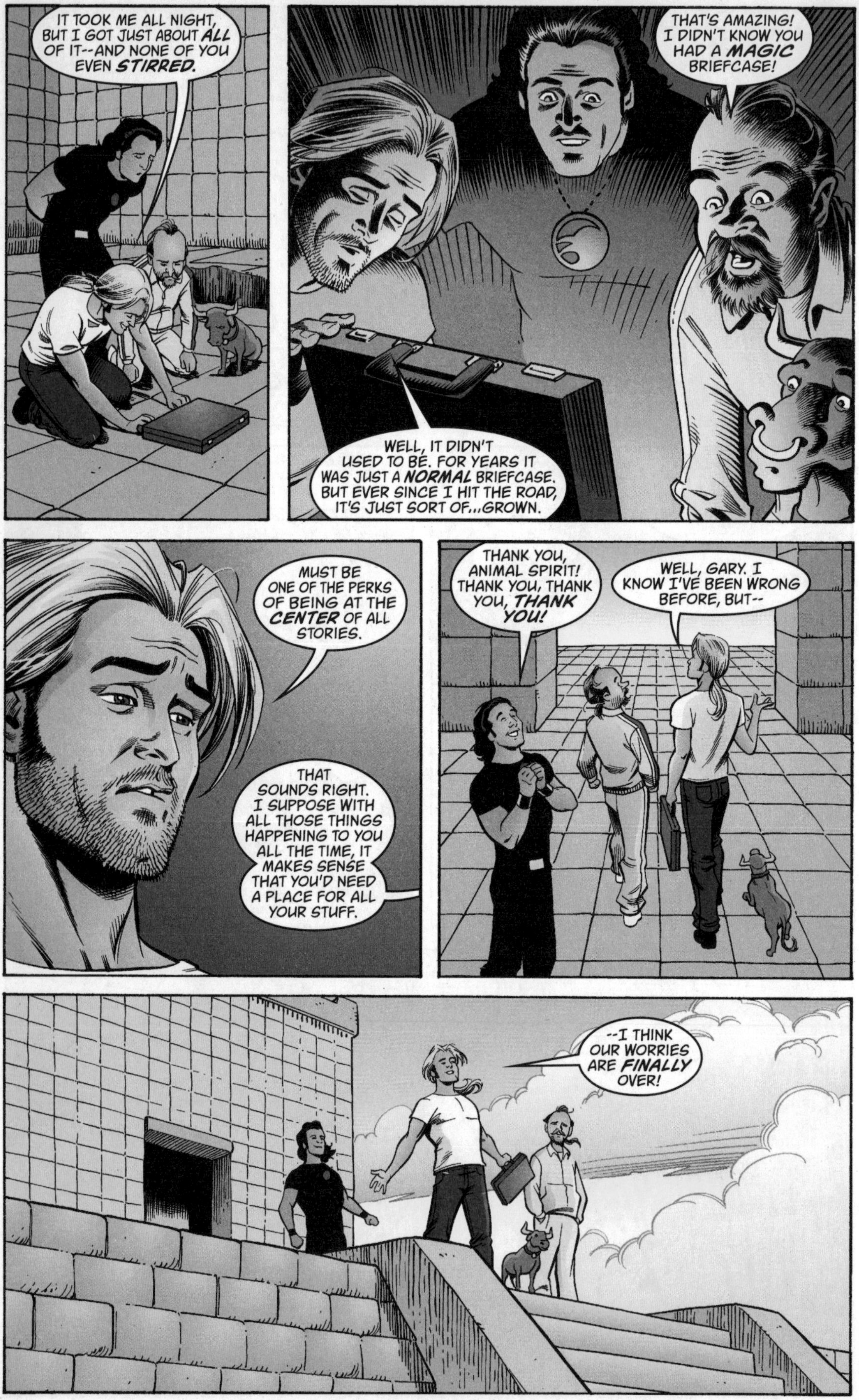
IT TOOK ME ALL NIGHT, BUT I GOT JUST ABOUT ALL OF IT--AND NONE OF YOU EVEN STIRRED.
THAT'S AMAZING! I DIDN'T KNOW YOU HAD A MAGIC BRIEFCASE!
WELL, IT DIDN'T USED TO BE. FOR YEARS IT WAS JUST A NORMAL BRIEFCASE. BUT EVER SINCE I HIT THE ROAD, IT'S JUST SORT OF...GROWN.
MUST BE ONE OF THE PERKS OF BEING AT THE CENTER OF ALL STORIES.
THAT SOUNDS RIGHT. I SUPPOSE WITH ALL THOSE THINGS HAPPENING TO YOU ALL THE TIME, IT MAKES SENSE THAT YOU'D NEED A PLACE FOR ALL YOUR STUFF.
THANK YOU, ANIMAL SPIRIT! THANK YOU, THANK YOU, THANK YOU!
WELL, GARY. I KNOW I'VE BEEN WRONG BEFORE, BUT--
--I THINK OUR WORRIES ARE FINALLY OVER!

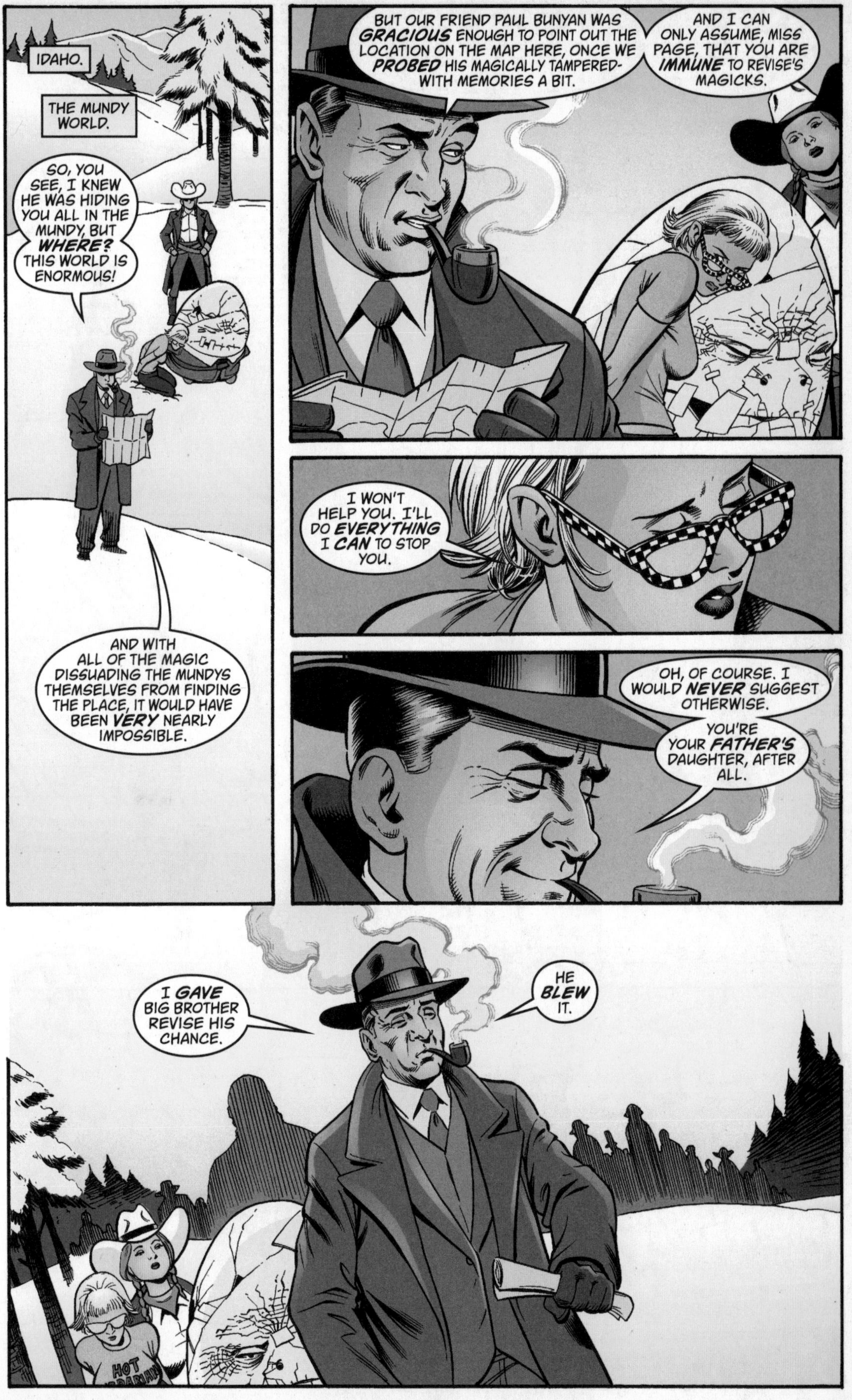
IDAHO.
THE MUNDY WORLD.
SO, YOU SEE, I KNEW HE WAS HIDING YOU ALL IN THE MUNDY, BUT WHERE? THIS WORLD IS ENORMOUS!
AND WITH ALL OF THE MAGIC DISSUADING THE MUNDYS THEMSELVES FROM FINDING THE PLACE, IT WOULD HAVE BEEN VERY NEARLY IMPOSSIBLE.
BUT OUR FRIEND PAUL BUNYAN WAS GRACIOUS ENOUGH TO POINT OUT THE LOCATION ON THE MAP HERE, ONCE WE PROBED HIS MAGICALLY TAMPERED-WITH MEMORIES A BIT.
AND I CAN ONLY ASSUME, MISS PAGE, THAT YOU ARE IMMUNE TO REVISE'S MAGICKS.
I WON'T HELP YOU. I'LL DO EVERYTHING I CAN TO STOP YOU.
OH, OF COURSE. I WOULD NEVER SUGGEST OTHERWISE.
YOU'RE YOUR FATHER'S DAUGHTER, AFTER ALL.
I GAVE BIG BROTHER REVISE HIS CHANCE.
HE BLEW IT.

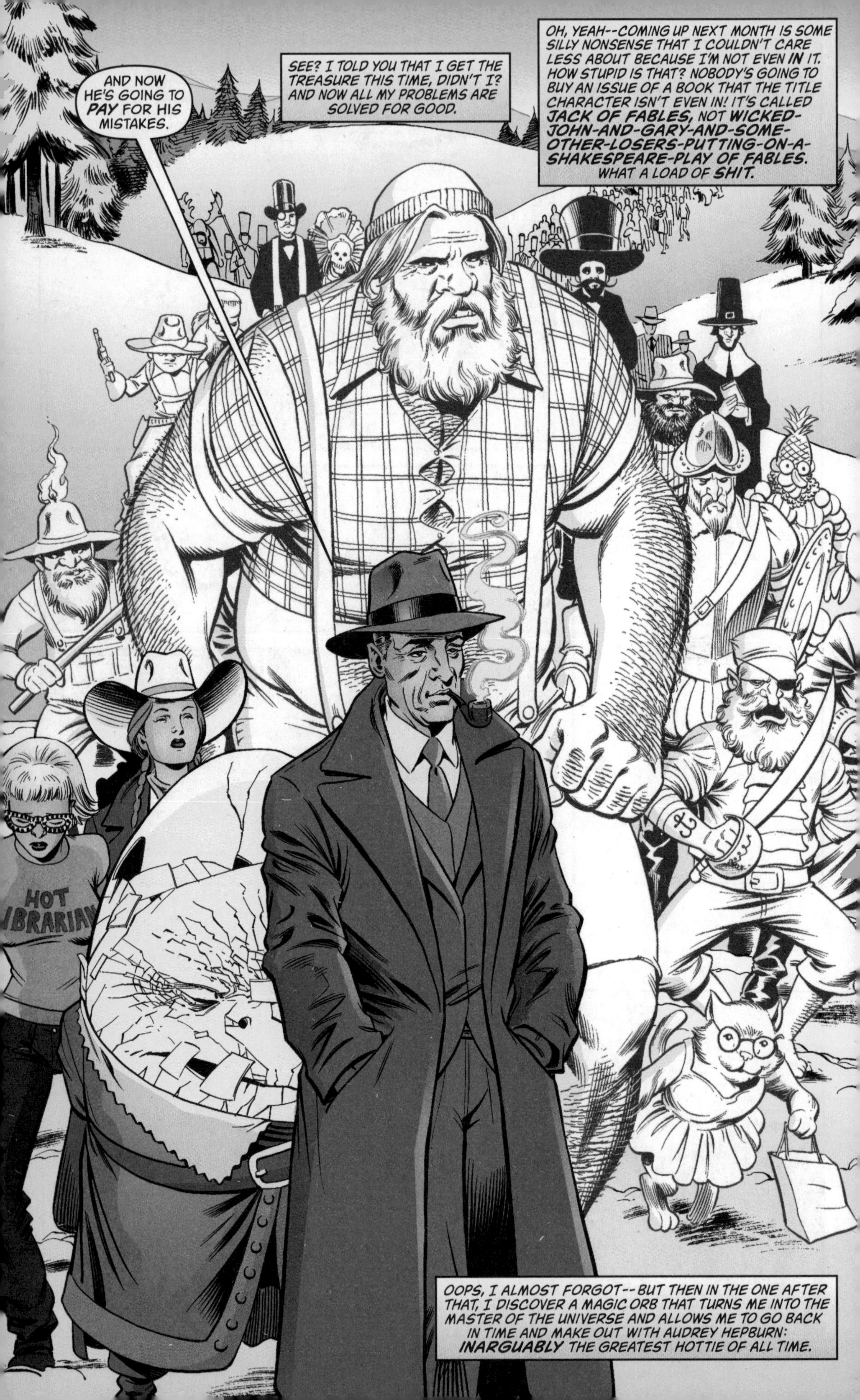
AND NOW HE'S GOING TO PAY FOR HIS MISTAKES.
SEE? I TOLD YOU THAT I GET THE TREASURE THIS TIME, DIDN'T I? AND NOW ALL MY PROBLEMS ARE SOLVED FOR GOOD.
OH, YEAH--COMING UP NEXT MONTH IS SOME SILLY NONSENSE THAT I COULDN'T CARE LESS ABOUT BECAUSE I'M NOT EVEN IN IT. HOW STUPID IS THAT? NOBODY'S GOING TO BUY AN ISSUE OF A BOOK THAT THE TITLE CHARACTER ISN'T EVEN IN! IT'S CALLED JACK OF FABLES, NOT WICKED-JOHN-AND-GARY-AND-SOME-OTHER-LOSERS-PUTTING-ON-A-SHAKESPEARE-PLAY OF FABLES. WHAT A LOAD OF SHIT.
HOT LIBRARIAN
OOPS, I ALMOST FORGOT--BUT THEN IN THE ONE AFTER THAT, I DISCOVER A MAGIC ORB THAT TURNS ME INTO THE MASTER OF THE UNIVERSE AND ALLOWS ME TO GO BACK IN TIME AND MAKE OUT WITH AUDREY HEPBURN: INARGUABLY THE GREATEST HOTTIE OF ALL TIME.

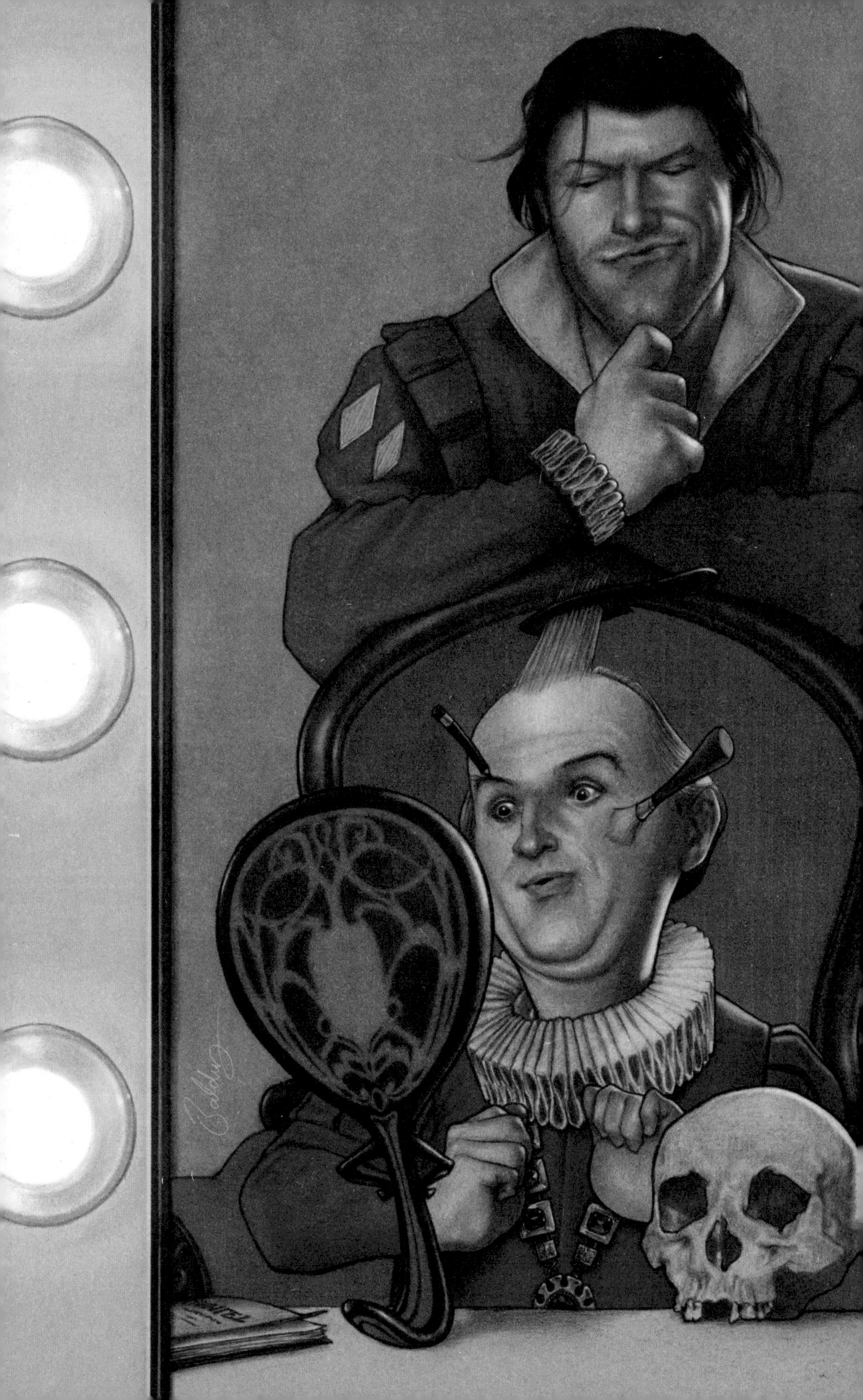

"You can cage the greatest Fable on Earth,
but **not** for long, friends."

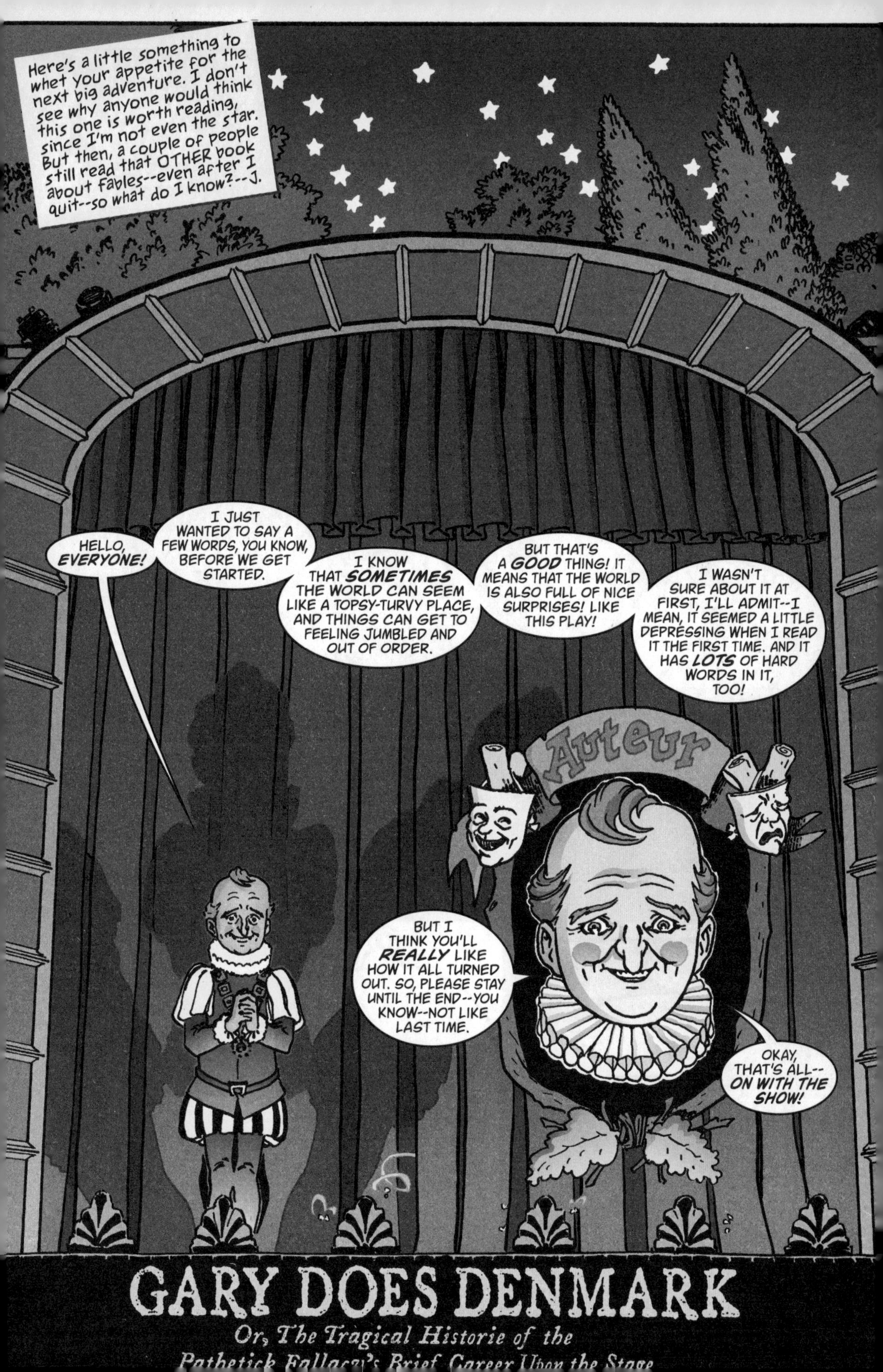

Here's a little something to whet your appetite for the next big adventure. I don't see why anyone would think this one is worth reading, since I'm not even the star. But then, a couple of people still read that OTHER book about fables--even after I quit--so what do I know?--J.
HELLO, EVERYONE!
I JUST WANTED TO SAY A FEW WORDS, YOU KNOW, BEFORE WE GET STARTED.
I KNOW THAT SOMETIMES THE WORLD CAN SEEM LIKE A TOPSY-TURVY PLACE, AND THINGS CAN GET TO FEELING JUMBLED AND OUT OF ORDER.
BUT THAT'S A GOOD THING! IT MEANS THAT THE WORLD IS ALSO FULL OF NICE SURPRISES! LIKE THIS PLAY!
I WASN'T SURE ABOUT IT AT FIRST, I'LL ADMIT--I MEAN, IT SEEMED A LITTLE DEPRESSING WHEN I READ IT THE FIRST TIME. AND IT HAS LOTS OF HARD WORDS IN IT, TOO!
Auteur
BUT I THINK YOU'LL REALLY LIKE HOW IT ALL TURNED OUT. SO, PLEASE STAY UNTIL THE END--YOU KNOW--NOT LIKE LAST TIME.
OKAY, THAT'S ALL--ON WITH THE SHOW!
GARY DOES DENMARK
Or, The Tragical Historie of the Pathetick Fallacy's Brief Career Upon the Stage

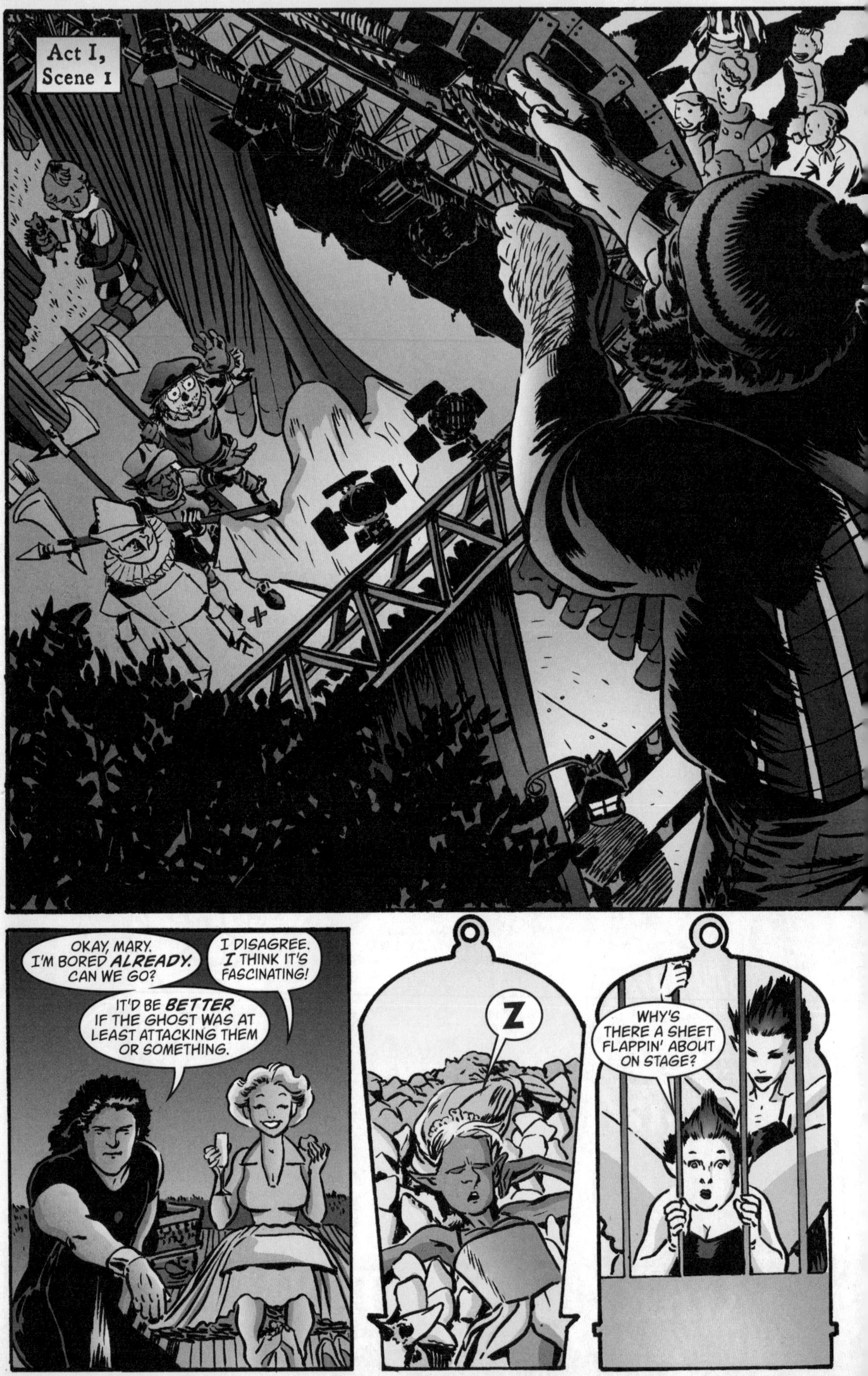
Act I,
Scene 1
OKAY, MARY. I'M BORED ALREADY. CAN WE GO?
I DISAGREE. I THINK IT'S FASCINATING!
IT'D BE BETTER IF THE GHOST WAS AT LEAST ATTACKING THEM OR SOMETHING.
Z
WHY'S THERE A SHEET FLAPPIN' ABOUT ON STAGE?

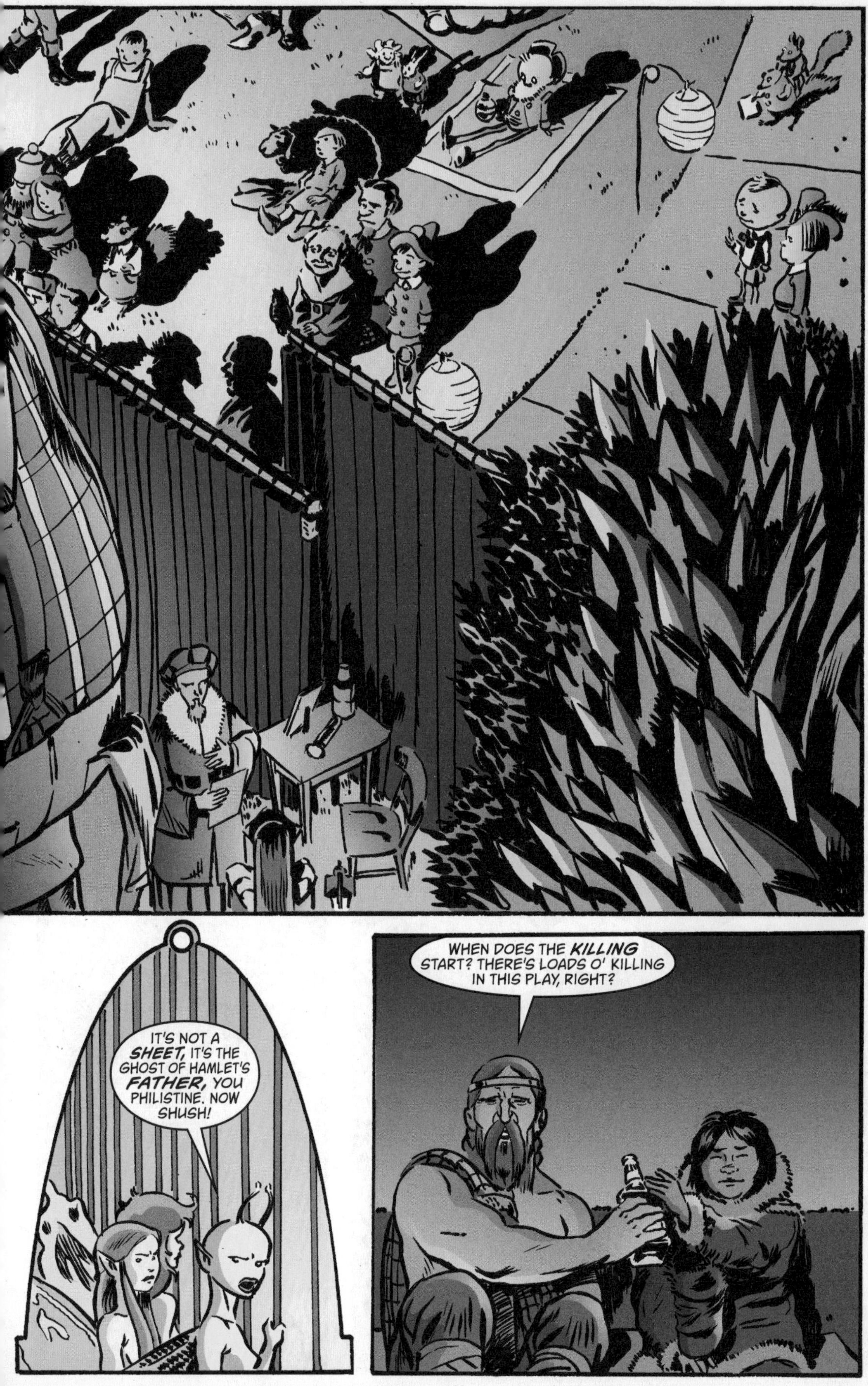
IT'S NOT A SHEET, IT'S THE GHOST OF HAMLET'S FATHER, YOU PHILISTINE. NOW SHUSH!
WHEN DOES THE KILLING START? THERE'S LOADS O' KILLING IN THIS PLAY, RIGHT?

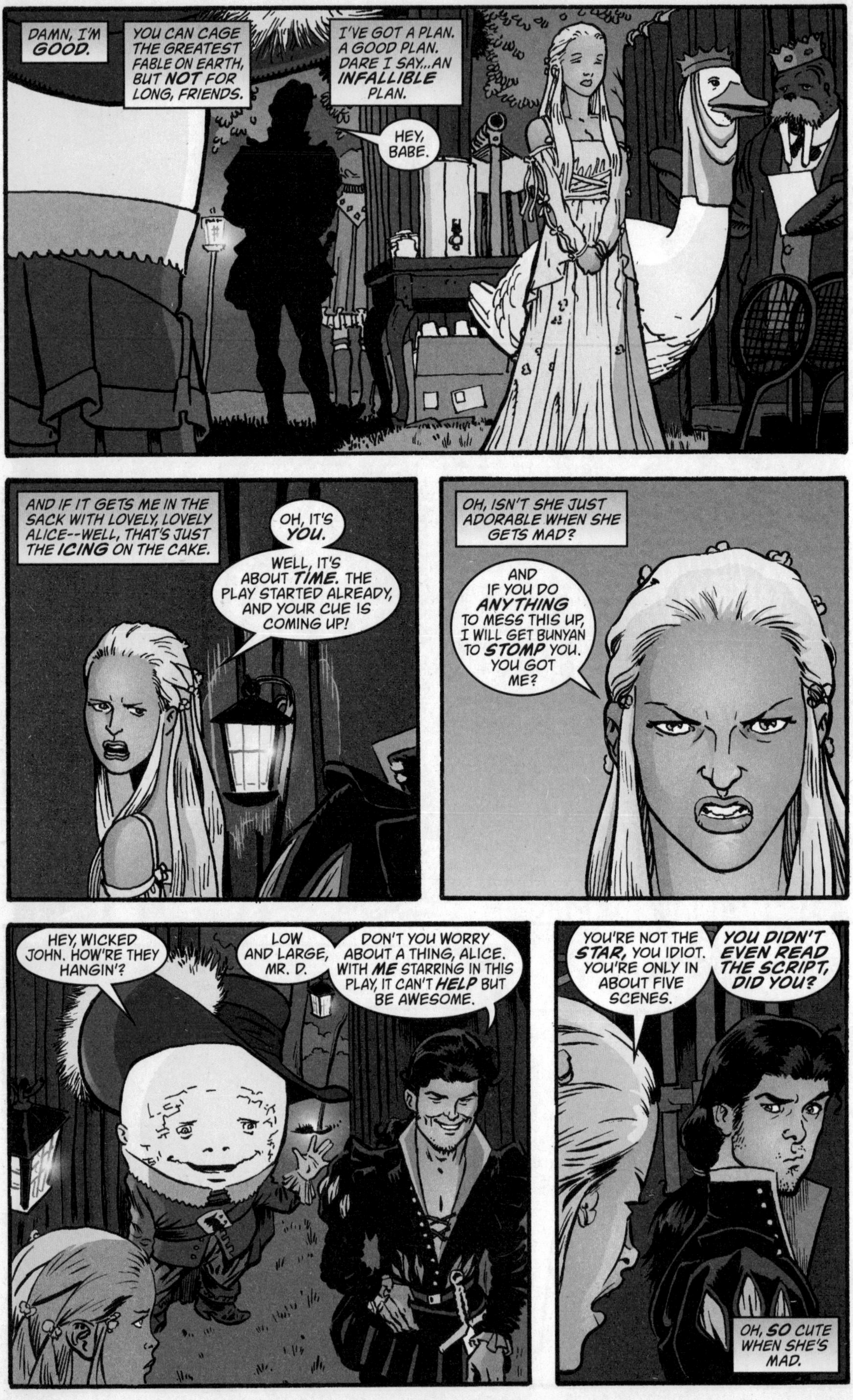
DAMN, I'M GOOD.
YOU CAN CAGE THE GREATEST FABLE ON EARTH, BUT NOT FOR LONG, FRIENDS.
I'VE GOT A PLAN. A GOOD PLAN. DARE I SAY...AN INFALLIBLE PLAN.
HEY, BABE.
AND IF IT GETS ME IN THE SACK WITH LOVELY, LOVELY ALICE--WELL, THAT'S JUST THE ICING ON THE CAKE.
OH, IT'S YOU.
WELL, IT'S ABOUT TIME. THE PLAY STARTED ALREADY, AND YOUR CUE IS COMING UP!
OH, ISN'T SHE JUST ADORABLE WHEN SHE GETS MAD?
AND IF YOU DO ANYTHING TO MESS THIS UP, I WILL GET BUNYAN TO STOMP YOU. YOU GOT ME?
HEY, WICKED JOHN. HOW'RE THEY HANGIN'?
LOW AND LARGE, MR. D.
DON'T YOU WORRY ABOUT A THING, ALICE. WITH ME STARRING IN THIS PLAY, IT CAN'T HELP BUT BE AWESOME.
YOU'RE NOT THE STAR, YOU IDIOT. YOU'RE ONLY IN ABOUT FIVE SCENES.
YOU DIDN'T EVEN READ THE SCRIPT, DID YOU?
OH, SO CUTE WHEN SHE'S MAD.

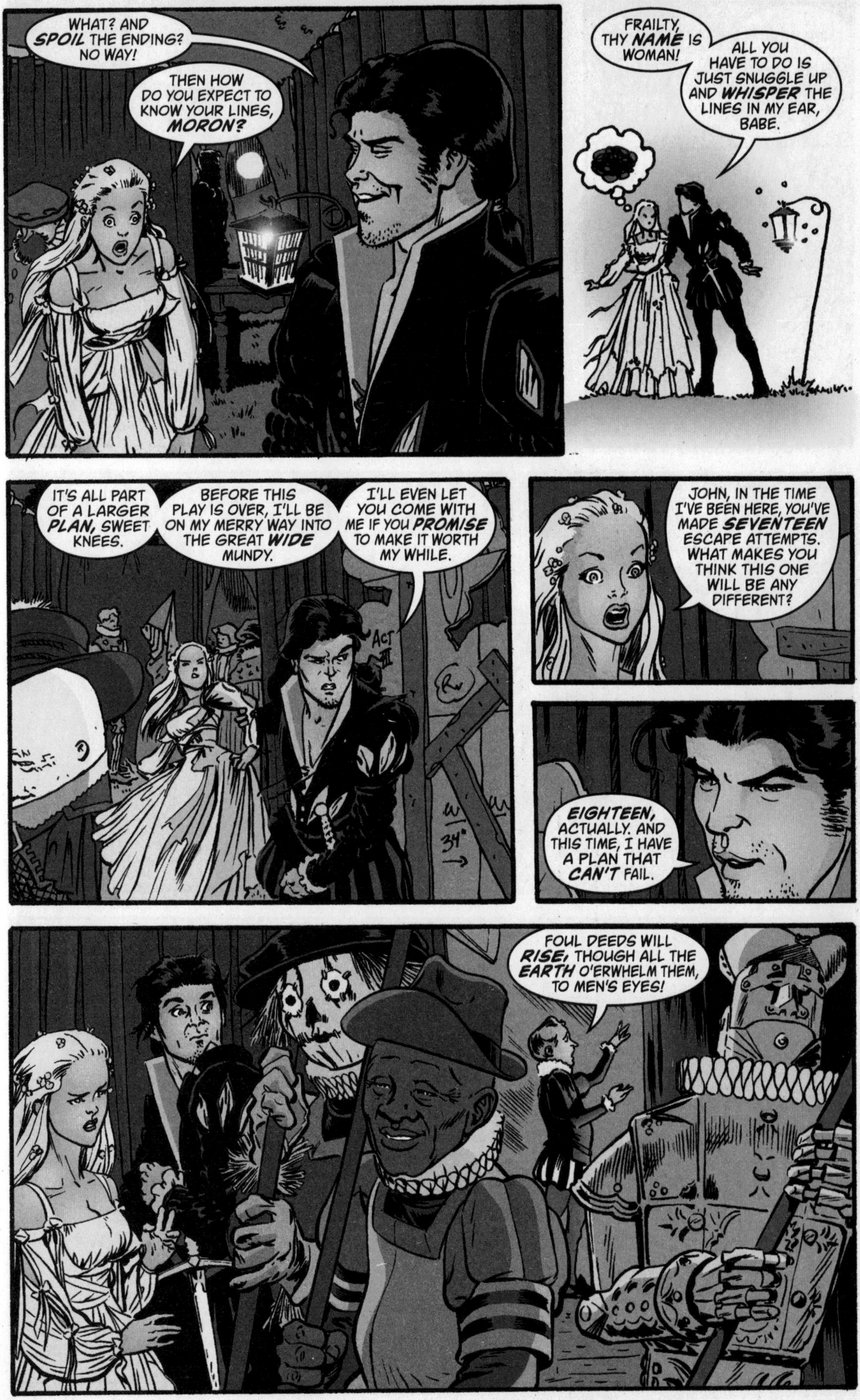
WHAT? AND SPOIL THE ENDING? NO WAY!
THEN HOW DO YOU EXPECT TO KNOW YOUR LINES, MORON?
FRAILTY, THY NAME IS WOMAN!
ALL YOU HAVE TO DO IS JUST SNUGGLE UP AND WHISPER THE LINES IN MY EAR, BABE.
IT'S ALL PART OF A LARGER PLAN, SWEET KNEES.
BEFORE THIS PLAY IS OVER, I'LL BE ON MY MERRY WAY INTO THE GREAT WIDE MUNDY.
I'LL EVEN LET YOU COME WITH ME IF YOU PROMISE TO MAKE IT WORTH MY WHILE.
JOHN, IN THE TIME I'VE BEEN HERE, YOU'VE MADE SEVENTEEN ESCAPE ATTEMPTS. WHAT MAKES YOU THINK THIS ONE WILL BE ANY DIFFERENT?
EIGHTEEN, ACTUALLY. AND THIS TIME, I HAVE A PLAN THAT CAN'T FAIL.
FOUL DEEDS WILL RISE, THOUGH ALL THE EARTH O'ERWHELM THEM, TO MEN'S EYES!

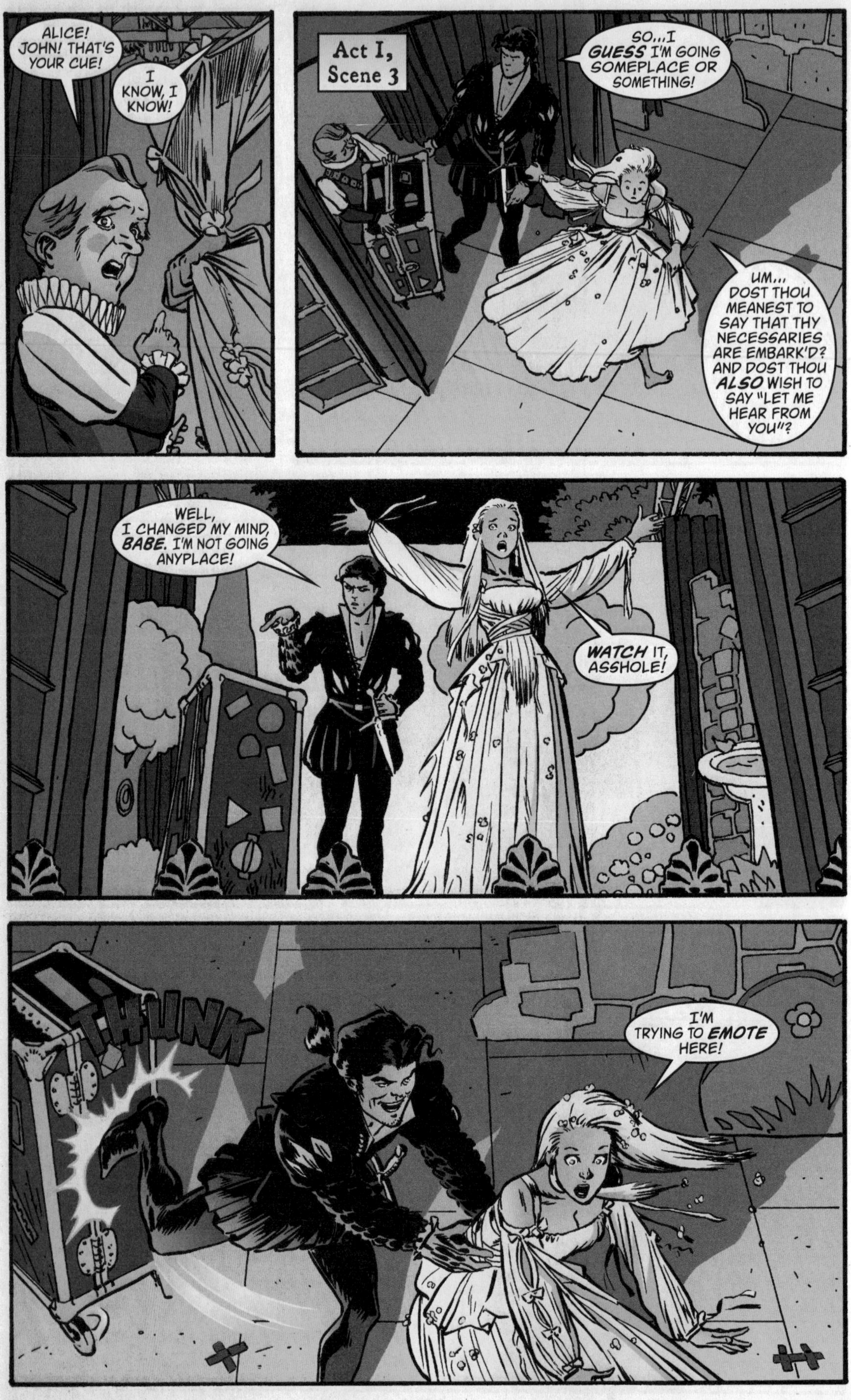
ALICE! JOHN! THAT'S YOUR CUE!
I KNOW, I KNOW!
Act I, Scene 3
SO...I GUESS I'M GOING SOMEPLACE OR SOMETHING!
UM... DOST THOU MEANEST TO SAY THAT THY NECESSARIES ARE EMBARK'D? AND DOST THOU ALSO WISH TO SAY "LET ME HEAR FROM YOU"?
WELL, I CHANGED MY MIND, BABE. I'M NOT GOING ANYPLACE!
WATCH IT, ASSHOLE!
THUNK
I'M TRYING TO EMOTE HERE!

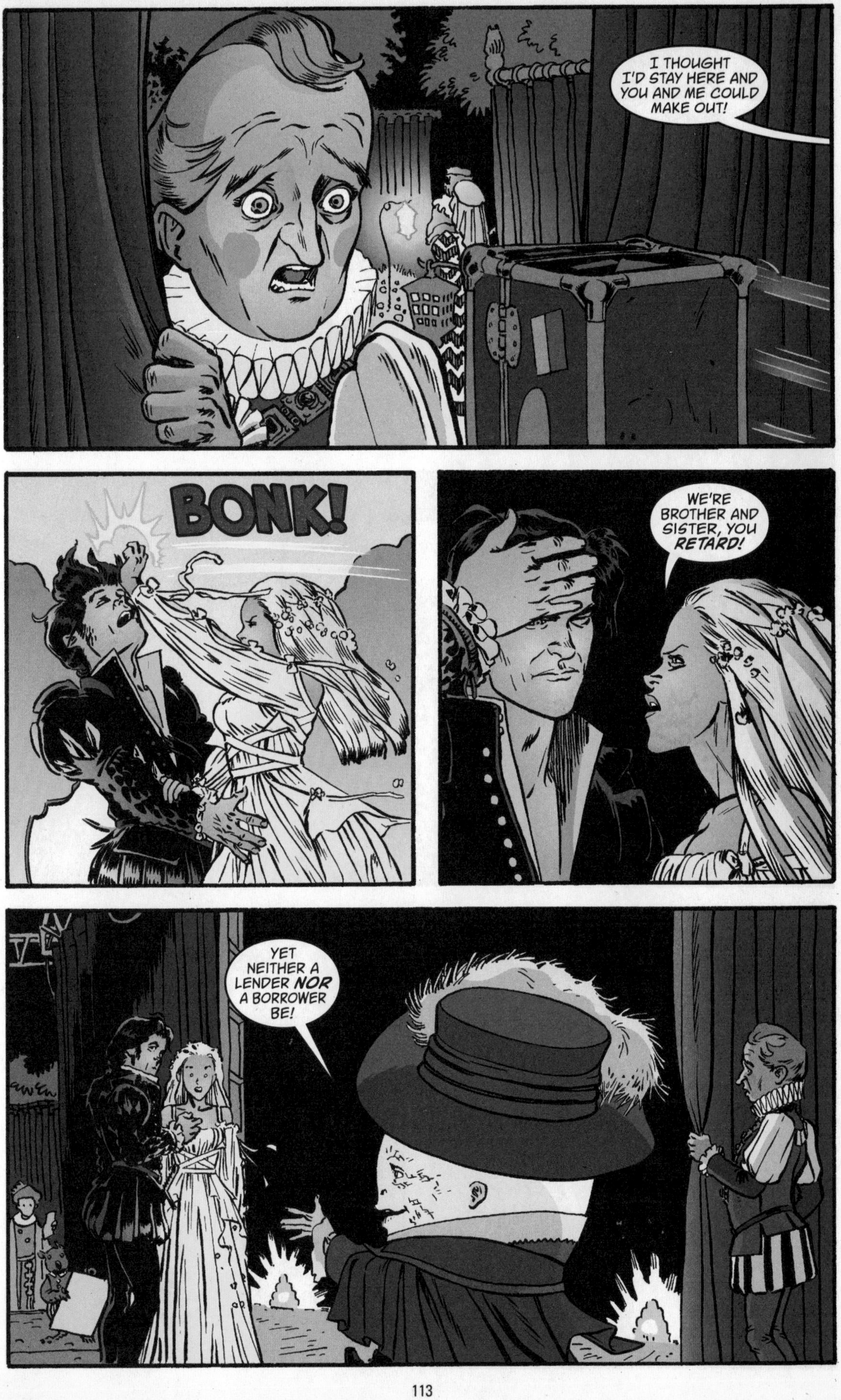

I THOUGHT I'D STAY HERE AND YOU AND ME COULD MAKE OUT!
BONK!
WE'RE BROTHER AND SISTER, YOU RETARD!
YET NEITHER A LENDER NOR A BORROWER BE!

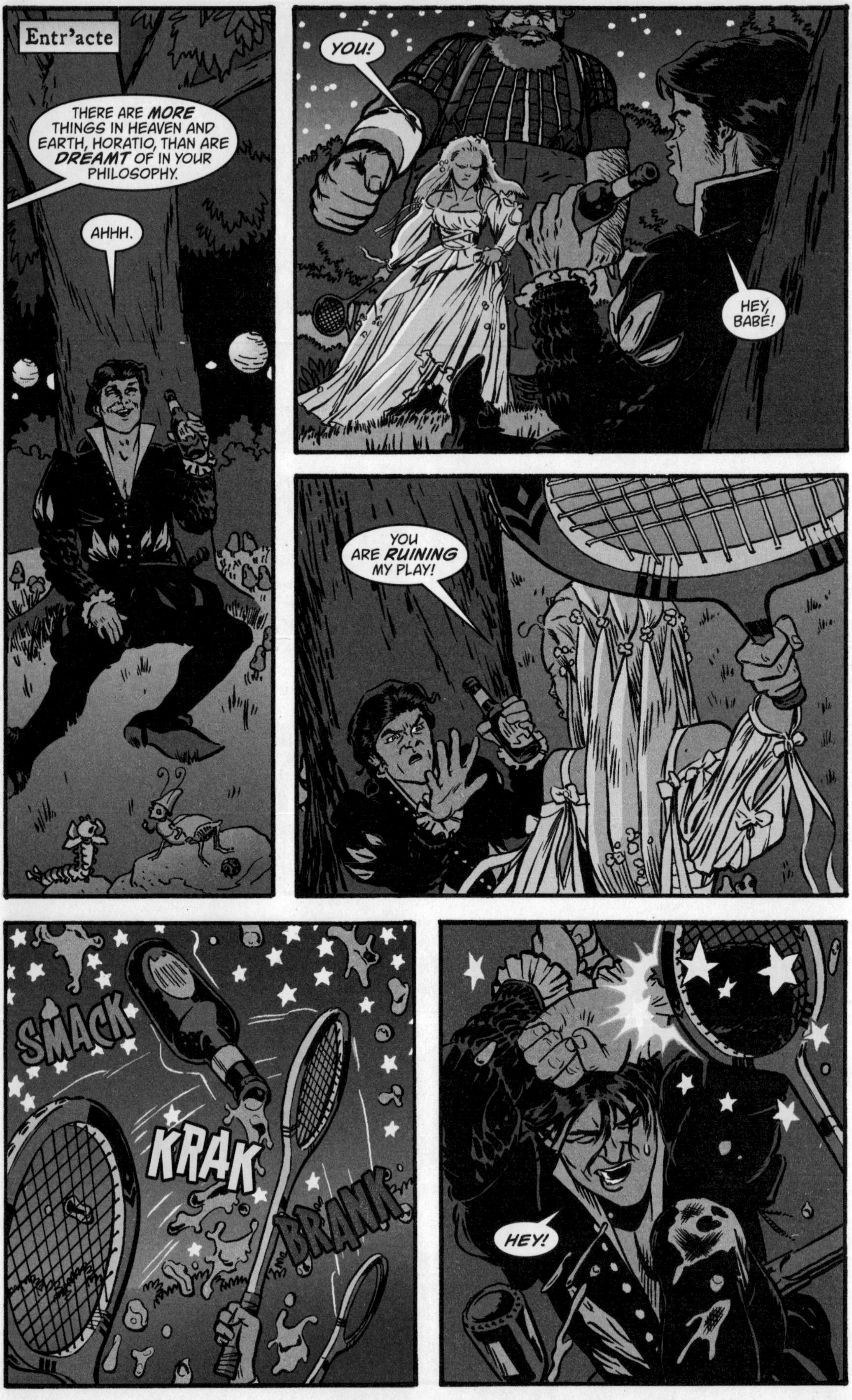
Entr'acte
THERE ARE MORE THINGS IN HEAVEN AND EARTH, HORATIO, THAN ARE DREAMT OF IN YOUR PHILOSOPHY.
AHHH.
YOU!
HEY, BABE!
YOU ARE RUINING MY PLAY!
SMACK
KRAK
BRANK
HEY!

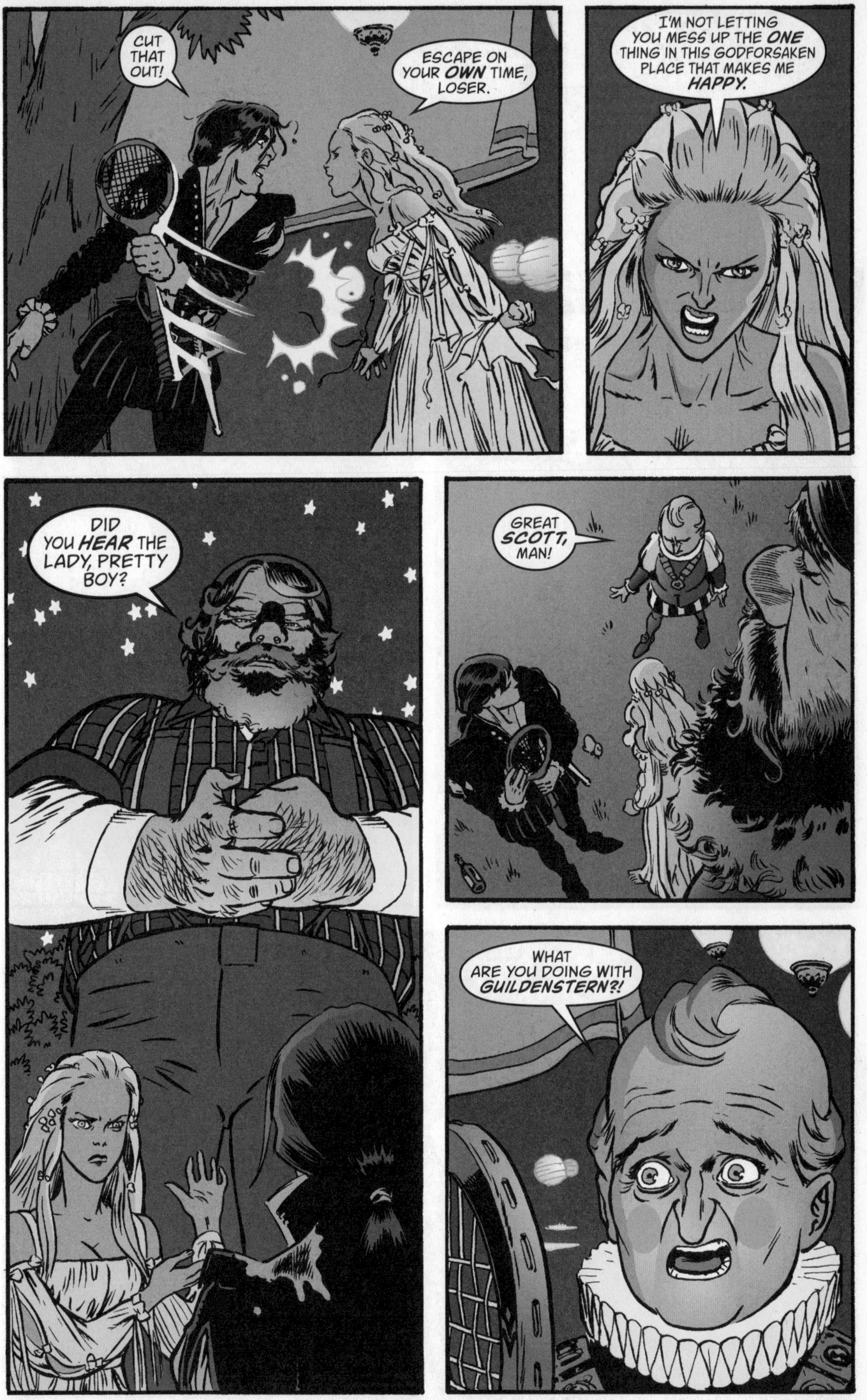
CUT THAT OUT!
ESCAPE ON YOUR OWN TIME, LOSER.
I'M NOT LETTING YOU MESS UP THE ONE THING IN THIS GODFORSAKEN PLACE THAT MAKES ME HAPPY.
DID YOU HEAR THE LADY, PRETTY BOY?
GREAT SCOTT, MAN!
WHAT ARE YOU DOING WITH GUILDENSTERN?!
WHAT

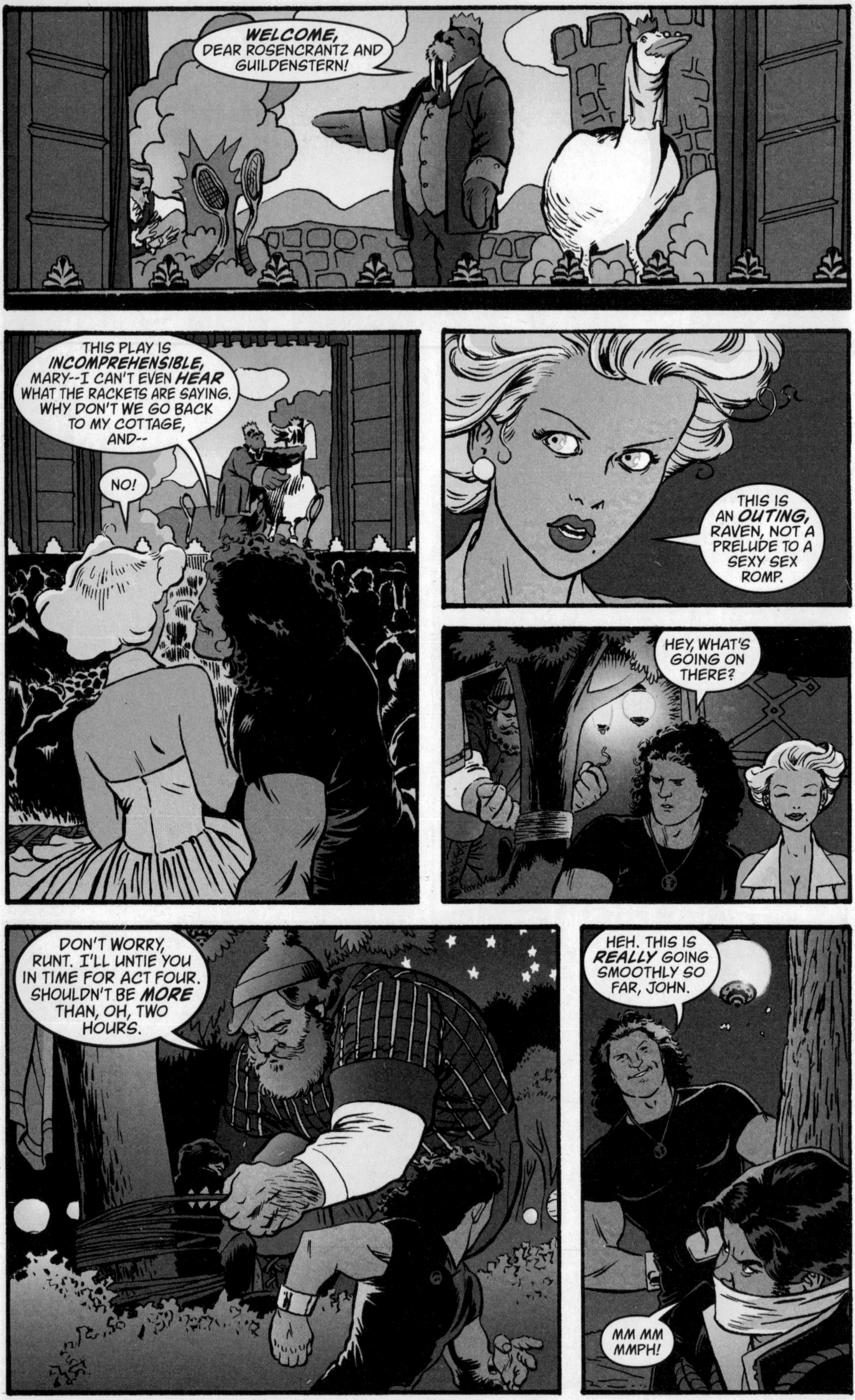
WELCOME, DEAR ROSENCRANTZ AND GUILDENSTERN!
THIS PLAY IS INCOMPREHENSIBLE, MARY--I CAN'T EVEN HEAR WHAT THE RACKETS ARE SAYING. WHY DON'T WE GO BACK TO MY COTTAGE, AND--
NO!
THIS IS AN OUTING, RAVEN, NOT A PRELUDE TO A SEXY SEX ROMP.
HEY, WHAT'S GOING ON THERE?
DON'T WORRY, RUNT. I'LL UNTIE YOU IN TIME FOR ACT FOUR. SHOULDN'T BE MORE THAN, OH, TWO HOURS.
HEH. THIS IS REALLY GOING SMOOTHLY SO FAR, JOHN.
MM MM MMPH!

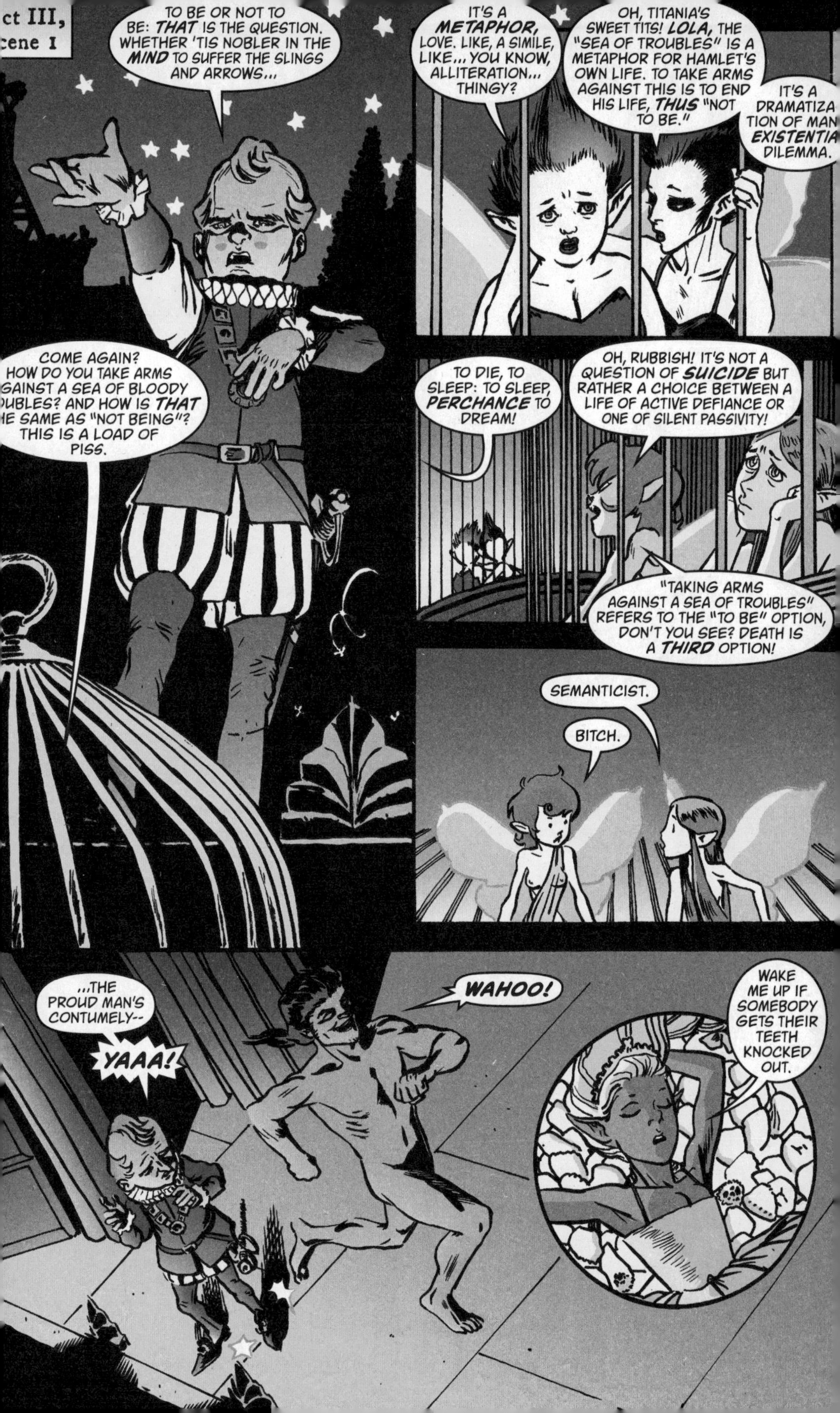
ct III,
cene I
TO BE OR NOT TO BE: THAT IS THE QUESTION. WHETHER 'TIS NOBLER IN THE MIND TO SUFFER THE SLINGS AND ARROWS...
COME AGAIN? HOW DO YOU TAKE ARMS GAINST A SEA OF BLOODY OUBLES? AND HOW IS THAT HE SAME AS "NOT BEING"? THIS IS A LOAD OF PISS.
IT'S A METAPHOR, LOVE. LIKE, A SIMILE, LIKE... YOU KNOW, ALLITERATION... THINGY?
OH, TITANIA'S SWEET TITS! LOLA, THE "SEA OF TROUBLES" IS A METAPHOR FOR HAMLET'S OWN LIFE. TO TAKE ARMS AGAINST THIS IS TO END HIS LIFE, THUS "NOT TO BE."
IT'S A DRAMATIZA TION OF MAN EXISTENTIA DILEMMA.
TO DIE, TO SLEEP: TO SLEEP, PERCHANCE TO DREAM!
OH, RUBBISH! IT'S NOT A QUESTION OF SUICIDE BUT RATHER A CHOICE BETWEEN A LIFE OF ACTIVE DEFIANCE OR ONE OF SILENT PASSIVITY!
"TAKING ARMS AGAINST A SEA OF TROUBLES" REFERS TO THE "TO BE" OPTION, DON'T YOU SEE? DEATH IS A THIRD OPTION!
SEMANTICIST.
BITCH.
...THE PROUD MAN'S CONTUMELY--
YAAA!
WAHOO!
WAKE ME UP IF SOMEBODY GETS THEIR TEETH KNOCKED OUT.

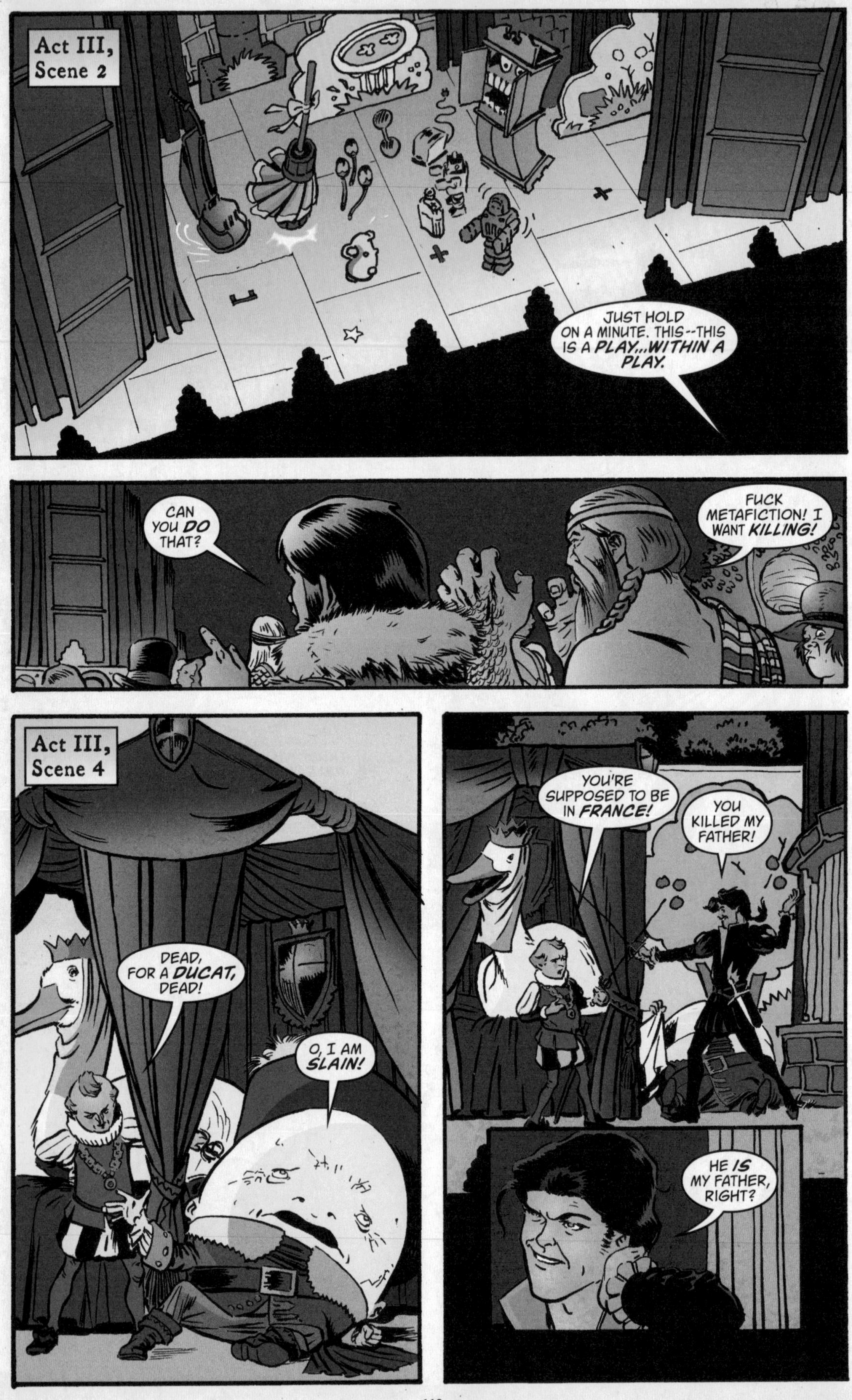
Act III, Scene 2
JUST HOLD ON A MINUTE. THIS--THIS IS A PLAY...WITHIN A PLAY.
CAN YOU DO THAT?
FUCK METAFICTION! I WANT KILLING!
Act III, Scene 4
DEAD, FOR A DUCAT, DEAD!
O, I AM SLAIN!
YOU'RE SUPPOSED TO BE IN FRANCE!
YOU KILLED MY FATHER!
HE IS MY FATHER, RIGHT?

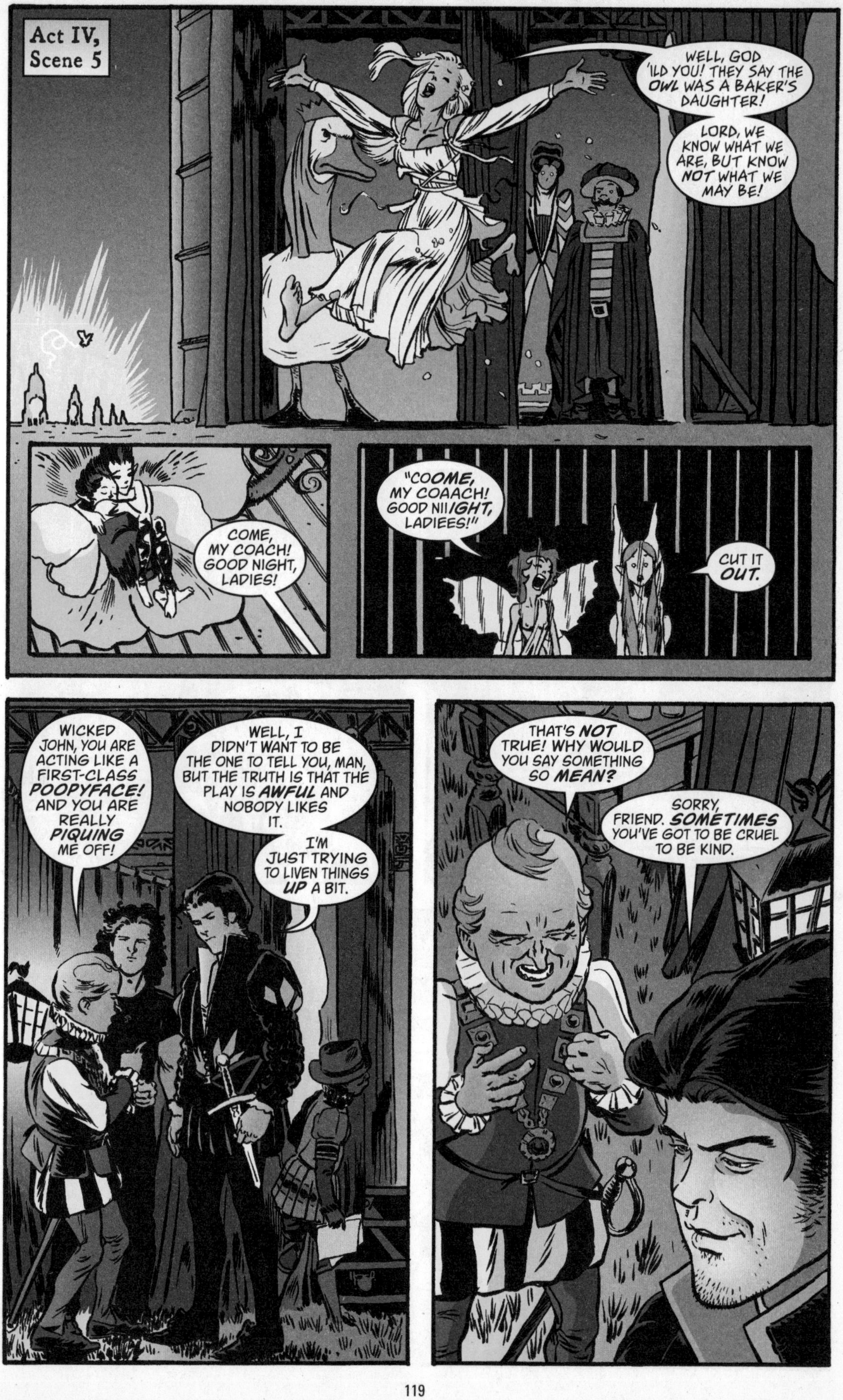

Act IV, Scene 5
WELL, GOD 'ILD YOU! THEY SAY THE OWL WAS A BAKER'S DAUGHTER!
LORD, WE KNOW WHAT WE ARE, BUT KNOW NOT WHAT WE MAY BE!
COME, MY COACH! GOOD NIGHT, LADIES!
"COOME, MY COAACH! GOOD NIIGHT, LADIEES!"
CUT IT OUT.
WICKED JOHN, YOU ARE ACTING LIKE A FIRST-CLASS POOPYFACE! AND YOU ARE REALLY PIQUING ME OFF!
WELL, I DIDN'T WANT TO BE THE ONE TO TELL YOU, MAN, BUT THE TRUTH IS THAT THE PLAY IS AWFUL AND NOBODY LIKES IT.
I'M JUST TRYING TO LIVEN THINGS UP A BIT.
THAT'S NOT TRUE! WHY WOULD YOU SAY SOMETHING SO MEAN?
SORRY, FRIEND. SOMETIMES YOU'VE GOT TO BE CRUEL TO BE KIND.

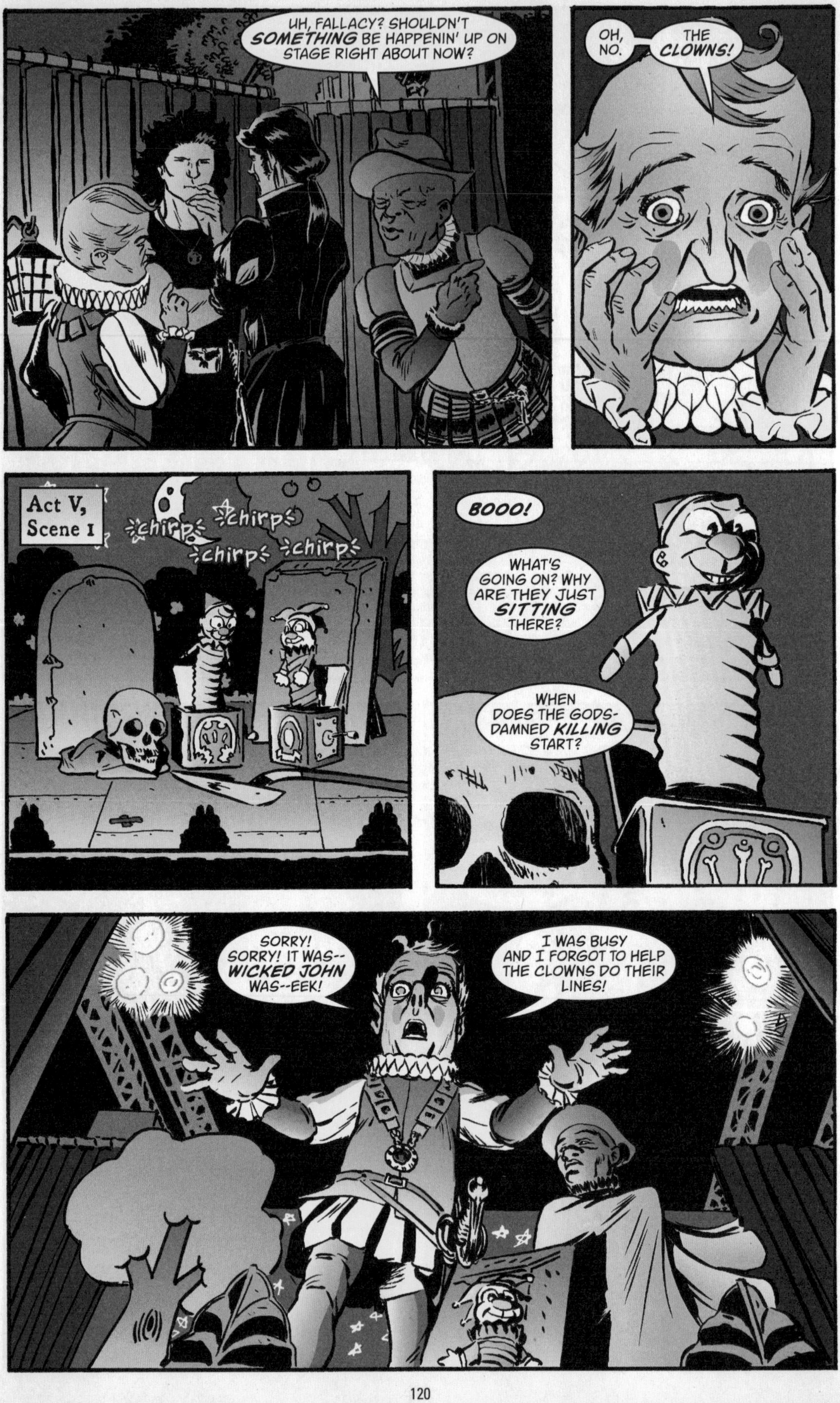
UH, FALLACY? SHOULDN'T SOMETHING BE HAPPENIN' UP ON STAGE RIGHT ABOUT NOW?
OH, NO.
THE CLOWNS!
Act V, Scene I
chirp
chirp
chirp
chirp
BOOO!
WHAT'S GOING ON? WHY ARE THEY JUST SITTING THERE?
WHEN DOES THE GODS-DAMNED KILLING START?
SORRY! SORRY! IT WAS-- WICKED JOHN WAS--EEK!
I WAS BUSY AND I FORGOT TO HELP THE CLOWNS DO THEIR LINES!

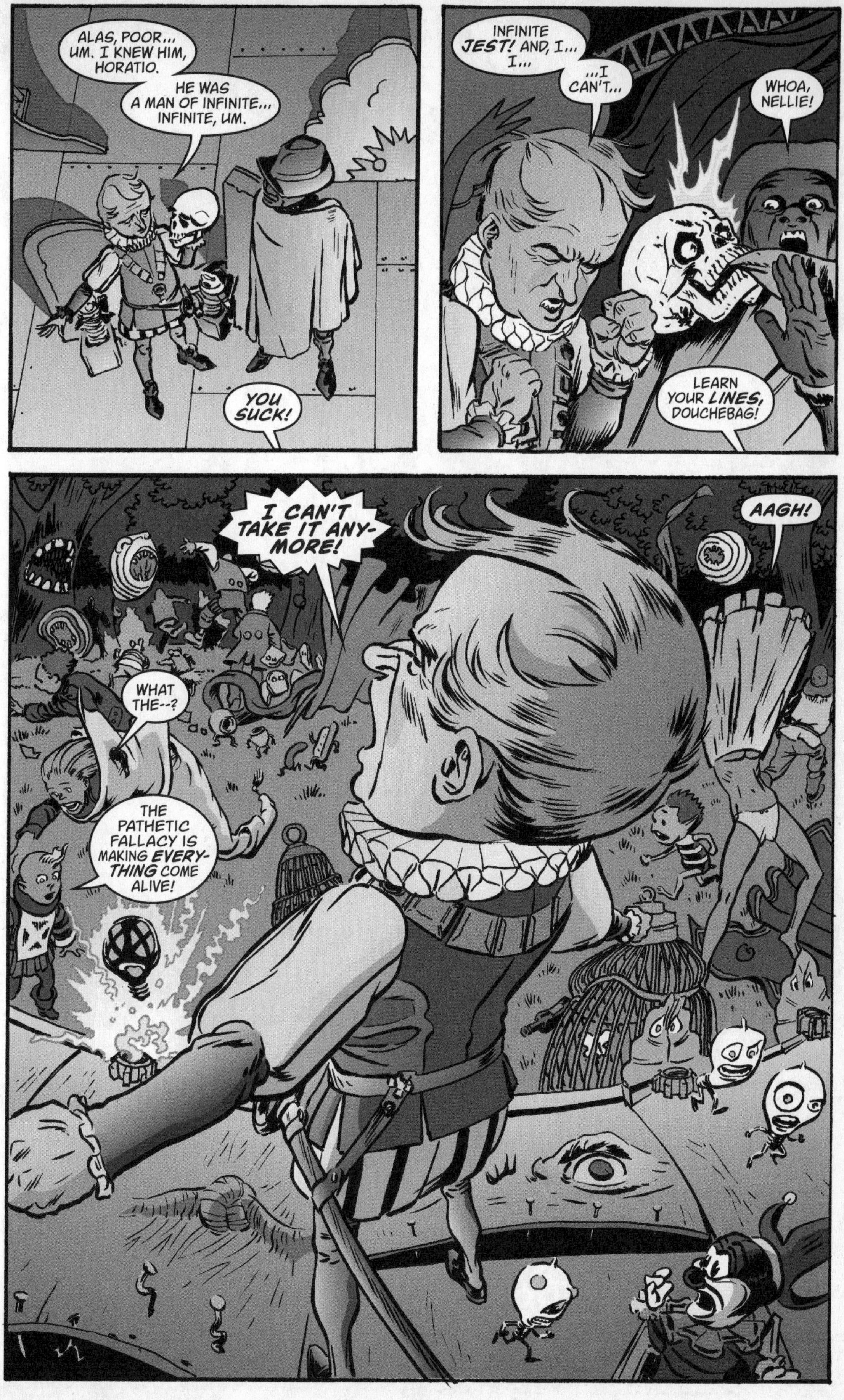
ALAS, POOR... UM. I KNEW HIM, HORATIO.
HE WAS A MAN OF INFINITE... INFINITE, UM.
YOU SUCK!
INFINITE JEST! AND, I... I...
...I CAN'T...
WHOA, NELLIE!
LEARN YOUR LINES, DOUCHEBAG!
I CAN'T TAKE IT ANY-MORE!
AAGH!
WHAT THE--?
THE PATHETIC FALLACY IS MAKING EVERY-THING COME ALIVE!

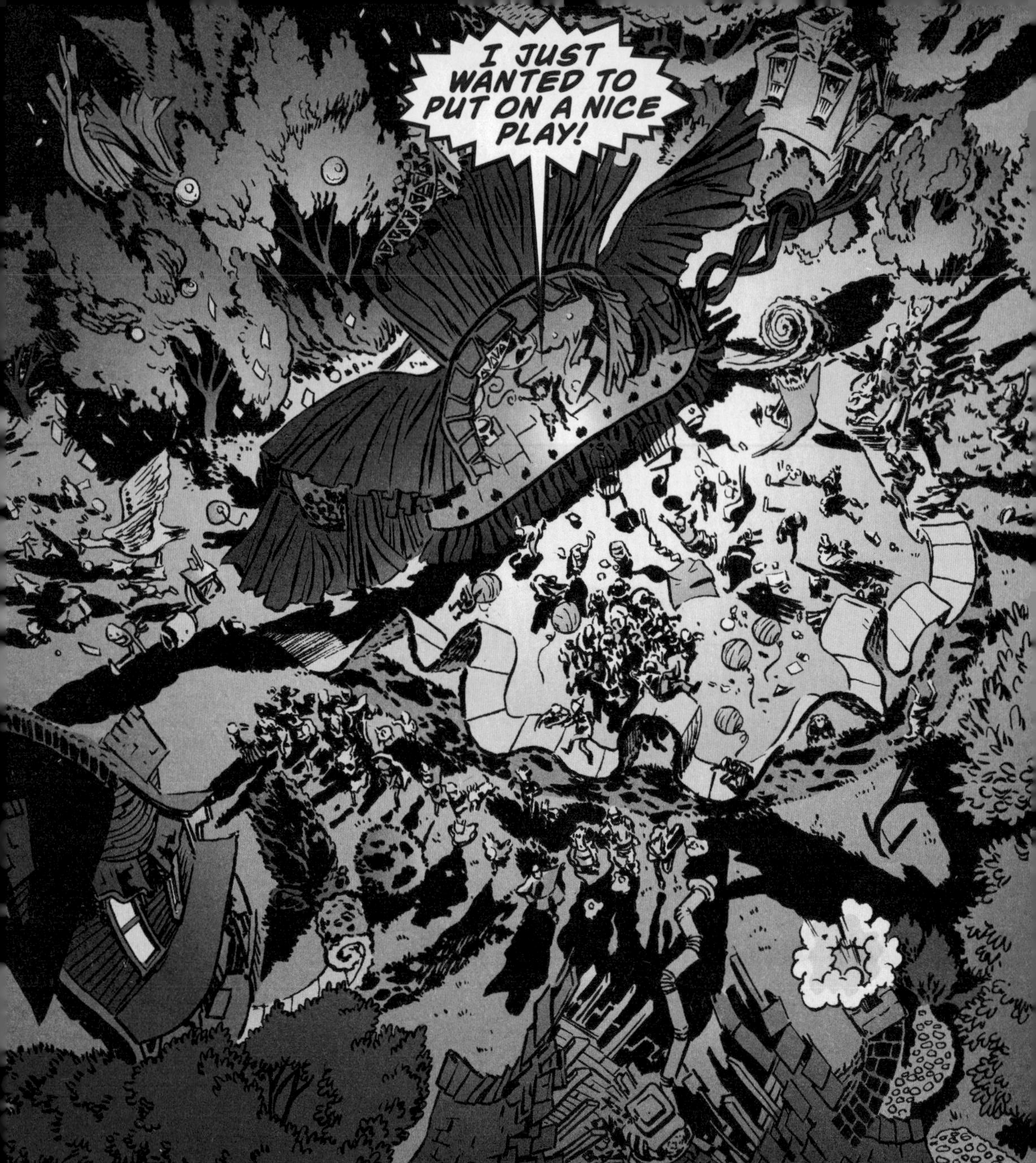
I JUST WANTED TO PUT ON A NICE PLAY!

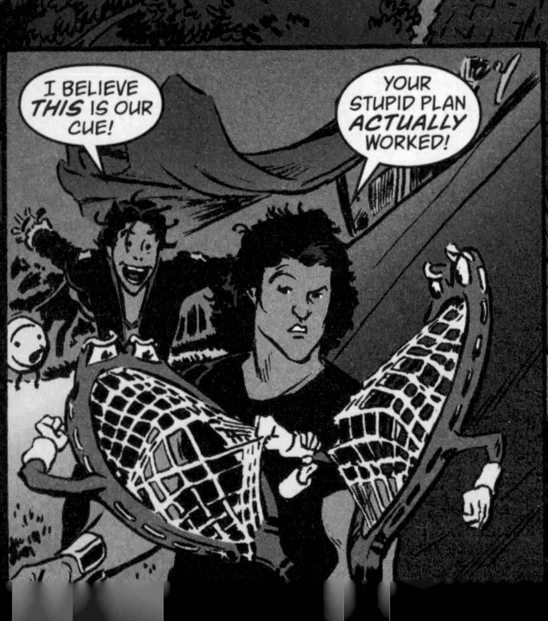
I BELIEVE THIS IS OUR CUE!
YOUR STUPID PLAN ACTUALLY WORKED!

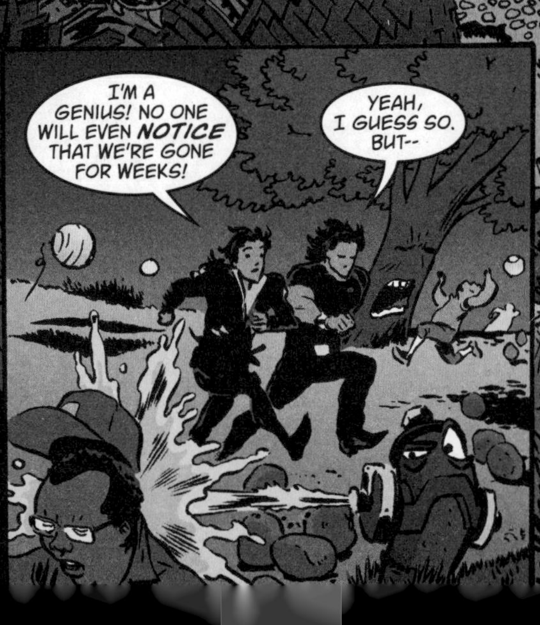
I'M A GENIUS! NO ONE WILL EVEN NOTICE THAT WE'RE GONE FOR WEEKS!
YEAH, I GUESS SO. BUT--

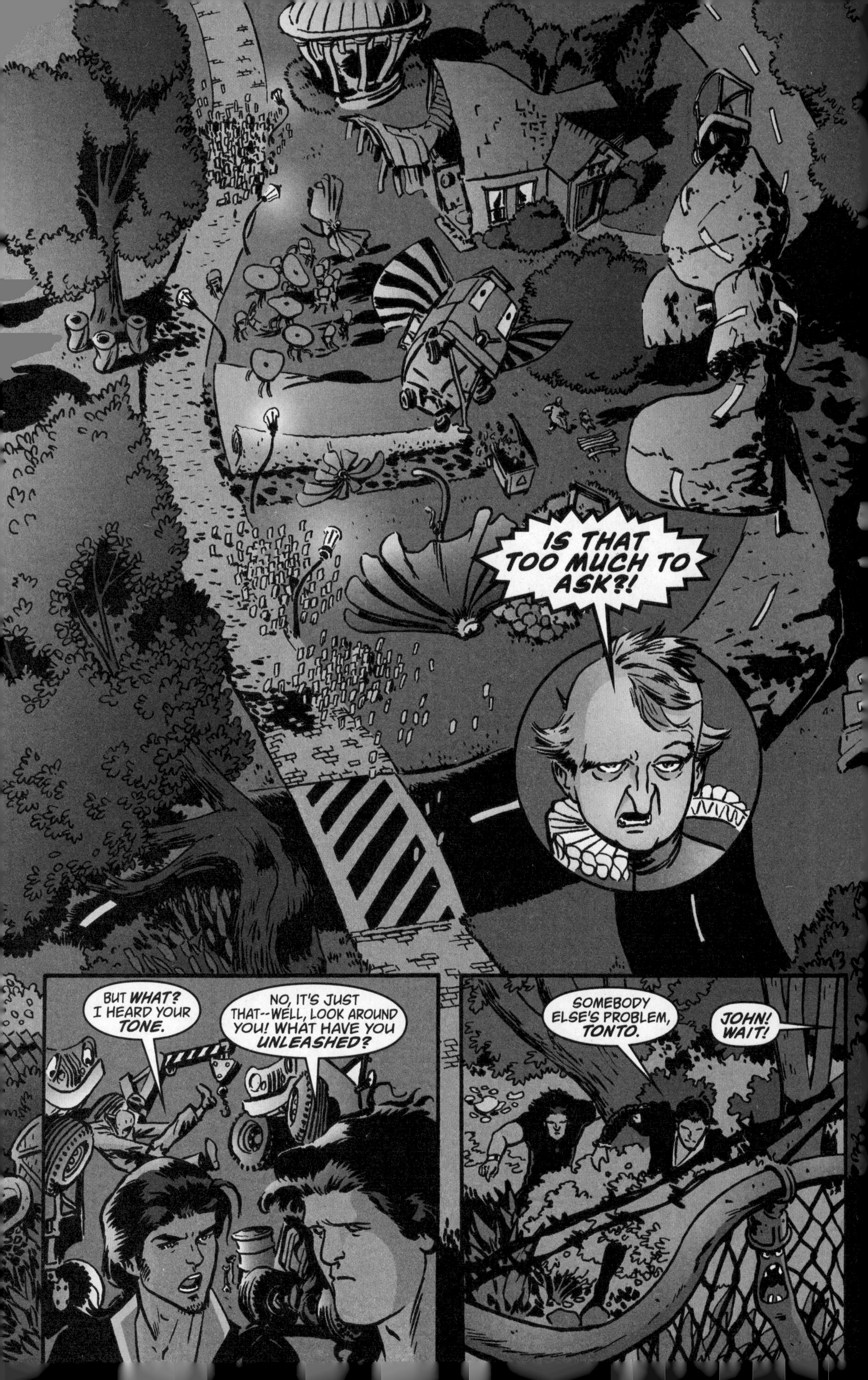
IS THAT TOO MUCH TO ASK?!
BUT WHAT? I HEARD YOUR TONE.
NO, IT'S JUST THAT--WELL, LOOK AROUND YOU! WHAT HAVE YOU UNLEASHED?
SOMEBODY ELSE'S PROBLEM, TONTO.
JOHN! WAIT!

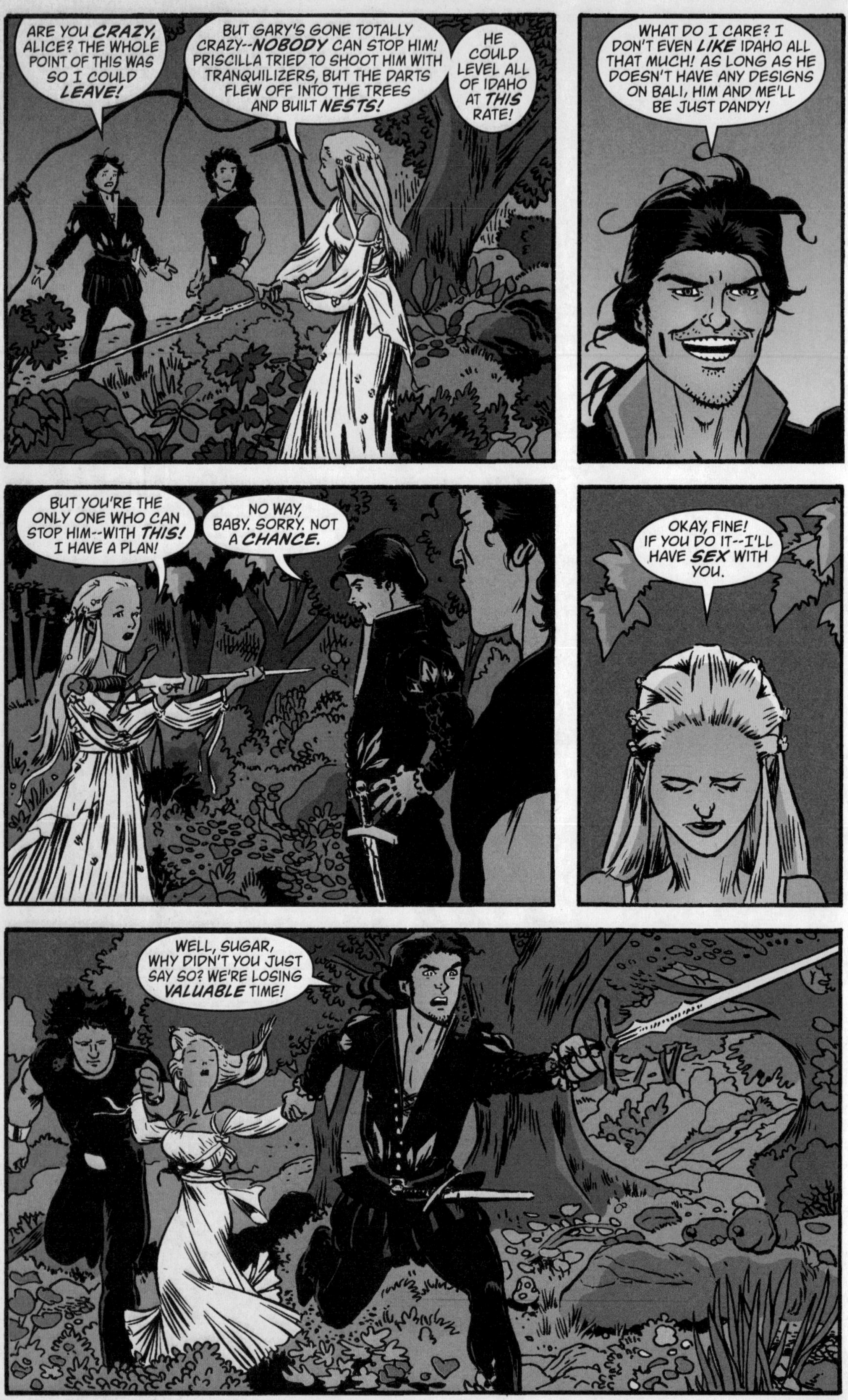
ARE YOU CRAZY, ALICE? THE WHOLE POINT OF THIS WAS SO I COULD LEAVE!
BUT GARY'S GONE TOTALLY CRAZY--NOBODY CAN STOP HIM! PRISCILLA TRIED TO SHOOT HIM WITH TRANQUILIZERS, BUT THE DARTS FLEW OFF INTO THE TREES AND BUILT NESTS!
HE COULD LEVEL ALL OF IDAHO AT THIS RATE!
WHAT DO I CARE? I DON'T EVEN LIKE IDAHO ALL THAT MUCH! AS LONG AS HE DOESN'T HAVE ANY DESIGNS ON BALI, HIM AND ME'LL BE JUST DANDY!
BUT YOU'RE THE ONLY ONE WHO CAN STOP HIM--WITH THIS! I HAVE A PLAN!
NO WAY, BABY. SORRY. NOT A CHANCE.
OKAY, FINE! IF YOU DO IT--I'LL HAVE SEX WITH YOU.
WELL, SUGAR, WHY DIDN'T YOU JUST SAY SO? WE'RE LOSING VALUABLE TIME!

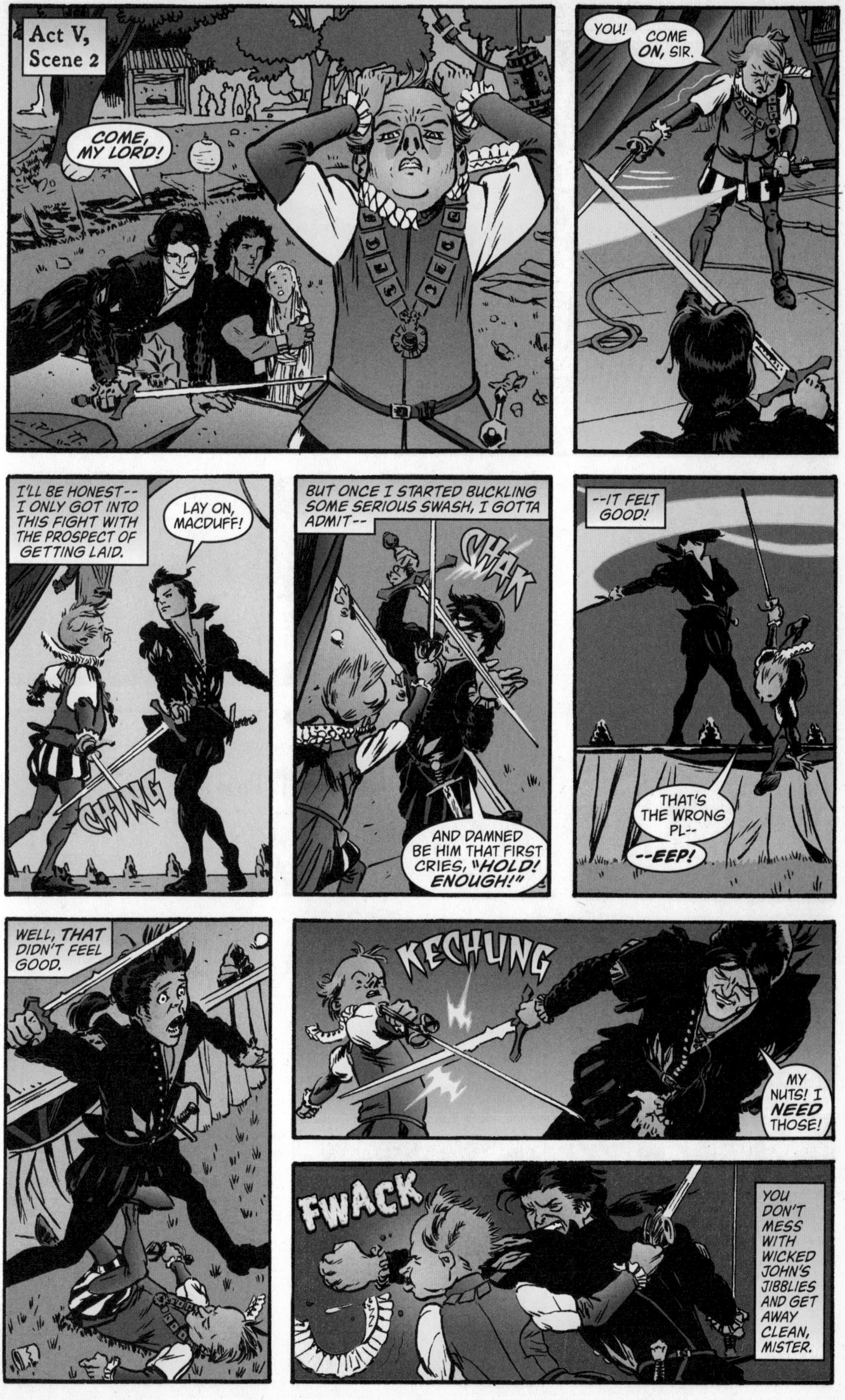
Act V, Scene 2
COME, MY LORD!
YOU!
COME ON, SIR.
I'LL BE HONEST-- I ONLY GOT INTO THIS FIGHT WITH THE PROSPECT OF GETTING LAID.
LAY ON, MACDUFF!
CHING
BUT ONCE I STARTED BUCKLING SOME SERIOUS SWASH, I GOTTA ADMIT--
CHAK
AND DAMNED BE HIM THAT FIRST CRIES, "HOLD! ENOUGH!"
--IT FELT GOOD!
THAT'S THE WRONG PL--
--EEP!
WELL, THAT DIDN'T FEEL GOOD.
KECHUNG
MY NUTS! I NEED THOSE!
FWACK
YOU DON'T MESS WITH WICKED JOHN'S JIBBLIES AND GET AWAY CLEAN, MISTER.

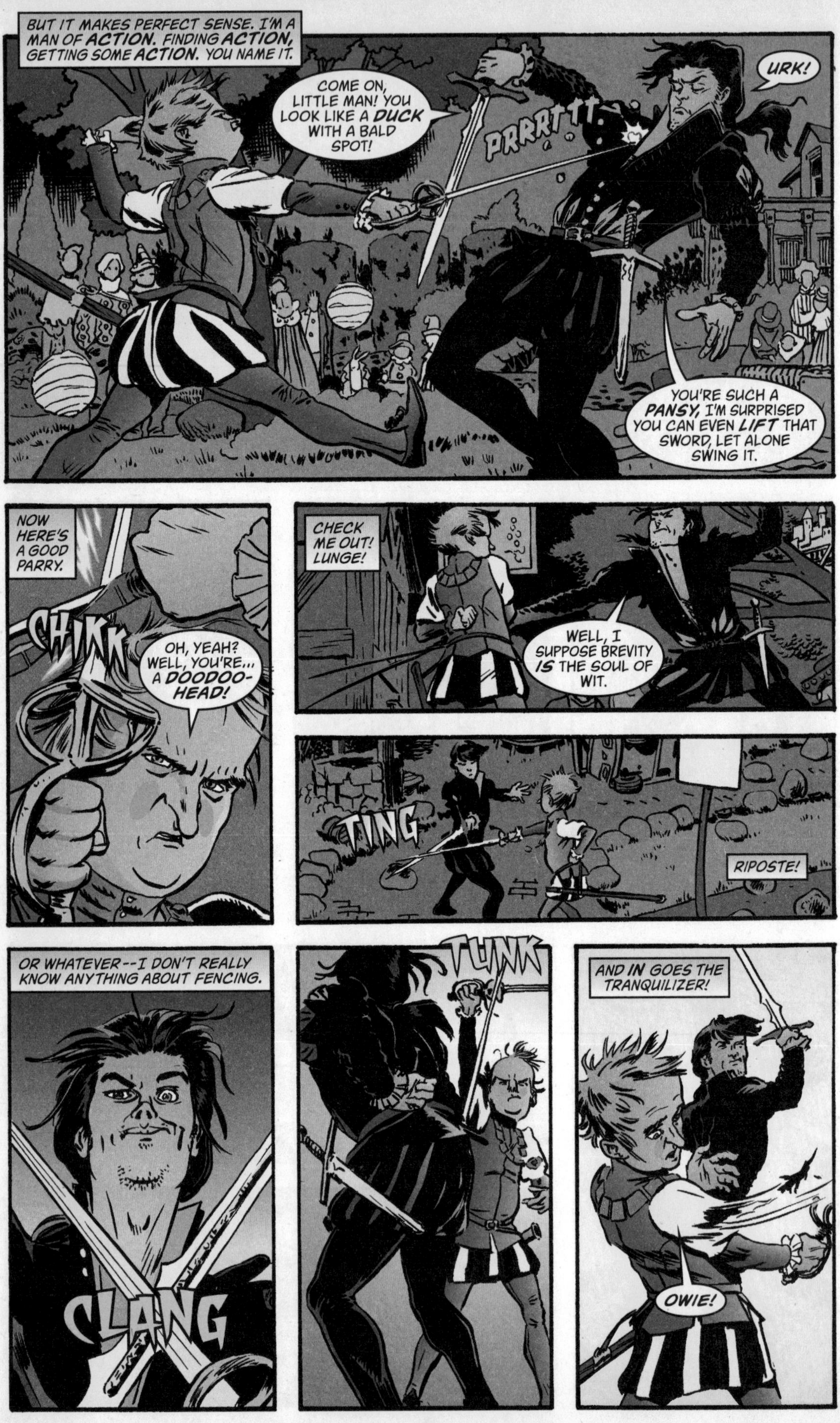
BUT IT MAKES PERFECT SENSE. I'M A MAN OF ACTION. FINDING ACTION, GETTING SOME ACTION. YOU NAME IT.
COME ON, LITTLE MAN! YOU LOOK LIKE A DUCK WITH A BALD SPOT!
PRRRTTT
URK!
YOU'RE SUCH A PANSY, I'M SURPRISED YOU CAN EVEN LIFT THAT SWORD, LET ALONE SWING IT.
NOW HERE'S A GOOD PARRY.
CHIKK
OH, YEAH? WELL, YOU'RE... A DOODOO-HEAD!
CHECK ME OUT! LUNGE!
WELL, I SUPPOSE BREVITY IS THE SOUL OF WIT.
TING
RIPOSTE!
OR WHATEVER--I DON'T REALLY KNOW ANYTHING ABOUT FENCING.
CLANG
TUNK
AND IN GOES THE TRANQUILIZER!
OWIE!

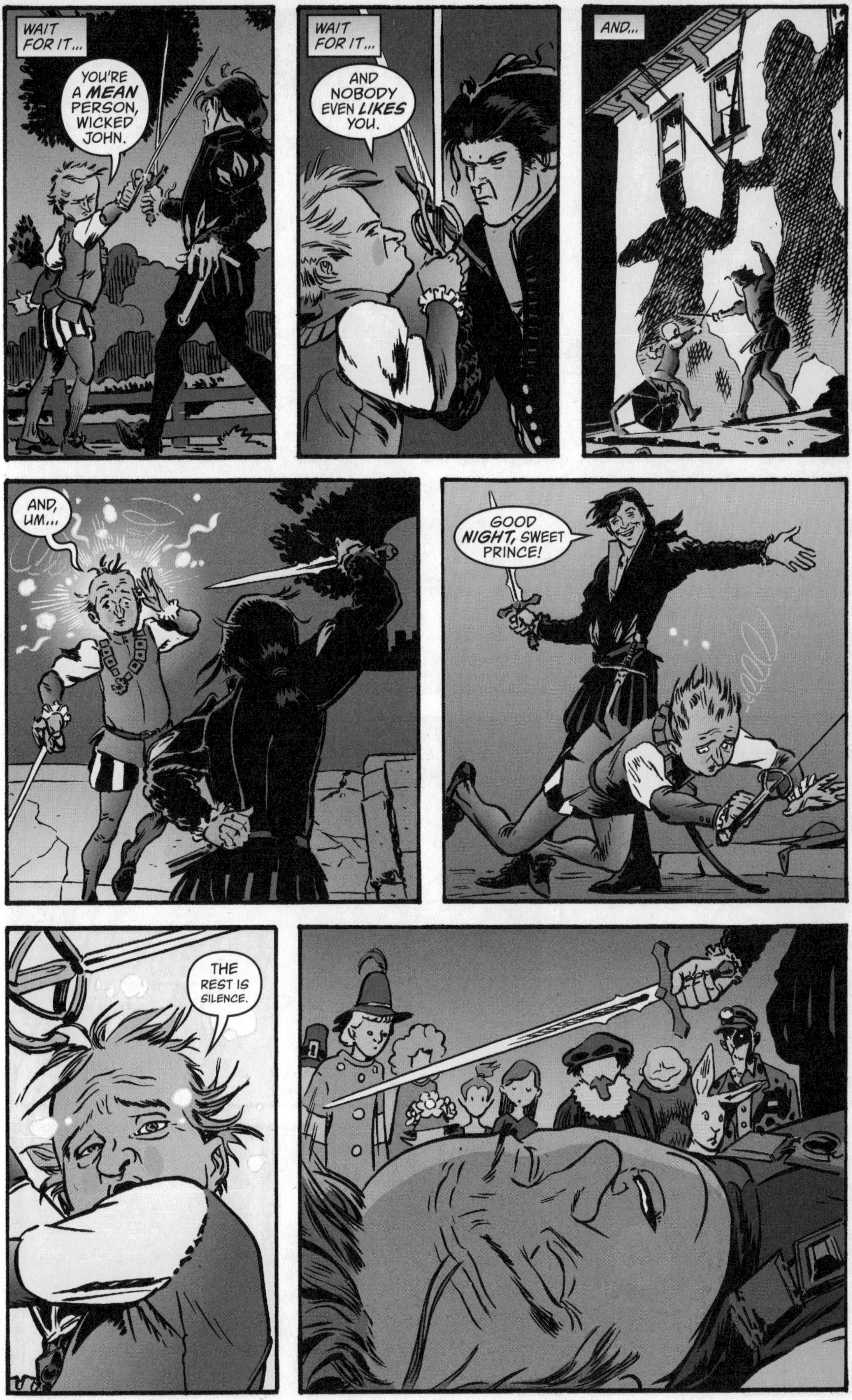
WAIT FOR IT...
YOU'RE A MEAN PERSON, WICKED JOHN.
WAIT FOR IT...
AND NOBODY EVEN LIKES YOU.
AND...
AND, UM...
GOOD NIGHT, SWEET PRINCE!
THE REST IS SILENCE.

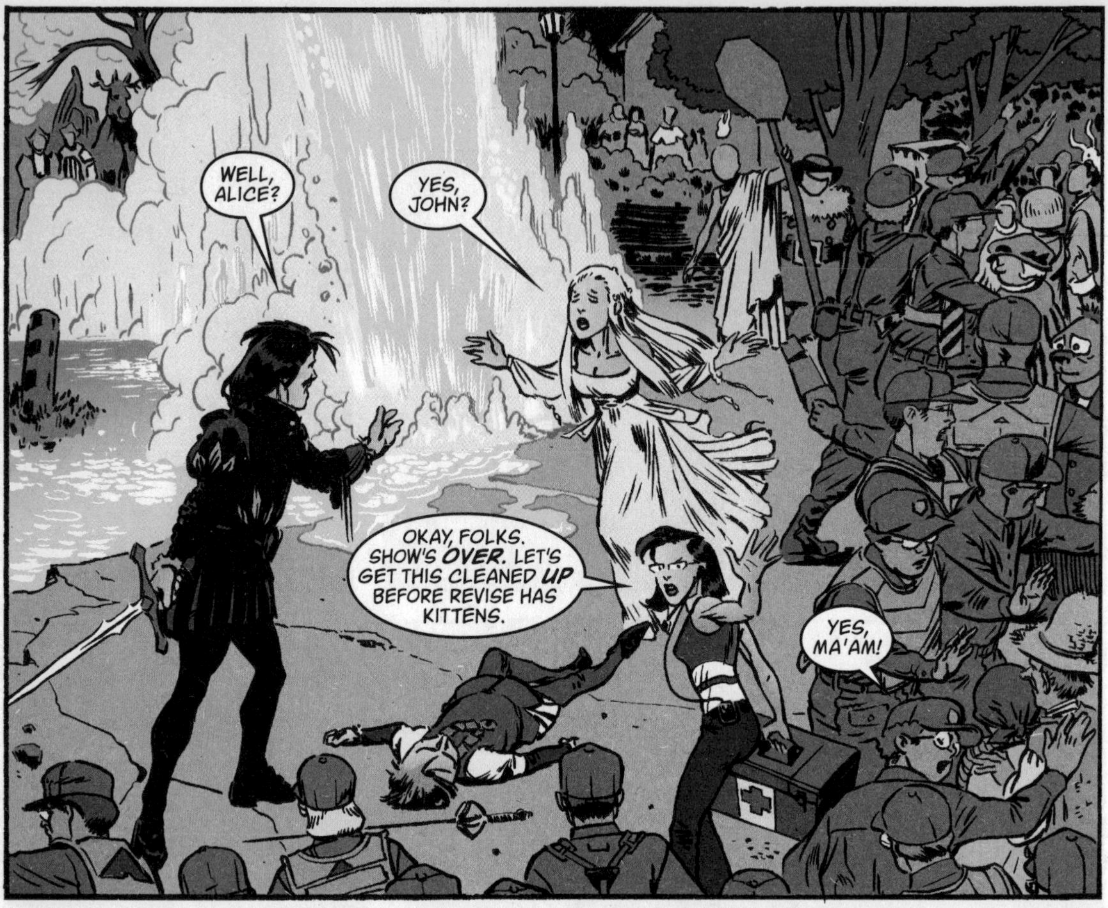
WELL, ALICE?
YES, JOHN?
OKAY, FOLKS. SHOW'S **OVER.** LET'S GET THIS CLEANED **UP** BEFORE REVISE HAS KITTENS.
YES, MA'AM!

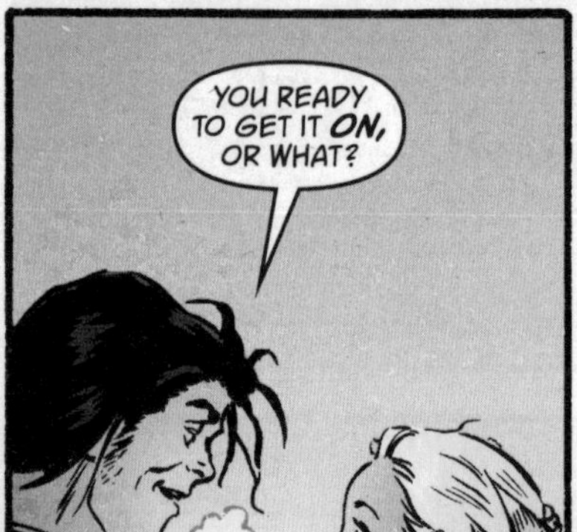
YOU READY TO GET IT **ON,** OR WHAT?

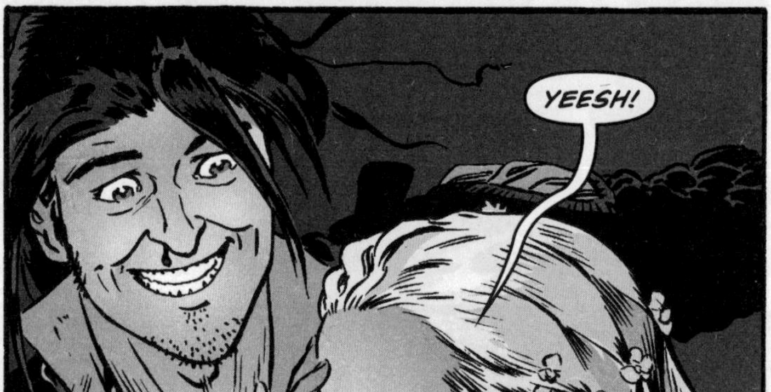
YEESH!

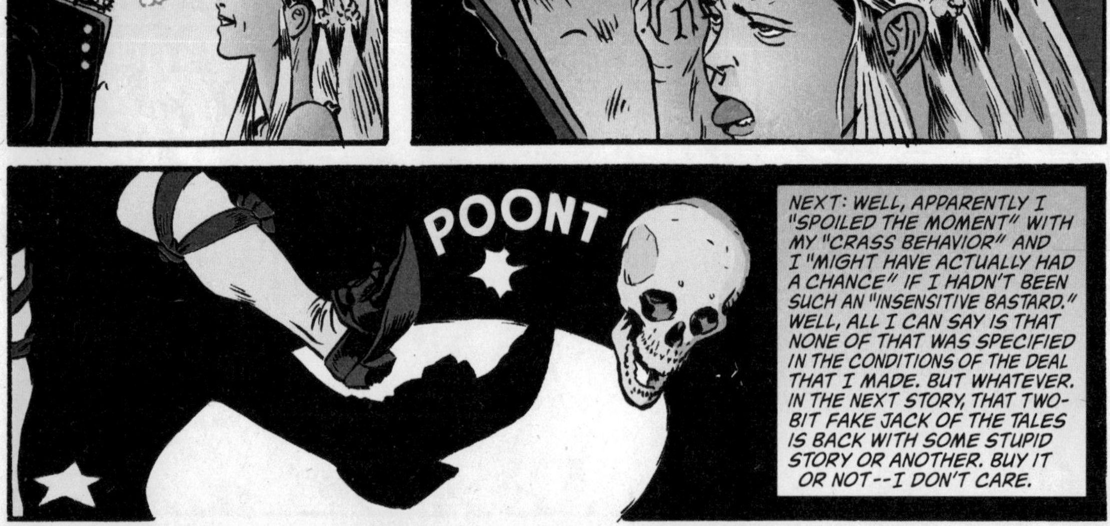
POONT
NEXT: WELL, APPARENTLY I "SPOILED THE MOMENT" WITH MY "CRASS BEHAVIOR" AND I "MIGHT HAVE ACTUALLY HAD A CHANCE" IF I HADN'T BEEN SUCH AN "INSENSITIVE BASTARD." WELL, ALL I CAN SAY IS THAT NONE OF THAT WAS SPECIFIED IN THE CONDITIONS OF THE DEAL THAT I MADE. BUT WHATEVER. IN THE NEXT STORY, THAT TWO-BIT FAKE JACK OF THE TALES IS BACK WITH SOME STUPID STORY OR ANOTHER. BUY IT OR NOT--I DON'T CARE.